Considered Action for Curriculum Improvement

Prepared by the
ASCD 1980 Yearbook Committee

Arthur W. Foshay,
Chairperson and Editor

Association for Supervision and Curriculum Development
225 North Washington Street • Alexandria, Virginia 22314

Editing:
  Ronald S. Brandt, ASCD Executive Editor
  Melva B. Jones, Staff Editor
  Nancy Olson, Senior Editor

Cover Design:
  PREP, Inc.

Stock Number: 610-80186
Library of Congress Catalog Card Number: 80-50621
ISBN 0-87120-099-6

Contents

Foreword

There can be no simple treatment of curriculum. The subject is complex and vast, defying easy definition. In the following pages, curriculum is analyzed in terms of its many parts—theory, structure, content, and implementation.

Curriculum must be concerned with *subject*. What do we want students to learn? What do they need to know in order to live life to the fullest? They need to read, to write, and to compute. They should be able to express themselves creatively in vocations and avocations. They need to be able to participate in a democracy and to earn a living that will bring them joy, satisfaction, and self-respect.

Curriculum must be concerned with *system*. How can we manage the process of education so it is humane, accessible, and exciting? The disciplines must be organized so as to be independent, yet related; discreet, yet balanced. Traditional structures and new organizational concepts must be analyzed with the learner always in the forefront. Systems are worthwhile when they serve people and nurture those for whom they are designed; school systems are designed for students.

Curriculum, the complex network of what to teach and how to teach it, exists for students. Educators can become so enmeshed in technology, philosophy, and management that they forget the focus of their endeavors —whom they are serving. We must constantly strive to educate in a manner that will humanize, personalize, and civilize. An educated person is one who knows the difference between the mundane and the important, between satiation and satisfaction, between escape and recreation. The educated person understands self as well as society, and reaches a level of fulfillment that allows freedom from elitism and pseudo-sophistication. The educated person is free.

In this Yearbook, we have the components of the ideal curriculum— that delicate balance among knowing the subject, knowing the system, and knowing the student. The authors call for quality curriculum that will fulfill the learner; effective curriculum that will stimulate the learner; and valid curriculum that will prepare the learner to deal with society and self. What greater goal could be devised?

BENJAMIN P. EBERSOLE
ASCD President, 1979-80

iv

Introduction
Arthur W. Foshay

THE ATTEMPT HERE is to bring up-to-date a constant theme in ASCD yearbooks—how curriculum workers may do their work. What we offer is the combined judgment of a number of curriculum workers. The judgments are based in part on what has been said and thought about curriculum work and in part on the experience and understandings of reality the writers have.

Considered action for curriculum improvement is based in part on theory and in part on experience. We have organized the present yearbook accordingly. The first three chapters (by English, Holman, and Grannis) deal with the culture of the school and were influenced somewhat by the work of Sarason. The next four (by Walker, Foshay, Connelly and Elbaz, and Gay) deal with certain aspects of curriculum theory. The final three (by English, Czajkowski and Patterson, and Weiss) deal with certain aspects of the way it all is.

The book is addressed primarily to the ASCD audience, which consists mainly of people directly involved in curriculum work in school systems. These people are the object of many conflicting pressures—to accommodate the often ignorant demands of the popular press, to respond to the needs teachers have to make sense out of what they are doing and wish they were doing, to meet the sometimes idealistic hopes of boards of education, and to make the whole affair operate efficiently and economically. We hope the ASCD audience, whether it is experienced in curriculum work or not, will find useful suggestions in these pages. If curriculum workers are not to be whipped from one fad to another, they will need to understand the school milieu, to know what the models of curriculum development are, to understand talk about the curriculum, and to be acquainted with some of the main concepts that govern the field. They also will need practical suggestions that put the writing and talk, the models, and the concepts into action within the schools as they are.

Translating theory into practice has never been easy. We hope we have helped in this difficult process here.

Section One.
The Culture of the School

WE BEGIN WITH a consideration of the school as a culture. So to consider it may make it seem a little less strange to those who enter it as participating adults. The officials of a school see it in entirely different terms from those of the students or the general public.

From the inside the school is, first of all, a public organization. In chapter 1 Fenwick English sees it this way. As a student of organizational behavior and as an experienced school superintendent, Dr. English considers in some depth the effect of school-community relations on the school. Readers of his chapter should come away with an increased understanding of the nature of community pressures.

A view of the school culture from the inside is offered in chapter 2 by Evelyn Lezzer Holman. Leaning heavily on Sarason's important book and on her own professional experience, Mrs. Holman offers a view of the internal workings of the school that is realistic yet theory oriented.

In "Classroom Culture and the Problem of Control," Joseph Grannis offers a stimulating account of current thinking about and practice in the actual operation of classrooms. He calls attention to malpractice and to built-in limitations (see his eloquent statement on herding) and offers a vision of classroom practice that is at once inspiring and practical.

There we have it: the school in the community, the school as a whole, the classroom—all from the point of view of the school as a culture.

1

The Dynamics of School-Community Relationships

Fenwick W. English

SCHOOLS AND COMMUNITIES exist in a state of dynamic tension. As a subsystem of the larger community, a school district exerts resources to balance its relationship with the community and at the same time maintain an internal balance of its own. A school district can be provoked by both internal and external pressures. This chapter focuses on the *external* pressures and balance.

The boundary between a school system and its community is somewhat fuzzy. School system and community relationships appear to remain tranquil as long as the school system does not stray too far or too long from the dominant attitudes of its community. An attitude is a kind of predisposition to react a certain way to specific stimuli. On the other hand, an opinion is a kind of belief that a person can hold without any deep emotional reaction.[1] School practices that are compatible with parental and community opinion will be tolerated and perhaps accepted. However, those that do not conform to the attitudinal core of beliefs may evoke strong reactions and countermeasures.

Like most human systems, schools create buffers so as to avoid excessive meddling from external forces. The first school system buffer is the board of education which is confined (in theory) to dealing only with policy decisions and not operational ones. This means that even if a policy is changed, the eventual impact may be operationally small. If a school board develops a policy about the priorities of basic skills, the decision may not change anything programmatically.

A second buffer is the official school curriculum. The curriculum represents the "core technology" of schools.[2] As such it contains a fair

---

[1] H. B. English and A. C. English, *A Comprehensive Dictionary of Psychological and Psychoanalytic Terms: A Guide to Usage* (New York: McKay, 1958), as cited in *Scales for the Measurement of Attitudes,* by Marvin E. Shaw, and Jack M. Wright (New York: McGraw-Hill, 1967), p. 5.

[2] James D. Thompson, *Organizations in Action* (New York: McGraw-Hill, 1967).

1

share of technical language and jargon. One of the many symbolic functions of the curriculum is to discourage interference by the community in the actual operations of a school or school system. The curriculum is therefore a barrier or buffer to extensive citizen meddling. Citizens will often take it more seriously than professionals, who may secretly ignore it. However, in a conflict situation both professionals and citizens will go to war as if a small word altered here and there will lead to an enormous impact. The curriculum is a political symbol in this respect. It stands for the territorial perquisites of educators to actually decide, often arbitrarily, what will be taught and under what conditions.

Citizens are not without recourse and, if mobilized properly, can eventually prevail in almost all situations of conflict. Their first recourse is with the board of education. Citizen actions may force the board to comply, or citizens may elect new members committed to a certain point of view. Once the board has been altered, the community may seek to influence the chief school officer or to control the structure of the system by providing him/her with a set of directives or by changing superintendents.

The preceding set of actions is an example of what may happen when an "errant school system" crosses the "zone of tolerance" of the community.

In reality, the zone of tolerance concept says, no superintendent or school board can obtain approval from the community for policies which conflict with predominant community preferences. If the board and its administration persist in enacting policy outside the bounds of the public needs and desires, they risk open conflict with the community.[3]

Factors Which Govern School-Community Conflict

Large school systems are not any more prone to conflict with their communities than small ones if the communities are relatively homogeneous. Because larger systems usually include more citizen heterogeneity in terms of the dominant value structure of attitudes, more conflict may be produced. Size per se, however, is not the key determinant. As any community becomes more diversified and shifts occur in citizen attitudes (not opinions), consensus becomes more difficult at the policy level. The "zone of tolerance" is more difficult to identify in heterogeneous communities. Great diversity presents a real governance problem and a broader "zone of tolerance," yet the school system may have fewer options for fear of offending any minority within the larger community.

Another factor which may influence the level of possible conflict is the amount of information the community actually has about the schools. An extremely knowledgeable community would be able to provide much

[3] National School Boards Association, *What Do We Know About School Boards?* (Evanston, Ill.: National School Boards Association, 1975), p. 8.

clearer directions to its elected officials. A less informed electorate may create the conditions in which the "zone of tolerance" is again larger, but when attention is focused on a specific subject, the electorate may actually be very much more discriminating.

In 1974 the National School Boards Association commissioned the Gallup Poll to examine the level of information among the general public about school board operations. The Poll revealed that fully 63 percent of the general public could not name one action by their local school boards; 22 percent did not know what the role of the school board was; 40 percent of the sample thought that the PTA had responsibility for running the public schools as opposed to 58 percent who thought the school board had the responsibility.

While the word *curriculum* was not used in asking the respondents about areas of authority of boards, two items within the curriculum area were included: deciding what textbooks to use and what subjects should be taught. Of the adults responding, 31 percent indicated that they thought boards should have a "great deal of authority" in deciding what textbooks to use, 35 percent felt "a fair amount of authority," 5 percent said "no authority," and 29 percent "did not know." In the area of subject determination, 30 percent indicated that boards should decide with "complete authority" what subjects should be taught, 35 percent indicated "a fair amount of authority," 5 percent said "no authority," and 30 percent "didn't know." [4]

A board of education may not be representative of a community. Shifts in the electorate may take place after elections. There may be times when a board is operating on a past understanding with its constituencies, and either the understanding is no longer functional or the constituents themselves have changed. The wider this disparity may be, the more misleading board approval of school district actions may be. However, at some point in time the dissonance between the community and the school district must again come into some kind of balance.

Even when this disparity is no longer a problem, the possible lack of representativeness of boards of education raises other interesting questions about possible conflict. Boards have typically represented a small section of the community. A 1969 study conducted by the University of Michigan and University of Oregon [5] indicated that the socioeconomic characteristics of board members were: 90 percent male, 96 percent white, 47 percent 1–4 years of college, 68 percent 40–59 years of age, 85 percent Protestant,

---

[4] National School Boards Association, *The People Look at Their School Boards* (Evanston, Ill.: National School Boards Association, 1975), p. 8.

[5] Pennsylvania School Boards Association, data cited in PSBA Bulletin 40 (September-October 1976). The PSBA was comparing Pennsylvania board characteristics with the national data. In Pennsylvania the board was 81 percent male, 98 percent white, 21 percent 1-4 years of college, 71 percent 40-49 years of age, 68 percent Protestant, and 63 percent Republican.

and 44 percent Republican. Boards are therefore not representative of the population at large; they are considerably underrepresentative of women, racial minorities, noncollege graduates, and non-Protestant religious inclinations.

Areas/Issues Which Portend Conflict

Perhaps the most explicit list of sensitive areas in which community attitudes may portend conflict with those in the school curriculum was developed by a citizens' group in the Kanawha County, West Virginia, textbook rebellion. The list of taboo postures was signed by 12,000 citizens after multicultural textbooks were adopted by the board of education. The list provides a synopsis of trouble and conflict experienced in the rest of the nation, but none elsewhere has been on quite such a scale of magnitude as in West Virginia. Paraphrased somewhat, no text or curriculum would be supported if it:

1. Raised questions about the sanctity of the family unit;

2. Questioned belief in a Supernatural Being or a power beyond man;

3. Demeaned, encouraged skepticism, or fostered disbelief in the political system described in the Constitution;

4. Downgraded the economic system referred to as *free enterprise;*

5. Encouraged disrespect for the laws of the nation, the state, and its subdivisions;

6. Fostered disbelief in the history and heritage of the U.S.;

7. Advocated, suggested, or implied that traditional rules of grammar and vocabulary of the English language were not proper;

8. Dealt with religion in any manner or supported programs that fostered religious disbelief. The denial of supernatural forces is a form of religion and must also be unconstitutional.[6]

Several additions could be made to the list including the rejection of any book which used profanity, encouraged racial hatred, did not encourage loyalty to the United States, or defamed any of the nation's founders by misrepresenting their motives or ideals. Among the targets of parents in Kanawha County were:

. . . textbooks' use of open-ended questions to encourage independent thought and analysis on the part of students. Parents have complained that questions concerning the students' feelings, their experiences, and their home life constitute an invasion of privacy. They have contended, also, that students

[6] National Education Association, *Kanawha County, West Virginia: A Textbook Study in Cultural Conflict* (Washington, D.C.: National Education Association, February 1975), pp. 18-19.

should not be asked what they think or how they should behave; they should be told what to think and how to behave.[7]

A publication from the John Birch Society similarly repeated the attitude:

If you want to please a "Liberal," turn over a rock so he can luxuriate in the ooze of his country's imagined shortfalls. Never mind that this is the greatest country on earth, whose noble ideals should be taught to our youth. Let him damn those ideals and wallow instead in gutter culture and ghetto language with revolutionaries, rapists, and prostitutes for his heroes. But please, keep him away from our children.[8]

Three years later in Montgomery County, Maryland, a wealthy suburb of Washington, D.C., a parent group called CURE (Citizens United for Responsible Education) protested to the school board to remove from the curriculum a book called *The Learning Tree* by Gordon Parks. CURE objected to the sexually explicit language and profanity experienced by the book's central figure, a 12-year-old black boy growing up in Kansas City.

In a heated dialogue with the leader of CURE, a board member asked the group whether it would ban Shakespearean plays, the Bible, or "even *Madame Bovary*" because of sexually explicit language. The CURE leader responded that "Shakespeare's sex is not explicit or vulgar." [9]

A parent group in Frederick County, Maryland, tried to have the book *Grendel,* a modernization of the English classic *Beowulf,* banned. The group charged that the book used "vile and vulgar language" and promoted "a negative view of life." [10]

The preceding examples show how some school systems' actions involving certain issues have gone beyond communities' "zones of tolerance" and resulted in school-community conflicts. The "zone of tolerance" concept also includes conflict initiated by the community and thrust upon the schools. For example, in Marion County, Indiana, the West Clark Community School Board adopted a textbook called *A Search for Order in Complexity* after public pressure was applied. The text, developed by the Institute for Creation Research, attempts to present findings which refute evolution and support biblical creationism. The Marion County Superior Court ruled that the use of the book in the public schools was contradictory to 200 years of constitutional government.

Clearly, the purpose of *A Search for Order in Complexity* is the promotion and inclusion of fundamentalist Christian doctrine in public schools. The

[7] Ibid., p. 35.

[8] John Hoar, "Parents Revolt When Textbooks are Propaganda," *American Opinion* (November 1974).

[9] Janis Johnson, *"The Learning Tree* Survives Assault by Montgomery County Parents Group," *Washington Post,* 20 June 1978.

[10] Maureen Dowd, "Book Censorship: Dead in Libraries, Alive in Schools," *Washington Star,* 22 January 1978, sec. B.

publishers, themselves, admit that this text is designed to find its way into the public schools to stress Biblical Creationism.[11]

In the same year that the Marion County, Indiana, case was decided, the Dallas Independent School District officially adopted *A Search for Order in Complexity* as a source book for high school biology students. On a six to three vote, the board split along racial lines in approving. All the white members voted to accept it, and the minority members opposed it.[12]

There are also cases in which both the schools and the community majority apparently find a practice acceptable, but it is deemed unacceptable by a minority. For example, a national survey conducted by the Anti-Defamation League of B'nai B'rith found that a majority of American public schools still ignore the spirit of the First Amendment. The survey was conducted in 103 communities in 31 states and the District of Columbia and indicated that 91.5 percent of those responding said their schools conducted holiday concerts with religious content, most often Christian. One-third of the respondents said that the schools in their communities used "prayers, hymns, and biblical selections or taught biblical principles such as the account of Creation in Genesis." [13]

Implications for Action

Not only are school-community relationships dynamic and tension filled, but they are also *transactional*. Each partner in the dyad expects to get something from the other:

Why then should school people want to be responsive to what they consider virtually insatiable, potentially less-informed, and legally non-accountable communities? The big carrot in eliciting responsiveness from school people is the support of their clientele. That support is no longer freely given. It is exchanged for something.[14]

Communities need schools to provide children with the results of schools' instructional programs. Children require skills, concepts, and knowledges to make their way in society and to find the keys to self-fullfillment and the good life. Schools need the support of their communities

---

[11] Hendren v. Campbell, 11 Ind. 5 (Sup. Ct. Marion County) cited in National Association of Biology Teachers, *A Compendium of Information on The Theory of Evolution and the Evolution-Creationism Controversy* (Reston, Va.: National Association of Biology Teachers, June 1972), pp. 1-2.

[12] "Dallas Schools Pick Disputed Textbook for Biology Class," *The New York Times*, 28 January 1977.

[13] Irving Spiegel, "First Amendment Violation Seen in School's Religious Practices," *New York Times*, 30 April 1976.

[14] Dale Mann, "Some Cheerful Prospects for Schooling and Public Involvement," paper prepared for the National Forum of Leaders of Educational Organizations, Washington, D.C., 6 November 1978, pp. 9-10. (Mimeographed.)

to maintain their services and functions and to grow as viable social institutions/organizations.

While the schools could engage in more practices that exclude parents and communities, increased isolation would lead to decreased support, even with a monopoly on the services they perform. If the people come to believe that the services are faulty or are not important, the community will reduce the level of financial support directly or indirectly. Therefore, while schools must exert organizational energy to maintain independence, they risk isolation and abandonment if they are too successful. So schools have sought to find various ways to channel such involvement in a constructive manner, without having to forfeit any of their perceived or actual prerogatives. A review of some of these ways is presented.

The Methods of Involvement

Ad Hoc Community Advisory Committees. At various times school districts have formed advisory committees to study a particular curriculum or program problem. Most often these relate to mandated federal and/or state requirements for input by parents and other citizens. For the most part few such groups are ever organized in areas where the school district already has a solid consensus in the community. They are usually formed as a political response to a touchy subject such as sex education, religion in the schools, textbook screening or guideline development, changing school boundaries or closing schools.

School systems appear to use such groups as sounding boards, stalking horses, or lightning rods. They allow the school system to explore alternatives to delicate issues which other subgroups in a community may find politically and educationally offensive. If the reaction is negative, the resulting antagonism is directed to the ad hoc committee and its work or recommendations, rather than to the school system or its staff.

The disadvantage of ad hoc committees, from a community perspective, is that problems are narrowly defined and time is limited. Sustained examination of an educational program or curriculum is often impossible under such circumstances. From a school system's perspective, a disadvantage is that effort is expended to keep ad hoc groups on target, i.e., to keep them from straying away from their approved domain.

A strategy called *fencing* is used for this purpose. Fencing is defining what problems are acceptable to the school system and thus, by definition, the possible solutions. However, should any group stray too far and not be corrected, a report can be politely accepted (and the symbolic function of involvement fulfilled) or quietly studied to death. A repugnant recommendation may also be fenced off by not assigning it to anyone or to any department or area in particular for action. It simply slips through the cracks of the table of organization and eventually becomes irrelevant. Given enough time, any prepared plan or report has within it enough information which needs to be dealt with immediately so that the plan will begin a kind of decaying process at a certain point, no matter how soundly conceived or reasoned it was originally.

Even if a school system approaches the use of community ad hoc committees with a sincere interest, the fact is that they are rarely spontaneous creations. They are usually initiated by the school district, the responsibilities are defined by the school district, and the membership may also be selected by the district.

These groups may be contrasted with community committees that form from a common dissatisfaction with some aspect of the school system. Some examples are parent groups which organize because they are concerned with safety to and from school and want to obtain a traffic signal at a dangerous intersection or because they are concerned with the actual or intended use of a controversial textbook in the educational program or school library. A taxpayers' group may organize to restrain or reduce school taxes. These groups are ad hoc as well, but their objectives, scope, and membership are not usually dictated by the school system.

Sooner or later such groups must confront or contact the school system, i.e., attempt to impact the system's behavior. Such contacts may consist of meetings with teachers, principals, the superintendent, or the board of education. The actual transaction may be acrimonious or conciliatory. The school system, however, is usually on the defensive because it has had no opportunity to define the turf or predetermine the focus of the group's agenda. The school system is therefore usually *reacting*. The "zone of tolerance" is defined in the reaction rather than by the initiation of the district.

Permanent Groups/Committees. Another method the community may use to become involved in the affairs of a school district is to assume a variety of roles in such groups as the PTA, school principal's council, superintendent's human relations committee, etc. These groups may have a permanent life beyond any role incumbent and may continue because of system-community tradition or demand. Some may be required by some form of legislative mandate.

Ombudsman/District Outreach. Though by no means a dominant form of involving citizens, the ombudsman idea has been tried in some school districts. The ombudsman may be a professional or a knowledgeable community person who helps citizens cut through the red tape and official channels of the school district. The ombudsman may initiate action as a kind of system outreach or merely respond to calls for help by frustrated parents or citizens.

Polls, Surveys, and Needs Assessments. Many school districts have attempted to formalize involvement of their communities by systematically developing polls, surveys, opinionnaires, or needs assessments. Needs assessment is the most formalized of the procedures.[15] However,

---

[15] Fenwick W. English and Roger Kaufman, *Needs Assessment: A Focus for Curriculum Development* (Washington, D.C.: Association for Supervision and Curriculum Development, 1975).

while it has shown much promise as the most sophisticated of the forms of involvement, it is not without problems.

The first difficulty that arises in using a needs assessment is the language barrier. Education has developed a specific and technical language which can be related to specific practices or activities much more easily than general language can. The technical language has meaning for practitioners, but considerably less for laypersons. To successfully involve the community, needs assessments, as well as polls and surveys, must be divested of jargon and much technical language. But while laypersons may then respond, their responses become too general for the educator. Whatever the results, however, educators are responsible for the translation into practice. If the results are so general as to provide a great level of variance in interpretation, disagreements within the school district can and often do arise regarding how to implement the community's feelings and perceptions. Some of the problems stem from attempting to determine exactly what the community was trying to communicate because more than one practice or activity may be involved. Information obtained in such needs assessments (and polls and surveys) becomes embroiled in system politics and may never be applied.

However, specific responses from the community may threaten the position of minorities. When vague objectives predominate, the impact of a minority viewpoint can be much larger than the actual numbers of people might dictate. For this reason, those in positions of power may not desire ranking of objectives, outcomes, or practices that they perceive not to be in the best interests of their groups.[16] In this case, language specificity may be more a matter of political impact and power than of simply developing curriculum from specific and validated outcomes. It has long been understood by diplomats in developing workable peace treaties that general language enabling more than one logical interpretation may be necessary for the parties involved to support any agreement.

Another problem with polls, surveys, and needs assessments is that of proper sampling of the groups to be involved. Some knowledge of statistics is required in order for the results to be considered a valid response.[17]

The question of what topics to include in polls and surveys can also be a problem. Community groups most often do not want to focus on the outcomes or results of school district operations. Rather, most prefer to consider the "solutions" such as specific subjects, grouping methodologies, textbooks, and instructional materials or take up matters such as class size, teacher salaries, or administrator popularity. Professionals rightly consider these issues as matters involving expert judgment. A turf problem is in-

---

[16] Fenwick W. English, "The Politics of Needs Assessment," *Educational Technology* 17 (November 1977): 18-23.

[17] Fenwick W. English and Roger Kaufman, *Needs Assessment: Concept and Application* (Englewood Cliffs, N.J.: Educational Technology Publications, 1978).

evitably produced. While educators may not resist having communities define the results, i.e., learner growth, communities may feel too constricted and not understand the relationship between means and ends. Communities may come to feel used by surveys restricted to results and perceive that such instruments have little use in helping citizens "run the schools" in harmony with their value structure. If citizens are blocked by a survey that doesn't ask them their feelings about open classrooms, they may perceive that questions about the priorities of reading goals are useless.

Thus, some questions used in polls and surveys may involve tensions between communities and their schools because of language, politics, and values. However, questions can be asked about technical innovations or changes unless such innovations portend shifts in values as well. An auto-

Table 1. The School-Community Transactional Relationship			
	STAGE/LEVEL	COMMUNITY BEHAVIOR	SCHOOL SYSTEM BEHAVIOR
ZONE OF TOLERANCE	Stage 1 Initiating	—Informal requests to meet with system officials —Petitions to meet with officials/board on identified problems	—Public discussions; call for a committee —Call for individual citizen response by letter or telephone —Circulation of a poll, survey, needs assessment
	Stage 2 Cooperative	—Dialogue; presentation of facts, agendas; trust building	—Dialogue; presentation of system viewpoints and perceptions —Receipt of recommendations and suggestions; action taken which is in harmony with the community
ZONE OF TOLERANCE			
ZONE OF SCHOOL SYSTEM-COMMUNITY TOLERANCE VARIANCE	Stage 3 Warning	—Verbal protests —Letters to the editor —Demonstrations —Circulation of petitions which call for action or support desired solutions	—Press conferences with prepared statements —Confrontations by system officials in public and private meetings
	Stage 4 Rebuke	—Use of ridicule; call for ousters —Organized protests and demonstrations which call for recall, i.e., action to remove officials —Calls for investigations —Petty harassment	—Legal maneuvering and advertising —Posting of notices to define/confine responses —Reduce access to system information/officials —Confined speaking time at public meetings
	Stage 5 Sanction	—Legal action; injunctions —Special elections to change officials —Militant action to pressure officials; sabotage of day-to-day operations	—Exclusion of groups from all but legally required meetings —Isolation of group —Organization of a counter group of supporters —Legal maneuvers; injunctions

mated attendance accounting system will not be resisted unless it is perceived to be excessively costly. The community value system may be that taking attendance is good (a value) but that it is too costly (a conflicting value). Computerized school scheduling may be considered appropriate until or unless it contradicts the value of schooling by creating open time during the school day when students may not be required to be in class. Flexible scheduling as an innovation in the late sixties was unappealing to citizens not because it was inefficient or ineffective as a tool per se but because unscheduled or open time contradicted various citizen perceptions about what constituted a proper school environment. Some communities simply could not tolerate students on the lawn during the school day. Many conventional school schedules are today computerized without controversy because they do not incorporate open time.

Some Signs of Trouble Between School Systems and Communities

The dynamic partnership between a school system and its community is one in which both parties require influence and authority to secure something from the other. Signs that trouble may be brewing between the partners may initially be subtle and confused with everyday activities. As the signals become more severe, they may be exacerbated by external pressures such as a new tax law or curriculum requirements in the form of minimum competencies, or by pressures resulting from an unpopular superintendent or internal dissent and militant teacher demonstrations.

Table 1 indicates some tentative signs of five hypothetical but distinct stages of school-community relations. Stage 1 indicates typical behavior when either partner initiates actions to involve the other in a transaction. When each party is functioning in the other's "zone of tolerance," relationships are cooperative and productive (Stage 2).

However, when a partner leaves the other's "zone of tolerance," warning signs may be issued and Stage 3 is entered. A community or subgroup within a community may begin Stage 3 by filing petitions which make demands for specific ends to practices or requests for performance of an action. There may be verbal protests at board meetings, PTA gatherings, and/or letters written to the editor of the newspaper.

The school system issues warnings by holding official press conferences denouncing the critics by passing along information, or by answering charges made by the subgroup of community representatives. It should be noted that the decision to engage in actual confrontation is usually a considered one for a school system. Occasional outbursts by district officials when they may be publicly goaded are not considered the same type of response as a press conference in which statements are made for the public media.

Each partner may resort to stronger actions when Stage 4, the rebuke or reprimand level is entered. The rebuke stage is a censure level and is different from the sanction level (Stage 5). The rebuke stage is marked by a community's underlying acceptance of the officials of the system although the community may want to block, nullify, or initiate an action or change.

At the Stage 5 sanction level, there is a deliberate attempt to remove officials or force a change by direct application of legal or nonlegal actions. While a school system is not without recourse at this most violent stage, it is considerably weakened in terms of the actual alternatives which can be selected. Extralegal means open to the community or its subgroups cannot usually be considered by the school system at all since there are more rules, regulations, and laws governing system officials and their conduct than citizens.

In reality the stages shown in Table 1 probably overlap and are not discrete and separate spheres of action and choice as shown. In addition neither a community nor a school system moves from one to the other stage smoothly and in progression. It is quite possible that either partner may skip several stages and proceed to the most violent level immediately.

Probing Community Confidence Levels in the School District

It would be difficult to differentiate the cause and the effect in the relationship between any community's "zone of tolerance" with the school system and its confidence in the ability of the school system to produce quality education. Confidence in the schools may be a result of the perceived quality of education in the school system, or it may be the cause of a wide "zone of tolerance." In the latter case, the zone may be larger because the community believes the schools are doing a good job and know what they are doing. However, if the schools are perceived to be of low quality, then the community may keep a watchful eye and allow only a very small range of tolerance for deviating from its basic attitudinal value set.

Data regarding public perception of national or local educational quality are hard to come by. Most of the information comes from national polls. A Harris Poll on confidence in U.S. institutions showed that more respect, and less cynicism and suspicion, was found towards the Presidency, Congress, higher education, and the medical profession. Two institutions that declined in confidence were the public schools (from 48 percent to 43 percent) and law enforcement (from 37 percent to 36 percent).[18] Another Harris Poll indicated that while 40 percent of a national sample thought that the quality of life had improved over the past ten years, 88

---

[18] William Claiborne, "Confidence In Institutions Up Strongly," *Washington Post*, 5 January 1978.

percent felt that "achieving quality education for children" was still a top priority.[19] A Gallup Poll on current levels of happiness indicated that white females were the "happiest" segments of the U.S. population. Education was an important variable: 46 percent of respondents with a college education indicated that they were "very happy" as compared with only 42 percent with a high school background and 29 percent with only a grade school education.[20]

On a more localized level, a University of Pittsburgh survey of six neighborhoods within that city indicated that the quality of schools topped the list of complaints about city services. The study concluded with the comment that "unless people's perceptions of a poor quality public school system can be dispelled, the city is going to have a difficult time holding on to its younger, better-educated and more upwardly mobile families."[21]

It is difficult to draw sweeping conclusions about confidence in public education, but at best, it can be said that there are no indicators showing high levels of satisfaction with the public schools at the present time. When reacting to such data, it is far easier for educators to complain about the public's lack of information, its apathy, or its stereotypes than to consider taking positive steps to improve confidence in public schools. The solution is not an expensive PR effort to convince any community that the existing quality of education is indeed the best ever. Rather, the answer seems to be disseminating information that the public considers relevant indicators of educational quality. To date, the only available data have been national SAT scores or press results about local student performance on other standardized tests. While educators complain that such instruments or procedures are inadequate measures at the best, they have offered very few alternatives which have generated any measure of public support. Individual classroom teacher tests, pupil-teacher contract work, pupil self-evaluation, live student performances before audiences, or simulations—none of these have generated much lay support as effective substitutes for national tests. They seem unlikely candidates to perform this function, particularly when public confidence in the schools has apparently ebbed.

Restoring Public Confidence: Rebuilding School-Community Trust

How do public agencies deal with the variety of charges leveled against them? How do they even know whether criticisms are valid or not? Agencies can and do use their own staff to investigate alleged problems, but there is

[19] Louis Harris, "Forty Percent Think the Quality of Life Has Improved Over 10 Years," *Washington Post*, 3 August 1978.

[20] George Gallup, "Whites, Women, Educated View Selves as Happiest," *Washington Post*, 25 December 1977.

[21] Paul Ayars, "Schools Top List Of Residents' Complaints, Study Shows," *Pittsburgh Post-Gazette*, 11 October 1978.

always the question of self-interest. How can the public be assured that the agency will look objectively at its own programs? And how can the public be sure that the agency will tell the truth, the whole truth and nothing but the truth when it tells its side of the story.[22]

The Los Angeles Board of Education established the Independent Analysis Unit as an internal response to providing the citizens and the Board with data about the actual operations of the school system. One of the expressed functions of the Unit is to restore confidence of the public so that they can believe what they are told about the school system.[23]

Another promising alternative to both externally administered standardized tests and the type of internal analysis provided in Los Angeles is the external EPA, i.e., the Educational Performance Audit. An EPA is the equivalent of a financial audit, but it is an audit of the educational programs of a school district. It seeks to provide an estimate of the degree to which any selected array of programs and/or curricula provides an *optimum* solution to the district's stated goals and objectives. It provides the best estimate of the degree to which a school system is utilizing its resources.

An EPA will provide a community answers or approximations to the following questions:

1. To what extent is the range of objectives for students adequate to provide directions for the school system's selection and deployment of its resources?

2. Is the given range of programs the best or optimum answer to the stated or assumed educational requirements?

3. What search strategies and what criteria were used by the school system in selecting and/or designing the programs?

4. To what extent are the existing or planned programs working?

5. In what ways can the school system become more *responsive* to the requirements of the community and become an effective educational entity for its clients?

The major parts of an EPA are:

1. *Review of Goals/Objectives of Instruction.* The major policy and operational statements of the school system are reviewed. The analysis reveals the extent to which they can adequately serve as a proper focusing device by which educational/instructional programs can be shaped, implemented, evaluated, and improved over time.

2. *Evaluation of Programs and Curriculum.* The major programmatic thrusts of the school system are reviewed in order to determine how or

---

[22] Roger L. Rasmussen, "The Independent Analysis Unit: A Mechanism for Increased School District Accountability," paper presented at the Summer 1978 Annual Convention of the American Association of School Administrators, Minneapolis, Minn., 10 July 1978, p. 2. (Mimeographed.)

[23] Ibid., p. 10.

whether they fit the specified instructional objectives. Programs and curriculum are reviewed to evaluate the degree to which they include or exclude goals/objectives and to estimate the existing level of effectiveness at the time of assessment.[24]

3. *Analysis of the Instructional Support Systems.* The review process considers the adequacy of the instructional support systems. Investigated are the level of support services and the degree to which current deployment patterns are responsive and effective in delivering the range of programs necessary to effectively reach the objectives of instruction. Such analyses review the table of organization, descriptions of jobs, division of labor, definition of work, work flow, adequacy of communication in assigning work, and current evaluation procedures. These are evaluated, and ways they can be improved are suggested.

4. *Review of the Decision-Making Data Base.* A critical aspect of an EPA is an assesssment of the existing data base for decision making and consideration of ways in which the system can become more effective and efficient by using relevant data in decision making.

5. *Recommendations for Policy and Operational Guideline Improvement.* The recommendations in an EPA include specific new or revised policies and operational guidelines by which the performance of the school system *as a system* can be improved.

An EPA indicates to the community, board of education, administration, and staff the current strengths and weaknesses of the various programs of the school district in terms of whether they are reaching their stated instructional targets. It provides an in-depth picture of the capability of these programs to successfully muster the existing range of resources to reach the school system's goals. In essence, an EPA is a content analysis of the educational programs of a school system with a public report as to the degree to which the programs can be expected to make a difference in the lives of the students the system is expected to serve. Just as in the case of an external financial audit, the independence of the auditor from the pressures and influence of the system and of the community helps establish a kind of objective measure to which public confidence can be attached.

The Concept of Macrochange

Community attitudes and opinions can represent major problems for school districts in terms of public tolerance of and confidence in the schools. *Macrochanges,* significant movements involving attitudes and opinions in the larger society, finally penetrate to the operational level in the school. Edward Wynne cites few such macrochanges in American educa-

[24] Fenwick W. English and Frank L. Steeves, "Curriculum Evaluation," in *Secondary Curriculum for a Changing World*, 13 (Columbus, Ohio: Charles E. Merrill, 1978), pp. 295-316.

tion.[25] Among these are the common school movement of the first half of the nineteenth century, the progressive education movement, the post-Sputnik curriculum reforms, and the school desegregation and compensatory education thrusts of the late fifties and early sixties.

Wynne shows that the South did not successfully integrate its schools until there had been widespread shifts in the attitudes of the general population regarding desegregation. He cites a 1942 opinion poll which indicated that only two of five white adults considered blacks equal and a 1956 poll which showed four of five. A dramatic shift occurred between 1963 and 1965; the number of white Southern parents who indicated they would not object to blacks' attending white schools changed from 38 percent to 62 percent. It was this shift which accounted for increased desegregation of Southern school systems.

It may be in the issue of integration and busing that the politics of educational change in terms of conflict is most amply illustrated. Boards follow community opinion shifts. Where significant segments of the community resist integration, there is conflict. In describing the antibusing marches in Boston, a newspaper account indicated that as the marchers rolled past various distinct neighborhoods, the people were wearing colored armbands. Green stood for South Boston, purple for Hyde Park, red for Dorchester. The school board chairman wore an arm band of many colors, and so did longtime antibusing advocate Louise Day Hicks.[26] In her own statement in *The New York Times* decrying the necessity for busing, Mrs. Hicks said:

> Just a quick glance at modern school-curriculum guides will give the least sophisticated among us an idea of just what is happening. Motherhood and fatherhood are evidently now obsolete. Instead, a professional group, teachers, salaried by the state, is now attempting to instill values formerly taught in the home. . . .
>
> As a result, the last bastion of the nuclear family, the city neighborhood, has been turned into a battleground where parents have decided to make their last stand in defense of their God-given responsibility to control the destinies of their children until they are mature enough to assume the same role for their children.[27]

Just as the South apparently said "Never" to the 1954 *Brown* decision, so "Southie Still Says Never" in South Boston.[28] The change of membership and direction of the board of education occurred in the process of integrating the Boston schools. At the same time a federal judge put vio-

[25] Edward Wynne, "Outsiders and Insiders: Public and School Macrochange," in *The Politics of School Accountability* (Berkeley, Calif.: McCutchan Publishing Corp., 1972), pp. 101-24.

[26] John Kifner, "Busing Opponents Protest in Boston," *New York Times*, 4 April 1974.

[27] Louise Day Hicks, "Marching," *New York Times*, 3 May 1976.

[28] "S. Boston Youngsters March Against Busing," *Boston Globe*, 25 October 1976.

lence-prone South Boston into receivership and became involved himself in the selection of administrators of those schools, going over the authority of the board of education.

Considered Action: Guidelines for Curriculum Developers

Unfortunately, those involved in developing and changing curriculum in a school system cannot count on the school administration and/or board of education to offer much protection when school texts and curriculum stand in opposition to and threaten the majoritarian value system or perhaps even the value system of a strong minority subpublic in a community. Changes must first occur in the political and/or social systems before curriculum alterations which may be lasting are possible. Anaheim, Boston, Kanawha County, and countless other battles and conflicts provide documentation of the efforts of educators to take up the cause of attitudinal change with new texts and curricula in the public schools. These experiences ought to at least dispel the notion that there can be such a thing as a neutral or value-free text or curriculum. Values, as they may find expression in the schools, are *selective*. Even the choice of no value is a value-laden alternative which stands on as many assumptions as any other kind of instructional decision.

Some educators have coped with the realities of value differences by co-opting them, ignoring them, or shielding real intentions in vague language which can cover a multitude of purposes. If the term *behavioral objective* is found objectionable, then *performance objective* may be substituted. Such phrases as *individualized instruction, human relations, survival skills,* and many others allow some room for professionals to function, interpret, and reinterpret restrictive or biased viewpoints which may have been foisted upon them.

While some parents apparently desire value-free instruction, such as the three Rs, in the schools, this point of view itself is representative of a system of values in the sense that it is an assertion or denial of present school texts or curricula. There is no way the school can stay away from teaching values, whether by choice or by default.

Educators should have some notion of their community's "zone of tolerance." They should know what subjects, topics, or practices will lead to confrontation in the political arena; and they should have some idea of the real consequences of such a battle. Sometimes a hard choice will have to be made: whether to sacrifice a program in the name of progress so that a general awakening to the real issues will result or to sacrifice that same program and salvage whatever is possible from it until there is a significant shift in the community's political system. Both are hard decisions. Yet they are made all the time, and some, rather matter of factly.

As Mary Breasted so insightfully observed about sex education in Anaheim, public schools can rarely teach the whole truth about anything unless they live in perfect communities which are totally objective about life and its many values.[29] Few such communities apparently exist. Therefore the "zone of tolerance" will vary with each community's degree of consensus about what is acceptable.

Over the past 200 years, American opinion has undergone tremendous shifts. Attitudes have changed much more slowly. Only large movements, macrochanges, have resulted in any deep alterations in educational practice found in texts and curricula used in the majority of school systems.

Racist and sexist notions and practices are still to be found in schools, but they are diminishing, as they are in the larger society. Problems remain for the schools in parts of the nation that resist changing practices which reflect communities' racist and sexist attitudes. The whole truth is relative and evolving. It does not exist everywhere at once as an absolute standard for curriculum development or anything else.

Truth in school curricula is truth as found to be acceptable in the nation's political and economic systems. For that reason, politics is not only an essential ingredient of curriculum change, it is an essential element in defining the content and methodology of the curriculum at any given point in time. Curriculum conflict between school systems and their communities is first, last, and always political. There can be no realistic pure discussion of curriculum development in the schools sans serious consideration of what is ultimately acceptable to the community.

[29] Mary Breasted, *Oh! Sex Education!* (New York: Signet Books, 1971).

2

The School Ecosystem
Evelyn Lezzer Holman

VISITORS to various schools within the same school system are often struck by the diversity and unevenness of quality they find. Schools serving the same populations and seemingly following the same county program can be vastly different. To understand the differences and why they occur, an ecological view of the school is helpful. By studying the interacting components of the school ecosystem—principal, teachers, students, and community—we come to see the complex relationships that make each school unique and to discover the patterns and regularities that we often fail to note because they are so obvious. An ecological understanding can also help us work more effectively within the school and work to improve it.

In *The Culture of the School and the Problem of Change,* Seymour Sarason* provides an ecological view that forces the reader to confront the trees as well as the forest. By suspending one's values and simply describing "what is out there" in the schools, Sarason reminds educators, we often find new ways of viewing our schools.[1]

Elaboration of the Obvious

Sarason's way of looking at the obvious takes the form of a being from outer space who hovers in his space craft above a building (elementary school) and feeds observational data into a computer. This data bank reveals certain patterns. For five consecutive days the school houses many people, mostly little, and accommodates many activities; but for two days a week the building is empty. Why this pattern? Why a five–two, not a

---

* Sarason's example of using the first person to create a more informal discussion of the school will be followed in this chapter.

[1] Seymour B. Sarason, *The Culture of the School and the Problem of Change* (Boston: Allyn and Bacon, 1971).

19

four–three pattern? At regular intervals, which earthlings call a month, big people come together in the evening. The big people who were in front of the small people in the cubicles during the day do most of the talking. The other big people sometimes do what the small people do when they wish to talk: they raise their hands. What does this mean? How do we explain such regularities to this man from space? What seems obvious often has little rationale that we can articulate. Such regularities or patterns within the school often go unexamined until some change is contemplated. "The attempt to introduce a change into the school setting usually is an attempt to change a regularity that someone does not like."[2] According to Sarason, programmatic regularities such as bell ringing or length of math class are meant to effect behavioral regularities such as student attentiveness or performance on math tests; but "would academic and intellectual development be adversely affected (if mathematics were taught) four days a week instead of five?"[3]

The point is that our alternatives are limited if we cannot examine the regularities within the school and how they affect the school ecosystem. We can be so engulfed in tradition and habit that we cannot view present regularities as part of a galaxy of alternatives. The similarities between the school day and PTA meeting in the question-asking regularity may seem an elaboration of the obvious, but the implications of such programmatic regularities and their effects on teachers and students should be explored, since regularities seem to be the stuff that schools are made of.

One example of the implications of such regularities, and an argument for middle schools which can smooth students' transition from a neighborhood elementary school into the wider community of combined feeder schools, lies in this description of the obvious:

> In contrast to the elementary schools, the junior high schools are physically larger and contain more people. The students come from more than one neighborhood, they move more frequently from room to room, they have more teachers, and they have more freedom in that there is not one teacher who is their teacher and whose responsibility it is to oversee them. There is a host of new rules and regulations that the students must observe. The students are like people who have spent their lives in a small town and suddenly find themselves in a large, unfamiliar city.[4]

Curriculum Change and the Ecosystem

When contemplating change, it is prudent to ask, Are these changes intended to alter existing regularities or to become new regularities that will exist side by side with old ones? *Innovation* involves new regularities

[2] Ibid., p. 66.
[3] Ibid., p. 69.
[4] Ibid., p. 82.

that coexist with the old; *change* involves some altering of the existing regularities.[5]

Seeking change requires entering the ecosystem of the school at any one of several points:

1. Through the hierarchy or commitment of the de facto leadership;

2. Through the supporting community, by seeking to alter what it will support;

3. Through the materials of instruction, including the examination system;

4. Through the teachers, by altering their beliefs about what should be taught, to which students, and how;

5. Through the students (the clients) by altering the kind of student served by a school or a given school program.[6]

Such points include the components of the ecosystem: administration, staff, students, and community. The materials of instruction are selected by one or any combination of the components.

In considering change in the ecosystem, according to Foshay, four principles emerge. "First, innovation or change not comprehensible to the leadership of the school . . . will be trivialized or aborted."[7] As a teacher, I believed and experienced that the principal made the difference; so as a principal, I accepted that burden with all the ambivalence and guilt entailed. I sought to keep up with educational literature and never managed to do so when putting in the time the job required; I always felt the pressure of being "the key to the successful school." As a director and supervisor of principals, I still accept the conventional wisdom articulated by Foshay that the school cannot rise above "the level of sophistication of the principal; the quality of instruction cannot rise above the quality of the administrator's mind."[8]

The second principle is that successful change or innovation appears to come both "from the top down (thus being legitimated) and from the bottom up (thus being honest)."[9] Although the principal may see the classroom teacher as the key person in any change, teachers see the principal's stamp of approval as necessary to any new program or procedure. In facing the public and explaining change, the principal must legitimize what takes place in the school; but teacher support determines the honesty or need for such change.

Foshay's third principle—that "credit for the success of an innovation goes to its originator; blame for a failure is logged with the classroom

[5] Ibid., p. 109.

[6] Arthur W. Foshay, "Strategies for Curriculum Change," in *Essays On Curriculum* (New York: Columbia University, 1975), p. 95.

[7] Ibid., p. 130.

[8] Ibid.

[9] Ibid., p. 132.

teacher"[10]—illustrates a reason there is lack of motivation for teachers to change. The much-touted resistance to change on the part of teachers may reflect a firm grasp of this point. If change is to occur, teacher-proof materials and packaged programs are not the answers; such condescending approaches and attempts to circumvent teachers only alienate them. They then retreat behind negotiated agreements. A system of positive reinforcement which utilizes the internal reward system of the school provides a more effective approach.

Foshay's fourth principle, "Innovation must be locally verifiable and locally modifiable, at the classroom level,"[11] addresses the perceived conflict between theory and practice which teachers so often express. A neglected route of verification at the school level includes the obvious approach of listening to teachers. Just as we often fail to listen to students, we fail to be open-minded when teachers and parents express concerns.

When I was a principal working under budget restrictions, a multi-textbook approach usually precluded every child's having an individual textbook to take home; classroom sets were usually ordered by or for schools and shared by different classes. When teachers complained that valuable time was wasted by able students in reading assignments in class that could be completed at home, we curriculum experts labeled them inflexible. In trying to prevent a page-by-page rote curriculum which was not tailored to individual student needs, we questioned teachers' professionalism in needing the security of a textbook.

When parents echoed their desire for students to take home individually assigned texts, we explained our multitext curricula and decried any need for homework. Instead of truly listening to parent concerns and enjoying their involvement as a symbol of their caring and support of the school, we retreated behind jargon. We forgot that parents wanted homework not only because they had it when they were in school but also because it often became a family hour when reading was done in the home and the television was off. Parents could help their children and feel involved in their progress. They wanted to look at the books the students proudly brought home on the first day of school. In our attempts to protect children who could not do homework because they lived in a two-room trailer or because they worked at night, we often neglected opportunities for able children who could do homework and lost an opportunity for the concerned parent to feel he/she was parenting in the best sense of the word.

A middle ground with assigned text, not necessarily the same text for each child, and a wide variety of supplementary materials and media seems in hindsight a more prudent approach. We sometimes make our own problems by not listening and not finding the avoidable pitfalls.

[10] Ibid., p. 134.
[11] Ibid., p. 136.

Insiders and Outsiders: Stability and Change

Schools, under certain conditions, can become more vital than they currently are and . . . most of the reconstruction must occur school by school. This means that it will move forward on a broken front and not as part of a national grand strategy. But there must be help and support from outside. There must be created a productive tension between inner- and outer-directed forces.[12]

Anyone working in a school system quickly perceives that those in the schools firmly retain a concept of *insiders* and *outsiders,* with outsiders referred to as *they.* They includes anyone who does not understand the day-to-day frustrations confronting those within the schools. If a principal remains aloof from his/her faculty, he/she may become part of they. They also denotes any system or group making decisions about changes and regularities without understanding existing regularities or without considering the impact upon staff or students. The outsiders in turn feel that the insiders are antagonistic, rigid, or insecure. Often outsiders fail to consider the possibility that the staff acquired such skepticism through past dealings with outsiders who visited, formed judgments, and proclaimed their opinions far and wide.

If change is to occur, it must occur at the school level with synthesis and balance between inner- and outer-directed forces. In attempting change, we should be sure to understand the complex ecosystem and provide "feedback, acceptance and encouragement of a trustworthy source, some source whose praise is valued"[13]—preferably an insider. (One hopes, the principal.)

Ecosystem Components: The Principal

The key person is always the principal.

Foshay

As a principal, I believed that the most important characteristics for survival and success were a sense of humor, a sense of security, and a sense of perspective. As a supervisor of principals, my thoughts are the same: those principals who are respected and considered effective radiate a sense of security, humor, and perspective that sets them apart. The principal's authority remains in the public's mind if not always in the principal's own thoughts. Everyone visiting the school stops at or at least passes by the principal's office, and often a sign in the lobby demands that visitors report to the main office before proceeding. Few would argue with the statement that the principal virtually sets the tone of the school. If he/she radiates a relaxed, open, and secure manner, such an attitude permeates

---

[12] John I. Goodlad, *The Dynamics of Educational Change* (New York: McGraw Hill, 1975), p. 20.

[13] Ibid., p. 21.

the staff and infects students. Is this because such a principal gathers or attracts teachers who reflect the same qualities or because such a principal provides a climate where such attitudes are nurtured and can thrive? Probably both.

In the school ecosystem the principal's understanding assumes paramount importance; he/she must conceptualize the system, including many complex relationships, and must focus on needed change. The school's ability to change is determined by the principal's ability to synthesize the school's forces and to mediate inside and outside demands.

The principal plays a key role in the school's becoming a dynamic self-renewing place. Supreme among the components of his or her "span of control" was intellectual or conceptual management—that is, the ability to conceptualize the whole so as to visualize other possibilities and how specific steps and innovations might lead to them. This is not necessarily a personal thing; in fact, it virtually necessitates team effort and argues for staff processes . . . But it is the leadership responsibility of the principal to see that such management occurs, not now and then but as a continuing vital element of the school's functioning.[14]

"Principals' Principles"

In discussing "principals' principles," Glen G. Eye perceives the principal's major purposes as enunciating, stimulating, reinforcing, creating, and evaluating.[15] As the "enunciator of purpose," the principal ensures that all personnel understand the purpose and goals of the school. This role calls for a person who can interpret and enunciate that purpose in a clear and concise manner for parents and students. The principal's ability to articulate successfully the school's philosophy and purpose provides direction for staff and students and greatly determines the school's success in meeting its goals. Often the school's or system's philosophy remains a distant, meaningless listing of goals that few teachers understand how to translate into learning for students. Synthesizing and channeling efforts toward stated goals echoes an elaboration of the obvious; but few teachers, principals, students, or parents can clearly state their school's objectives. Just ask. In his dealing with educators, Goodlad laments that neither principals nor teachers were able to articulate clearly just what goals they thought to be the most important for their schools.[16] Helping to provide a process for arriving at consensus remains a major function of the principal. The principal mediates the delicate balance between school and school system purposes, translates the purposes into working reality, and provides staff members with a feeling they are working toward some worthwhile result that will benefit students.

[14] Ibid., p. 63.

[15] Glen G. Eye, "Principals' Principles," *Journal of Educational Research* 69 (January 1976): 189-92.

[16] Goodlad, *Dynamics*, p. 21.

The principal as "reinforcer" of accomplishments provides an avenue of reward and recognition for those working toward stated school purposes. "Notes of commendation elicit greater support of school policy than vigorous warnings about violation."[17] A positive approach encourages teachers to try harder and expand their professional know-how. We all want to be perceived as competent in our jobs and be respected as individuals; but too often principals, who we hope were teachers of the highest quality, forget the valuable classroom technique of reinforcing the good and positive. Forgetting that effective power need never be seen or used, principals sometimes erroneously perceive that superintendent, staff, students, or community will consider them ineffectual if they do not demonstrate their authority and control. The energy for change often lies in simply recognizing good teachers who can explain how they are working toward the school objectives and who receive reinforcement for doing so. Such teachers can provide a model and demonstrate good teaching more effectively than numerous bulletins on teaching techniques with which the principal floods the teaching staff. A principal who gives friendly greeting and praise to teachers for hard work and achievement encourages them to do likewise for the students. The principal's modeling for teachers provides a structured but secure and relaxed environment which ensures gradual spillover into the classroom. One quickly senses a spillover in schools when talking with staff and students who are working and thriving in such an atmosphere.

By creating a design or process for reaching goals, the principal encourages the professional staff to support needed changes. The imaginative administrator encourages an imaginative staff process in reaching consensus on goals and exploring all alternatives for reaching those goals. Although conflicts inevitably arise, an "open search for sound criteria and relevant evidence in conflict resolution will increase the principal's identity with the source of justice."[18] Solving problems together encourages a staff to consider all alternatives and feel ownership in the solutions; making defensible choices encourages teachers to be open and collaborative with parents as well as with students and each other.

The principal's role as "evaluator of product" entails a supervisory function that encourages increased voluntary scrutiny of the teaching process and continuous auditing of the learning of pupils. Evaluation of students or teachers must be seen as a continuous process. A principal's auditing of student performance as related to the school's goals encourages teachers constantly to monitor their own teaching behaviors and results. The principal who discusses his/her own role in reaching school objectives and who shares successes and failures with staff provides a model for such an ongoing process of evaluation throughout the school.

[17] Eye, "Principles," p. 191.
[18] Ibid., p. 191.

The principal must also be concerned with "consolidating people." An administrator considers timing and proper presentation before presenting new programs or making demands on a staff. Faculty meetings or presentations that are not unnecessarily long or disorganized provide a model that encourages teachers to make the best use of instructional time with students. An agenda for meetings followed by minutes or individual follow-up enables staff to flowchart goals and achievements. The principal should be able to communicate expectations clearly both in speaking and in writing, indicating what he/she perceives as the main goal of the effort, the levels of responsibility, the time table, the resources, and the limitations, while "monitoring the effort, but delegating responsibility."[19]

It is impossible to overemphasize the principal's role. While studying schools that did well on the Iowa Test of Basic Skills, the Maryland State Department of Education found a constellation of positive factors associated with high scores:

1. Strong principal leadership, e.g., schools "being run" for a purpose, rather than just "running";

2. Active participation by the principal in the classroom and instructional programs and teaching;

3. High expectations on the part of the principal with respect to student and teacher performance;

4. Perception by the principal of having control over the functioning of the school, the curriculum and program, and the staff.[20]

Goodlad echoes the key elements needed for successful schools: autonomy in the system; a sense of "mission, unity, identity and wholeness that pervades" the school; and a structure surrounding the school that is supportive. The principal is central to the attainment of the kind of school implied. She or he, far more than any other person, "shapes and articulates the prevailing ambiance and creates a sense of mission."[21]

Ecosystem Components: The Teacher

Successful teachers orchestrate 10 or more major contributions to learning in order to assist student progress. They include assuring that students understand directions before embarking on the task, maintaining momentum, keeping students involved, using positive reinforcement but not unrealistic praise, varying

[19] Margaret S. Dyer, "Mastering Change in Education: New Concepts in Leadership," *Educational Technology* (November 1976), pp. 57-58.

[20] Maryland State Department of Education, *Process Evaluation* (Baltimore, Md., 1978).

[21] John I. Goodlad, "Can Our Schools Get Better?" *Phi Delta Kappan* (January 1979): 346.

instructional techniques, alternating the length of learning episodes, providing regular and consistent feedback, and on and on.[22]

Few other jobs demand that one be enthusiastic, caring, and knowledgeable every 50 minutes with the same subject matter and the same people day after day. Teachers are expected to motivate, encourage, prod, challenge, and counsel students and at the same time demand and deserve respect. Directing large groups, giving individual attention, programming content, following lesson plans, checking papers as well as the lavatory, and keeping students moving in overcrowded halls between classes—or, at the elementary level, taking off snow boots, finding lunch boxes, wiping up milk spills, and supervising recess—these provide the daily fare of teachers. As a teacher, I felt the pressure of constantly planning for many different student needs and the emotional drain of dealing with students in need of love as much as academic training. Facing students' emotional deprivation as well as their intellectual deprivation and bearing responsibility for their intellectual growth seemed an awesome responsibility. As an idealistic young history and government teacher, I believed students needed a grasp of the past to put the present in perspective. How could they control the mechanisms of government without understanding its purpose and the reciprocal nature of our social contract? Believing, almost too fervently, that an educated populace remained the basis of our society's freedom, I felt I could help them not only to survive but to survive with understanding, intelligence, and hope—and I had one hour each day in which to accomplish such worthy goals.

The guilt and conflict resulting from not ever being able to give enough to fulfill the emotional and intellectual needs of five classes of over 30 human beings weigh heavily on the young teacher. I was always wondering how to challenge Tony, giving a kind word to Beth whose mother had just died, checking with Stan who was sleeping at the fire house because his father had thrown him out, or deciding whether to wake Joe even though he had worked late (he supported his mother but it looked bad to other students and the administration if I allowed him to sleep). All of this happened in a well-run school with sympathetic administrators in a supportive community with working class students whose parents wanted them to get a good education. One can only imagine the frustration and burnout rate of teachers working in inner-city schools or in schools with a nonsupportive administration or community.

Teachers are ill prepared for such realities. They are defeated by "their inadequate formal training for the realities of the classroom, their sheer ignorance of and lack of preparation for what life in a school would be, the demands and willingness to give and the consequence of sustained giving in a context of constant vigilance."[23]

---

[22] Ibid.
[23] Sarason, *Culture*, p. 172.

Drawing on his experience with young teachers, Sarason concludes:

First, by and large they are an eager, anxious malleable group searching rather desperately for some kind of acceptable compromise between the realities of the classroom and their fantasies about being able to help all children. Second, they are often torn between the perception that they must adhere to a schedule and a curriculum (and in some instances daily lesson plans are required) and their frequent feeling that they should depart from the routine. Third, they are quite unprepared both for the loneliness of the classroom and the lack of relationships in which questions and problems can be asked and discussed without the fear that the teacher is being evaluated. Fourth, when an evaluation-free relationship is available . . . a fair number of these young teachers are able to change, and sometimes dramatically so.[24]

My experience only confirms such observations. Only the strongest survive the first few years of teaching. At what cost to themselves or the students? Anyone sitting in a faculty lounge can sense those who have reached a level of frustration. Are teachers' comments in the faculty lounge a needed outlet for everyday stress, or are they professional cries for help with individual students or personal failure? Too often teachers' complaints about students are regarded as unprofessional rather than as attempts to find alternative ways of handling the student. In the lounge, such comments may elicit help from an experienced teacher. Why do we not formalize such needed sessions by providing seminar time in the school day for teachers to talk over mutual problems with other staff members or in-house resources? That teachers have trouble adjusting to a role which requires them to "serve as a combination traffic cop, judge, supply sergeant, and time-keeper" should be understandable, as should be the conflicts in the principal's role.[25] Teachers need help in coping with the dilemma inherent in a job that requires them to be "at once the executive (supervisory, directive, critical) and the intellectual guide and counselor (supportive, advisory, knowledge oriented)."[26] Such contradictory roles bring frustration to teachers, who often consider themselves inadequate to cope with the many situations they confront each day.

An obvious need exists to create a dynamic learning environment for teachers as well as for students. Attempts at inservice seem to offer too little too late. Teachers' remarks concerning inservice programs range from "a waste of time" to "an injection of inspiration with no lasting value." The problem lies partially in the absence of an overall cohesive plan—just a few days scattered here and there to inspire the troops. Teachers, who are told to make their classrooms interesting and appropriate to the instructional needs of individual students, find themselves herded into

[24] Ibid., p. 171.

[25] Philip W. Jackson, *Life in the Classroom* (New York: Holt, Rinehart and Winston, 1968), p. 15.

[26] Susan Kelchen Edgerton, "Teachers in Role Conflict: The Hidden Dilemma," *Phi Delta Kappan* (October 1977): 120.

mass presentations with little or no follow-up. Too often those leading the inservice are college oriented or are consultants remote from the realities of school demands. Too often the school administrators take no part in the inservice, revealing a great deal by their absence. Teachers, besieged with admonishments to provide for individual needs, to be accountable, and to provide for continuous progress of their students, find few models on inservice days and find no one concerned or accountable for their growth. Teachers frequently demand more involvement in inservice activities to protect themselves from arbitrary mass meetings offering simplistic solutions to complex problems. Teachers acutely feel the need for professional development, and their criticism of inservice reflects the quality of their experience rather than their professional interests. Inservice, to be effective, must be an integral part of each school, filling needs identified by that staff and led by both insiders and outsiders. Such comprehensive and meaningful inservice requires both money and staff for follow-up; the "band aid" approach only irritates the wound.

Each school requires some school-based specialist to whom the teachers confide weakness without fear of evaluation. Resource teachers from a school system's central office remain outsiders with little knowledge of the day-to-day problems and frustrations within a particular school. If the principal could be free to perform such a function, his/her evaluation duties would still remain; however, a master teacher who is able to work within the school, helping the principal design inservice around individual teacher teams or department needs and simply being available to listen to the problems of teachers, would provide the principal and staff with some practical expertise and help daily. The specialist's office could become a resource room for teachers, the "pedagogical service station" sought by Alexander and Goodlad, a place for teachers to "fill up" and recharge.[27] This master teacher who has the principal's ear and confidence would be a "counselor for teachers." With the myriad responsibilities of principals, the additional help of an in-house teaching specialist makes sense. Because of budget restrictions and overcrowded classes, school systems infrequently grant such "luxury" positions; however, such positions seem a necessity. Schools having adequate administrative help such as resource teachers or specialists, as well as team or departmental leaders with released time for helping teachers with their problems, seem to have fewer problems and better teacher and student morale. Unfortunately, too few schools enjoy such resources.

Teacher Concerns: Time

Most teacher complaints and concerns fall into the categories of either a lack of time or a lack of classroom management. Sarason states

[27] William M. Alexander, *MASCD Focus* (Fall Conference Maryland Association for Supervision and Curriculum Development, 1978).

that he "never met a teacher who was not aware of and disturbed by the fact that she had not the time to give some children the kind of help they needed."[28] An ungraded class may compound the organizational and management problems, for without additional staffing there is still one teacher with 30 students. Instructional aides are a mixed blessing: much organization and management are required to use them effectively. No wonder negotiated agreements are designed to protect teachers from encroachments upon their planning time, such as cafeteria or recess duty. Aides increasingly handle such duties, but administrators with little time to train and supervise aides often spend more time in the cafeteria than they do in the main office or with instruction.

Too often principals have no one to negotiate their cause and prevent the erosion of their professional time. Polarization of teachers and administrators easily occurs when lessening demands on one results in a heavier burden for the other. Teachers in overcrowded and understaffed schools find themselves in a vicious circle; overworked administrators are busy coping with daily crises and have little time to listen to teachers' concerns; teachers feel the administration remains aloof and unsympathetic.

This author conducted one survey of an overcrowded school in which 75 percent of the faculty stated that the administration "did not care" and that a majority of the student body had a "poor attitude." Students, too, responded that "teachers did not care" about them and did not take time to "pat them on the back" and give encouragement. Intervention in this debilitating circle of perceived isolation was obviously needed.

Teacher Concerns: Discipline

A biology class begins with the teacher reviewing lab proceedings and reminding students to fill in the lab worksheet. Several students continue private conversations in the back of the class; another boy reads a James Bond novel; two girls chat and comb their hair with only slight acknowledgment of the teacher's presence. Two boys coming late take seats near the back and continue their discussion in low tones. Several students near the front listen while thumbing through their lab workbooks, hunting for the lab report. The teacher ignores any lack of interest and continues to address the few who seem to be paying attention.

One hour later the same group of students enters a Shakespeare class. Students take their seats quickly, take out a copy of *Othello* and review their notes from the previous day. Students discuss the characters in the play in quiet but interested tones. When the teacher moves from the hall, closes the door, and seats himself in front of the semicircle of desks, all students are quiet, waiting for him to speak. "Yesterday, we discussed the character of Desdemona as typical or atypical of Shakespeare's heroines. Tom felt. . . . How many of you agree?"

[28] Sarason, *Culture*, p. 152.

Although both teachers have the same academic group (supposedly academic students are more easily controlled), the biology teacher acquires a reputation of being easy, and staff members label him as having little control; yet the English teacher enjoys a respected reputation of being interesting but hard, and fellow colleagues admire his discipline. What amorphous characteristics of the latter teacher make the young man reading James Bond say, "I'd never try that in his English class"? We say the English teacher has discipline. Such discipline remains so subtly integrated into the instructional atmosphere of the class as to defy its existence; it is recognizable only by the lack of any problems or distractions. Educators know that one can't separate discipline from instruction; however, in order to study class management and guide young teachers in how-to seminars, we isolate key elements. Young teachers often say "What would you do if such-and-such occurred?" when such a situation would probably not occur in an experienced teacher's classroom. However, the classroom structure or previous handling of more minor situations would have set the tone and prevented the incident. For example:

New teacher enters the classroom and students continue talking. "All right class, let me have your attention." A few students continue to chat. Raising her voice, "I said, let me have your attention. Quiet down." Murmurs continue but the teacher begins the lesson, talking over the underlying current of noise. Five minutes into the lesson, the conversation is too distracting to continue. Teacher interrupts the class to call down the students who are talking and then resumes her remarks. After a few moments, the students continue their distracting conversation. The teacher assigns detention and warns that offenders will be sent to the office if the talk continues.

The experienced teacher closes the door, walks to the center of the room and establishes eye contact with as many students as possible. Students look around the room at anyone still talking. A prolonged stare at one corner brings the desired eye contact and, smiling and relaxed, she begins the lesson. Five minutes into the lesson two students start a conversation; the teacher continues to talk but moves toward the offenders and proceeds with the lesson beside the conversationally minded students. Her proximity discourages further talk, and few students notice the teacher involved in discipline.

Shooting butterflies with rifles quickly turns the young teacher into a screamer or worse. A sparse repertoire of responses to student distractions can result in quick failure for the new teacher. But no one has taught her otherwise; she is left to her own devices after an hour-long faculty meeting to review the school's policy and procedure handbook and a quick departmental meeting to assign appropriate textbooks. Few administrators take the time to teach new staff the skills necessary for good discipline, and thus their administrative time becomes occupied by students sent to the office by teachers who lack basic discipline skills.

. . . Discipline is the morale obtained under institutionalized leadership. It is observable in the social interaction of the persons concerned, and it rests upon psychic arrangements in the minds of those persons. Discipline is partly personal influence and partly the social standing of the office. It is the resultant from the filtering of the teacher's personality through the porous framework of the institution.[29]

Although personality filters through the institution, teachers need training in the specifics of classroom management. Physical proximity to students, eye contact, quick response to possible distractions, and a wide variety of nonverbal or low-key responses can help the new teacher cure rather than contribute to discipline problems. It falls to the schools to train teachers in classroom management because that is where the students are and where those experienced teachers are who have the skills of classroom management. Observation of other teachers' skills remains unprofitable, however, without someone to point out the small details that make for a smooth-running classroom. New teachers are often amazed that the same students act so differently in an experienced teacher's class, but they lack the sophistication to see what actions on the part of the teacher cause the difference in student behavior.

Teacher as Model

Just as the principal sets the tone for the school, the teacher sets the tone for his/her students. A teacher who is interested in ideas often finds students eager to emulate that model. I can remember visiting an English class where two teachers were engaged in a debate over the character of Phinney in *A Separate Peace*. The students supported the view of their own teacher but were amazed that the two teachers had the intellectual openness and security to admit that the arguments of each were well grounded in the plot development. Such models of adults actively, excitedly involved in literature and the interpretation of character were rare; two teachers respecting the intellectual competence of each other without closure on who was right or wrong provided an invaluable model for students. Sarason notes that teachers "thinking about thinking, which is never made public, is precisely what the children are interested in and excited by on those rare occasions when it becomes public."[30] A student named Sharon, after seeing the play *1776* and discussing it with two social studies teachers and an English teacher, wrote a note and called the experience "the most exciting learning experience I ever had." The teachers were pleased but failed to recognize or capitalize on the potential for motivation and learning discovered. The obvious can so easily be ignored.

---

[29] Willard Waller, The *Sociology of Teaching* (London: John Wiley and Sons, 1932), p. 197.

[30] Sarason, *Culture*, p. 187.

Ecosystem Components: The Student

Over the last quarter of a century, dramatic changes in family stability have affected our nation's young. The threadbare social fabric surrounding the family seems unable to provide the emotional warmth and support students need to cope with their world. Divorce, illegitimate births, and desertions cause one in every six children to live in a one-parent home, usually with a mother who has little money or time to spend with her children. Even in two-parent homes, increasing job demands, commuting, and community obligations mean parents spend "less time working, playing, reading, and talking with their children."[31] Since the majority of mothers need to work, children returning from school find an empty house where they are left to their own devices. "Replacing parents, relatives, neighbors, and other caring adults are . . . television, peer groups, and loneliness."[32]

Television becomes the ever present baby-sitter, enabling tired parents to tune out their children and allowing children to succumb passively to a mental preoccupation with fantasy and make-believe at best—and sex and violence at worst. Most students own their own television sets, thus preventing adult-child confrontation over programs; and some families relegate children to watch television in their bedrooms while the traditional living room or family room is reserved for adult viewing.

Peer groups play an increasingly important role in the emotional fabric of students. Students finding few adults with whom to talk rely on each other for guidance in deciding right and wrong; conformity to group standards too often becomes the measure of good. With no one at home when they return from school, latch-key children receive little or no adult care and rely on each other for basic emotional needs.

Parents trapped by poverty, work demands, or the cult of individualism often fail to recognize their responsibilities and the frustration and loneliness of their children. Juvenile suicide and crime have tripled in the last 15 years; in some communities, drugs and alcohol abuse seem commonplace. From the segregation and loneliness of children emerge the alienation and hostility of the young adult.

For the ecosystem to survive, the components must interact and support the system. School provides only a small portion of the skills, attitudes, knowledge, and habits needed by students.

In the past, experiences in the home, the work situation, and the school made somewhat different contributions to the development of American youth. Most young people acquired their basic habits of orderliness, punctuality, and attention to work primarily through experiences in the home and work setting,

---

[31] Urie Bronfenbrenner, "The Disturbing Changes in the American Family," *Search* (Albany: State University of New York, Fall 1976), p. 5.

[32] Ibid., p. 6.

with the helpful supplementation of the school's regimen. They came to recognize the meaning and importance of the productive work through participating in family chores and through holding part-time jobs that often involved the close supervision and critical appraisal of their efforts.[33]

In the past, students were actively involved in family and community. Today, increased use of role playing in schools reflects a need to expand the limited experiences of students, but simulations cannot substitute for real social interaction. Schools must be an integral part of a community and provide for shared educational opportunities in that community.

Support Systems Needed

More school-based support must be established; more pupil personnel workers, school psychologists, and social workers are needed. Often a school of over a thousand students receives the services of a school psychologist or pupil personnel worker (home visitor) less than one-half day each week. Overlapping bureaucracies could be reduced if community-school liaison groups received adequate resources of people, money, and time to do the job. School counselors need to be trained to work with parents as well as children. With adequate funding, counselors and school personnel could run programs at night for parents who need help with their parenting skills. In the Gallup Poll of educational attitudes, three of four adults surveyed favored school-based night courses about handling children's problems and were willing to pay additional taxes to support such programs.[34] Presently many school personnel try to run parent programs in addition to the rigorous demands of the regular school day. In some schools teachers do not know the name of the pupil personnel worker or psychologist who services their school population. This statement is not meant as a reflection on services but a reflection on how too few resources are marshalled to help the students and their families.

Students and Skills

Since the College Entrance Board's announcement of the Scholastic Aptitude Test scores' decline, school systems and parents across the country have cried "back to the basics"; the three Rs of reading, writing, and arithmetic, not frills, have merited educators' attention. However, the problem does not lie in mastering basics alone. Student scores for spelling, punctuation, and reading recall show no decline; neither are basic arithmetic skills lacking. But students seemingly lack the higher complex skills of making inferences and analogies or the ability to organize concepts into coherent paragraphs.[35] Placing blame provides little help to students

[33] Ralph W. Tyler, "The New Emphasis In Curriculum Development," *Educational Leadership* (October 1976): 65.

[34] George H. Gallup, "Ninth Annual Gallup Poll of the Public's Attitude Toward Public School," *Phi Delta Kappan* (September 1977): 41.

[35] Christopher Jencks, "The Wrong Answer for Schools Is:," *Washington Post*, 19 February 1978.

or reassurance to parents. Rather than speculate over the decline, attack statistics, or take defensive postures, educators must demonstrate student mastery of the three Rs and progress to a broader view of skills. We must show parents that students need not only the three Rs but more—perhaps the three Cs: coding, critical thinking, caring.

Sharing civilization's wealth of knowledge, communicating and expanding that knowledge, and caring about the impact of that knowledge on ourselves, each other, and the world—these translate into the three Cs of coding, critical thinking, and caring. *Coding* includes the communication and computation processes or systems that encompass our human heritage of knowledge. Knowledge of the symbols that comprise language or communications systems, including mathematical equations and scientific formulae, is crucial for students seeking access to that heritage. The traditional three Rs of reading, writing, and arithmetic fall under coding. *Critical thinking* requires the incorporation of logic, decision making and problem solving as part of the daily fare for all students. An atmosphere of *caring*—caring for self, others, and our environment—must permeate our schools. Without students who care, all our knowledge and thinking signify nothing.

Coding: Communication and Computation. "Knowledge, in principle, is information that can be coded explicitly in a symbolic system."[36] To acquire information or to pass on knowledge, we must be able to decode the various symbolic systems. Any type of communication—listening, speaking, reading, writing, or nonverbal communication—requires decoding skills which enable us to understand the symbols that form the building blocks of knowledge, past experience, and culture. An understanding or decoding of $e = mc^2$ or H_2O enables us to manipulate, catalog, and mentally store the symbols necessary for thinking. Helping students to understand the coding process and tap the storehouse of human knowledge remains a basic aim of education. Literacy in various symbolic codes is the primary concern of education.[37] Before a student can think critically, understand the view of others, or test his/her concept of what another may be thinking or feeling, the student must grasp the codes so integral to our own or any civilization. Communication and computational skills receive, and rightly so, great emphasis in our schools. Most schools continue their commitment to filling any gaps in students' coding skills. Rather than retreating from teaching basic skills, educators continue to help each student acquire as much of the great reservoir of human knowledge as possible. In the past some educators thought that students drowned in a flood of symbols that they were unable to absorb, so teach-

---

[36] David R. Olson, "What is Worth Knowing and What Can Be Taught," *School Review* (November 1973): 42.

[37] Ibid., p. 35.

ers attempted to slow down and control the flow of factual information. This effort was interpreted as less emphasis on basic skills; however, the goal remained to facilitate the absorption and learning process, not stop it. Any code requires experience with the concepts symbolized. To pronounce the word *escalator* or read $e = mc^2$ does not ensure understanding or an ability to manipulate the code in the mind. The *act* of *actually* seeing an escalator may be necessary in the decoding process. Widening the experiential background of students through field trips and other exploratory activities helps students gain new symbols and requires them to catalog experiences and to communicate those experiences by using coding skills.

Critical Thinking. Whether it be serving well at tennis or thinking critically, any skill demands modeling and a system of responses regarding performance. If students are to think critically, teachers must model the intellectual process and be able to lead and explore alternatives with students. If intelligence is skill in the cultural medium, students must explore the culture, finding patterns and analogies; but they need intellectual leadership in doing so. Recent articles in educational journals express concern that teachers are too content oriented. Certainly a teacher must care about the student first, but after rapport and caring relationships are established, what do we teach a student but manipulation of content—whether it be vowels, analogies, or statistics? In order to lead the student in discovery, a teacher must model intellectual curiosity and be able to structure the content in many ways for different students' backgrounds. The teacher who does not easily manipulate content cannot present a concept in the many different ways good teaching requires.

I am reminded of an advanced statistics class where I finally conjured nerve to ask a question and to interrupt a professor who was busy filling the board with equations. He repeated his explanation, not once but twice, using exactly the same words; but my deficiency was not a listening problem. After class, another professor who could approach the problem in many ways quickly alleviated my frustration. The first professor was not too content oriented. He lacked the firm grasp of his field that allows complex problems to be related in simple terms with practical explanations to students of various needs and backgrounds.

The often heard but senseless dichotomy of elementary teachers being child oriented and secondary teachers being content oriented makes little sense. As a child reaches various levels of sophistication he/she must have teachers able to diagnose and prescribe for his/her needs at that level. Students who reach the formal operational level need exposure to content that allows for transfer and synthesis of previous learning just as students who have reading problems need special help. What is needed is a secure environment for all students to attempt and fail, to explore and retreat with constant encouragement that allows for the necessary practice in the skill of critical thinking. Seminars, discussion groups, and student involvement in decision making and problem solving all help students apply and transfer such skill. Students who complain of irrelevant courses and boredom within schools speak to the need for challenging students and involving our youth in the problems of the community and school. If students are to be able to perceive patterns, grasp limitless factual information, decide what questions to ask and what knowledge society must store and value, they must learn to think critically about today's problems. Administrators, counselors and teachers who model problem solving, consider alternatives, and listen respectfully to all points of view provide needed models of intellectual openness. One cannot become skilled in tennis without practice; and one does not learn to make decisions, solve problems, and think critically without practice.

Caring. Caring, a commitment to self and others, cannot be absorbed from an environment devoid of concern for students. Students need concerned adults as models. If administrators and teachers care about students and show they care, students will care about themselves, each other, and their world. A sense of community and concern must permeate the ecosystem of the school and be modeled by everyone with whom the student comes in contact, from the principal to the cafeteria worker. By working with the families and with the community, the schools can provide an extension of the caring function, which must be encouraged.

Ecosystem Components: Community and School

Schools must provide opportunities for parent involvement. Not *one* but *all* the communication avenues should be explored. Study groups provided by school staff to help parents and time set aside within the teacher's school day for parent talks on an informal basis help the home-school bond. Too often a phone call or contact with the school results from negative incidents or problems. Adjusting teachers' work hours so that parents can drop by school after work one day a week requires only minor schedule changes but pays off in strong school support by working parents. School-related questionnaires and newsletters provide parents with the feeling that they are an important and integral part of the ecosystem.

Family structure, ideals, and patterns of behavior should be supported and strengthened, not disrupted by school system decisions and actions. In an age characterized by rapid demographic change, high mobility, fluctuating values, and accelerating social change, it becomes increasingly important for children and their families to have islands of strength. A community with a sense of identity can provide a significant place for the development of both family and social bonds which bring together home and school to the mutual benefit of both.[38]

[38] Gordon Anderson, "Sense of Community," (Frederick, Md.: Board of Education of Frederick County) p. 2.

A feeling of ownership by the community and students reinforces identification with the school.

Family and community must be supported by school decisions. Redistricting, new schools, and boundary changes often work against the community. Two equally expensive proposals may produce decidedly unequal benefits in human terms. To build a more economical new school rather than to renovate an existing structure with community ties may be a huge loss in the human element. A renovated facility that enjoys the tradition and emotional investment of the community may be esthetically, historically, and humanly a better investment than a modern facility that does not enjoy the ownership of the community. One need not wonder why the school that enjoys community support, the school from which brothers and sisters, mothers and fathers have graduated, the school whose students identify with the facility seems to have less vandalism.

Case Study

Studies of curriculum change generally seek to account for success or failure in bringing about curriculum change. Many of the studies of curriculum change processes focus on formal planning as a determinant of success. Others emphasize the human factors. Still others point to the availability of resources of various types as a critical factor. Some concentrate on the organization and its social roles. Others concentrate on questions of participation and authority. All seek to disclose how the last steps between formal planning and actual delivery of a curriculum to school and classroom are, can be, and should be taken.[39]

That studies of curriculum change revolve around formal planning, availability of resources, organization, social roles, participation, and authority, as well as the human factor, indicates that all play an important role in change. How does interaction of such factors influence the ecosystem's balance? That some blend of the factors contributes to the relative success of change merits consideration. Without attempting to analyze the blend, the following case study illustrates one attempt at building a viable ecosystem.

Establishing a New Middle School: Old Mill Middle School North, Glen Burnie, Maryland

In 1975 the Anne Arundel County Board of Education in Annapolis, Maryland, adopted a middle school philosophy that included certain specific goals. The middle school philosophy culminated the work of a professional committee determined to provide a smooth transition and secure environment for the student between elementary school and senior high. The school was to reflect the needs of youngsters in sixth, seventh, and eighth grades rather than to imitate senior high school by being a junior

---

[39] Decker F. Walker, *Toward Comprehension of Curricular Realities* (Palo Alto, Calif.: Stanford University), p. 5.

high school. Night dances and activities, as well as competitive sports, were replaced by intramurals and after-school activities that were of a non-dating nature. A teacher guidance program that provided support for youngsters coming from neighborhood elementary schools into the larger middle school community was to be established; and more cooperation between home and school, with additional parent involvement was sought. Teachers who were cognizant and understanding of the middle school students' needs and were able to provide for those needs seemed necessary. Exploratory activities that broadened students' experiential background without causing fear of failure were to be encouraged. The middle school philosophy reflected a need for a departmental organization to articulate the skills and an interdisciplinary organization to integrate the skills, providing transfer and meeting individual student needs.

As a new middle school, Old Mill Middle School North enjoyed the luxury of a well-defined county program and a middle school philosophy established by county professional staff and supported by the board of education. Such prior planning paid dividends to all involved. The principal, who was a member of the county middle school committee and was appointed a year prior to the new middle school's opening, selected a staff committed to the philosophy and goals of the middle school. A commitment of staff to a philosophy does not preclude future differences of opinion, but it does ensure a common frame of reference for discussion. The availability of a central-purchasing agent to help order equipment and materials for the new building made it possible for the principal's time to be spent on curriculum, inservice, staffing, and student needs.

Because the new school necessitated a reassignment of feeder schools, much administrative time was devoted to building community identification and support for the concept of middle schools. Parents voiced anxiety for sixth graders leaving smaller neighborhood elementary schools and entering the large Old Mill complex. Besieged by media reports of drugs and discipline in larger schools, parents needed reassurance. The purpose of the middle school entailed protecting and keeping students "younger" by enabling the middle school youngsters to mature in an environment designed for them rather than in a miniature high school, a junior high. Adding to parental fears was the knowledge that the building would be the open space design that some parents associated with permissiveness. Coffee clatches at 7 a.m. and 7 p.m. in community homes provided opportunities for the principal to talk with parents and listen to their concerns, fears, and hopes. These meetings built a base of community support. Meetings with feeder school groups and talks to local organizations and civic associations furthered the concept of middle schools and allayed initial concerns of parents.

Departmental leaders, resource teachers, and counselors were chosen by the principal before February of the year prior to school's opening. They came from many schools in the county system but managed to meet and plan programs, discuss philosophy and goals, and order materials and equipment. Having insiders who understood, supported, and could articulate middle school goals provided the first step toward implementing and achieving school objectives. School leaders who could help teachers transform written philosophy and aims into reality by modeling the day-to-day expertise added invaluable support.

Teacher selection criteria included commitment to the middle school philosophy and a willingness to work on both departmental and interdisciplinary teams. Each teacher also accepted the role of teacher-advisor for a group of middle school students. Before being assigned to the Old Mill Middle staff, teachers currently in the county system received a class visit from the principal.

All teachers assigned to the school attended summer workshops prior to school's opening. Since county funding paid for only a one-week workshop for new schools and the staff felt more preparation time was needed, a two-credit workshop submitted to the Maryland State Department of Education permitted longer workshop time. Department or team leaders, paid for five additional work days during the summer, planned for immediate staff needs and formed the basic structure for an ongoing faculty inservice program. In addition, six staff members took a county-sponsored course on middle schools and developed Teacher Advisor Program (TAP) materials during the course.

Prior to opening, days were scheduled when parents could come in and meet with teacher-advisors and the interdisciplinary team responsible for their children. Student volunteers from the feeder schools acted as guides for parents and conducted student tours during August. Because students' first opinion of the school would influence parents' perceptions of the open-space middle school, every effort went into the first few school days. Highly structured plans reflected a concern with student adjustment. Hopefully, students felt comfortable but challenged. The important dimension resided in the process by which decisions involving all aspects of the school were made. Administrators meeting with departmental or team leaders on a daily basis for the first week allowed quick feedback as to what areas needed attention or where possible changes could avert problems. A collaborative feeling of making a good start and having a stake in the success or failure of the middle school concept spurred extra effort that overcame the frustrations of opening school two weeks late without many of the books and materials which had been ordered.

To encourage community involvement, on each Wednesday, after regular student dismissal, the interdisciplinary teams met to discuss program and student progress with parents. Parents appreciated the informal nature of such conferences and were reassured by the realization that they could drop by school without incurring red tape. Parent questionnaires, open house days, and newsletters all encouraged an open-door policy that delivered many parent volunteers to the school's doorstep. Volunteers received training conducted by the school's resource teacher. Parent-Teacher-Student Association and the Citizens Advisory Committee jointly sponsored monthly meetings that turned into seminars on parenting skills. The school psychologist provided evening courses for parents, and the school counselors held guidance sessions for parents, dealing with problems identified by PTSA questionnaires.

Approaching the parent-school relationship on many levels encouraged home-school cooperation. Welcoming parents to participate and view the working school did much to alleviate concerns. Inservice time devoted to teaching teachers how to handle controversial issues and parent complaints when they naturally occur provided teachers with background and an accepting attitude that reaped rich rewards in community support of the staff.

Each week the principal met with department heads to ensure an open organization and communication structure that encouraged a flow of concerns and shared decision making. Staff questionnaires provided input for inservice and faculty meetings devoted to instructional concerns. Bulletins discussed at departmental or interdisciplinary meetings led by the principal, resource teacher, or other in-house personnel met administrative needs. Utilization of consultants required prior planning with school committees and follow-up by school staff. The most effective inservice involved teachers' seeing their peers demonstrating behaviors supported by the school administration and leading to specific middle school objectives.

Resource teachers and department chairpersons worked in instructional areas and modeled desired teaching behaviors; but at the same time they managed to observe program, work closely with teachers, and also fulfill an administrative function. By removing uncooperative students from main instructional areas, assigning conference time or detention, and suggesting alternative ways of handling instructional or behavior problems to teachers, department chairpersons provided on-the-spot expertise. Such immediate access to a master teacher or someone with authority prevented all but the most serious problems from reaching the main office, thus allowing administrators time to work with teachers on instruction and curriculum rather than the small but time-consuming problems that prevent long-range planning.

At the end of the first year, the relative success in meeting goals seemed directly proportional to the amount of time and emphasis given the goals by the administration. Student questionnaires elicited positive comments toward the school. Asked what they liked most about school, students responded with "the teachers" and comments such as "we can talk to them" or "they listen." Other activities mentioned most often by students were TAP; mini-courses; field trips to the Port of Baltimore, the Smithsonian in Washington, and Historic Annapolis; or other activities revolving around the school's Bicentennial themes. Questionnaires sent to parents reflected strong support for the school staff. The staff's willingness to welcome parents each Wednesday afternoon and the interdisciplinary team organization were heralded by parents as strong points of the school. During the second year Old Mill Middle School North received mention by the Maryland Congress of Parents and Teachers, Inc. for work in school-community relations.

Expansion of special areas required adding new staff members at the end of the first year. Providing inservice for new teachers while continuing regular staff development proved a heavy but necessary burden. Weekly meetings for new teachers included inservice topics covered by the staff the previous year. Fortunately, Old Mill Middle School North became a teacher training center for the University of Maryland and part of a joint county-university effort to institute a middle school emphasis for teachers. This cooperative endeavor provided a school-trained, school-supervised, and school-evaluated pool of prospective teachers that alleviated problems of replenishing the middle school staff and provided the additional help of as many as 20 student teachers in the school.

Old Mill Middle North followed a process that enabled the components of the school to fuse in a viable ecosystem. It was buffeted by the same problems that confront most schools, but it held together with the strong interaction that makes the whole stronger than the parts.

3

Classroom Culture and the Problem of Control
Joseph C. Grannis

SCHOOL CLASSROOMS everywhere are different and the same. The tendency of educators and citizens to project their visions of a better life on the schools has, along with modern technology, contributed to a proliferation of designs for classrooms. We can point to classrooms that purport to be open or closed; nongraded or graded; oriented to individuals, groups, or a class as a whole; and concerned more with basics or with enrichment. For each of these and their combinations we can find a political and technical rationale. Classrooms vary also in their populations: teachers or pupils are of one or another gender, age, socioeconomic status, ethnicity, and aptitude. For these reasons one might expect strong differences between the cultures of various classrooms.

We observe also, however, that virtually all classrooms have in common certain features. Formally, these features include an expectation that teachers will inculcate in their pupils certain knowledge, skills, and standards of conduct; the daily, seasonal, and life-span time frame within which schooling is conducted; and the high ratio of pupils to teachers—high, that is, compared with the proportion of children or youths to adults that is found in most settings outside schools. Informally, classrooms are characterized by behavior patterns that include responses to these conditions—responses which, in the eyes of many observers, are more similar than dissimilar.

The formal conditions of schooling generate what we can call the problem of control in classrooms. Indeed, turning things around somewhat, we must ask whether classrooms are not themselves an adaptation to the problem of control in schooling. The core of the culture of a class-

NOTE: The development of this chapter was supported by the ERIC Clearinghouse on Urban Education, Teachers College, Columbia University, funded by the National Institute of Education. The points of view stated herein do not necessarily represent official position or policy of the National Institute of Education.

room is a teacher's and the pupils' responses to the problem of control. This will be our central argument. The argument assumes that this culture, what we have elsewhere called the structure of school experience, is the most powerful and enduring aspect of the curriculum of school and classroom.[1] The most clearly patterned and frequently recurring organizations of school and classroom life *are* the curriculum that observation discovers.

We shall begin by characterizing a standard classroom culture and examining the sources of the general problem of control. Later the chapter will turn to variations on this pattern and explore the significance of differences among pupils and between alternative designs for the classroom. Ultimately, one must ask how the problem of control in classrooms relates to problems of control in society at large. However, those analyses—of which there are many now—that immediately leap to the socializing and sorting functions of schooling overlook the more immediate origins of the problem of control in the peculiar ecology of schools themselves.

The Sameness of Classrooms

The point to be made first is not simply that all classrooms are alike, but that there is a standard classroom situation that is very difficult to alter. In the late 1960s Goodlad and Klein conducted observations in 150 classrooms, ranging from kindergarten through third grade, and about equally distributed between large and small proportions of disadvantaged children. (The term *disadvantaged* itself assumes a cultural standard.) About half of the sample schools were involved as single schools or as part of their districts in projects or activities supported by supplementary funds from local, state, federal, or private sources. The time, it will be recalled, stood toward the end of a decade and a half of rationalist school reform—team teaching and nongraded instruction, for which Goodlad had been one of the most outspoken proponents, and numerous national curriculum projects, including a variety at the elementary school level. Goodlad and Klein found a general pattern which is most sharply conveyed by the physical image of the classrooms they observed:

In regard to seating, the kindergarten rooms almost always provided some kind of table-and-chair arrangement, a pattern that faded until individual desks in rooms became equally uniform for the third grade. Similarly, the rug corners and reading circles of the first two years had virtually disappeared by the third and fourth.

The general picture is that of a play-like environment of the kindergarten, with considerable opportunity for freedom of movement and activity, giving

[1] Joseph C. Grannis, "The School As a Model of Society," *Harvard Graduate School of Education Bulletin* (Autumn 1967): 14-27. Reprinted in *The Learning of Political Behavior*, eds. Norman Adler and Charles Harrington (Glenview, Ill.: Scott Foresman, 1970); cf. Robert Dreeben, *On What is Learned in School* (Reading, Mass.: Addison-Wesley, 1968).

way to a much more restricted and circumscribed academic environment thereafter. By the third grade, materials and seating arrangements suggest a passive, immobile pattern characterized by seatwork and total group activity under teacher direction.[2]

Overall, reading in groups was the most frequent activity observed. Second most frequent was "independent activities," which, between kindergarten and third grade, shifted from physical movement, especially manipulation of objects, toward academic work. Arithmetic, language arts other than reading (writing, spelling, listening to stories, etc.), singing and music, and physical education made up the remainder of the activities that, together, constituted more than 85 percent of the classroom events observed. Goodlad and Klein did find variations in this pattern between the "regular" and the predominantly disadvantaged classes. Disadvantaged children spent proportionally more time than advantaged children in reading in first grade, but less time in reading in third grade. The disadvantaged third grade children also spent less time in singing and music, physical education, and independent work of a relatively creative sort or at least selected by the children from a set of options. They spent correspondingly *more* time in prescribed seatwork, in workbooks and so forth, which Goodlad and Klein characterize as "busy work." [3] Finally, the proportions of time spent in artithmetic were comparable for the different classes throughout the grades. These findings foreshadow those of other research that we will attend to later in the chapter. However, Goodlad and Klein end up giving greatest emphasis to the similarities between classes:

One conclusion stands out clearly: many of the changes we have believed to be taking place in schooling have not been getting into classrooms; changes widely recommended for the schools over the past 15 years were blunted on school and classroom door. Second, schools and classrooms were marked by a sameness regardless of location, student enrollment, and "typing" as provided initially to us by an administrator.

Third, there seemed to be a considerable discrepancy between teachers' perceptions of their own innovative behavior and the perceptions of observers. The teachers sincerely thought they were individualizing instruction, encouraging inductive learning, involving children in group processes, and so on. Fourth, "special," supplementary, and enrichment activities and practices differed very little from "regular" classroom activities. Fifth, general or specific classroom goals were not identifiable to observers. Instruction was general in character and not specifically directed to diagnosed needs, progress, and problems of individual children. Teachers shot with a shotgun, not a rifle. Sixth, the direction being pursued by the school as a whole was equally obscure or diffused.

Seventh, there appeared not to be a critical mass of teachers, parents, and others working together toward developing either a sense of direction or solutions to school-wide problems concerning them. Eight parallels number seven:

---

[2] John I. Goodlad and M. Francis Klein, *Behind the Classroom Door* (Worthington, Ohio: Charles A. Jones Publishing Company, 1970), p. 63.

[3] Personal communication from the authors. The increase in seatwork is implied but not explicated in *Behind the Classroom Door*.

school personnel appeared to be very much alone in their endeavors. Principals tended to remain in offices and hallways and not to intrude on sacred classroom ground in any direct way. Teachers, although alone and presumably free to teach in their classrooms, appeared to be bound to a common conception of what school is and should be.[4]

The highly teacher-dominated verbal interactions Goodlad and Klein observed "behind the classroom door" are very consistent with those observed a decade before by Hughes[5] in a sample of 41 both recommended and randomly selected elementary school classrooms. The more general behavior patterns are consistent with various observations in elementary school classrooms, ranging from Jackson's dispassionate *Life in Classrooms*[6] to Holt's polemical *How Children Fail*.[7]

At the junior and senior high school level, a similar variety of studies attest to the sameness of classrooms. The *Report of the National Panel on High Schools and Adolescent Education*,[8] to which a group of widely experienced and distinguished educators contributed, concluded that the organization of high schools around the classroom unit has tended to render them "inflexible in their adaptive capacity to encompass newer instructional forms and prodecures." Since these newer forms and procedures—at the high school level these include team teaching, the use of paraprofessionals, flexible scheduling, modules, mini-schools, and various inductive and experiential approaches to learning—have been meant to *break* the mold of the classroom unit, and in a limited number of cases have done so, it appears that organization around the classroom unit has tended to *resist* these changes.

Inside the standard high school classroom, most of what takes place overtly is talk, and most of the talk is by the teacher. The typical pattern of talk is teacher question/student answer/teacher reaction followed by teacher question. The questions generally ask for recall or extrapolation of knowledge, making minimal demands on students' critical, creative, or empathic capacities; and capacities of this sort that students do have are manifested more in their myriad ways of refining the classroom game than in what one first thinks of as critical, creative, or empathic activity.

Quotations from two first-hand accounts of life in secondary schools will illustrate these claims. Cusick participated in the student life of a comprehensive school that drew lower- to middle-class students from small

[4] Goodlad and Klein, *Classroom Door*, pp. 97-98.

[5] Marie M. Hughes and others, *A Research Report: The Assessment of the Quality of Teaching* (Salt Lake City: University of Utah, 1959).

[6] Philip W. Jackson, *Life in Classrooms* (New York: Holt, Rinehart & Winston, 1968).

[7] John Holt, *How Children Fail* (New York: Pitman, 1964).

[8] John H. Martin. (Chairman) *Report of the National Panel on High Schools and Adolescent Education*. Washington, D.C.: GPO, 1975.

towns and rural and suburban areas. One of the observations that sets the stage of his book is the following:

> Exceptions do occur, especially in classes where the students are divided into work units and carry out some prearranged experiment or project in co-operation with one another. There the teacher carries on his instruction by walking around, interacting with them encouraging one group at a time. But these are classes such as physics or chemistry labs where the lab manuals and texts lay out the step by step process to be followed, and there too the methods are structured and the answers set. It is not enough just to say simply that there were good and bad classes, good and bad teachers. The fact was that the teaching in all classes, science, math, English, language, was remarkably similar. The teacher would take care of his basic maintenance activity: take attendance, close the door, accept late slips, take out his book, and call the page number; then he would structure the activity by acting out the part of questioner, encourager, teller, and explicator, doing, of course, most of what there was to do while the students watched, waited, and responded to his cues. This was the way classes were conducted day in and day out.[9]

Herndon taught in an inner-city junior high school, "about 98 percent Negro, they had told me downtown in the district office, as if to say not entirely Negro." At one point, Herndon was frustrated by the failure of class discussions to lead to writing.

> The problem with 9D was to find out what they wanted done which needed the classroom, the school situation to do, which couldn't be done otherwise.[10]

Herndon was absent for a month. When he returned,

> 9D . . . greeted me with an indignant and sincere-sounding outcry. Mrs. A was a better teacher than I, she was a real teacher, I wasn't no real teacher, she really made them work, not just have them old discussions every day; no, man, they were learning spelling and sentences and all they was spozed to. Moreover she was strict and didn't allow fooling around—all in all they felt they'd been really getting somewhere. I looked in my grade book, up to now pretty empty of marks, and saw, sure enough, a whole string of grades after each name—mostly, however, F's and zeroes. Many of them had nothing but zeroes, which I took to mean they had been busy not-doing this important work. I pointed this out to the class, but it didn't matter. They had been back on familiar ground; strict teacher, no fooling around, no smart-off, no discussions about how bad school was, and plenty of work. That was, after all, what school was and they were in favor of it.[11]

The Problem of Control as Discipline

What school, or curriculum, *is* underlies all of these observations, which brings us back to the problem of control. On the surface, the prob-

---

[9] Philip A. Cusick, *Inside High School* (New York: Holt, Rinehart & Winston, 1973), p. 28.

[10] James Herndon, *The Way It Spozed to Be* (New York: Simon and Schuster, 1965), p. 100.

[11] Ibid., p. 102.

lem of control is *the discipline problem*. Numerous studies have found this to be among the most salient problems teachers themselves perceive. Waller,[12] using anecdotes collected from his students, interpreted life in the high school classroom as a constant struggle for control. Loss of control over their classes and loss of their jobs were the two things teachers feared most. The problem of control underlay even those classrooms in which the rows of children appeared to be the most orderly. The pupils could erupt at any moment, exploiting any weakness of the teacher. They might take off on a saying or gesture of the teacher, might destroy a rule by literalizing it, might introduce extraneous matter to disturb a discussion, and so on. The teachers who controlled their classes most successfully commanded without explanation, used punishment to define the situation of the student, manipulated pupils' social relationships, expressed anger quickly and maintained it until a crisis had passed, and appealed to the most relevant ideals and motives of their pupils.

Waller's account would apply to many classrooms today, though one might characterize others in more subtle terms. Most enduring are the dynamics of control that Waller analyzed: the "perilous equilibrium" of social order in the school, the social distance between teacher and pupil, the need for the teacher not to compromise this distance in the eyes of other teachers, and the roles pupils play in the classroom—clown, bully, goat, good boy, bad boy, teacher's helper and so on—some of them roles that developed in the children's primary groups, and others roles that are more unique to the classroom.

Smith and Geoffrey, some 35 years later, analyzed an urban eighth grade classroom in terms that are remarkably consistent with Waller's dynamics, especially considering that the conceptual framework of their analysis was painstakingly built by applying to their observations theoretical sources that were far removed from Waller, the spare and elegant sociological concepts of Homans. Smith and Geoffrey add to Waller a time perspective derived from their having observed with Geoffrey as the teacher for a whole year in a single classroom. Thus one sees in their account not only individual student roles—the court jester, the nonworker—but also an intricate process of interweaving the children's and the teacher's expectations as certain behavior sequences spiral to form the individual-in-the-role. Defining "classroom control" as "the relationship between teacher direction, usually verbal, and a high probability of pupil compliance,"[13] Smith and Geoffrey identified four stages of the teacher's establishing initial control. "Grooving the children" involved the teacher's stating the rules and commanding activities—without much explanation, but with enough warmth, humor, and pleasure in the activities themselves to infuse the

---

[12] Willard Waller, *The Sociology of Teaching* (New York: Wiley, 1932).

[13] Louis M. Smith and William Geoffrey, *The Complexities of an Urban Classroom* (New York: Holt, Rinehart & Winston, 1968), p. 67.

classroom "belief" systems with "sentiments" to form classroom "norms." "I mean it," "following through," and "softening the tone of classroom management" characterized the subsequent stages of establishing control.

As Waller emphasized, and recent studies have reaffirmed, it is not only the teacher who establishes control. A new teacher, especially, is socialized to the role of disciplinarian by other teachers and by the pupils themselves. McPherson identified four major strands of the self-image of the teachers in a school in which she herself taught: disciplinarian, director of learning, industrious worker, and one deserving just and equitable treatment.

The most clearly observable aspect of a teacher was her success or failure as a preserver of discipline.
"Successful teachers do not have problems."
"To have to send a child to the principal is to 'admit that you can't control the kids.'"
So it was in the area of discipline that the standards of role performance were clearest and that the attempts at social control by older over younger and newer teachers were most evident.[14]

Fuller summarized as follows the data reported in six studies that examined beginning teachers' problems without severely restricting the alternatives among which the teachers could choose:

As it is reported by these investigations, what we know is that beginning teachers are concerned about class control, about their own content adequacy, about the situations in which they teach and about evaluations by their supervisors, by their pupils and of their pupils by themselves.
The consistency of these findings is remarkable in the light of the different populations surveyed. The consistency lies not only in the similarity of concerns expressed but in the absence of concern about topics which are usually included in education courses: instructional design, methods of presenting subject matter, assessment of pupil learning, dynamics of child behavior and so on.[15]

On the basis of a range of studies, Fuller argued persuasively for a developmental conceptualization of teachers' concerns, going from a pre-teaching phase that is quite vague about the classroom to an early teaching phase of concern with self (as characterized above) to, finally, a phase of late concerns focused on pupil gain and self-evaluation as opposed to personal gain and evaluation by others. Fuller observed that a teacher could get "stuck" in the second of her three phases. From a more sociological and ecological perspective, we might hypothesize that the basic conditions of schooling that constitute the problem of control ensnare most teachers in Fuller's initial teaching phase.

[14] Gertrude H. McPherson, *Small Town Teacher* (Cambridge, Mass.: Harvard University Press, 1972), p. 31.
[15] Frances F. Fuller, "Concerns of Teachers: A Developmental Conceptualization," *American Educational Research Journal* 6 (1969): 210.

Lortie[16] discusses teachers' opinions, documented in other studies and confirmed by his own surveys, that education courses had not adequately prepared them to deal with the problems of classroom discipline and management. The courses were too "idealistic" and "out of touch with reality." Teachers learn to take the role of teacher largely through the 13,000 hours they spend in classrooms, on the average, *before* graduation, and then through their experience as teachers themselves. Teachers-to-be underestimate the difficulties of the role, but still there is not much shift in their conceptualization of it after entering the role. Lortie takes this fact to be evidence of the limited influence other teachers have on a given teacher's idea of *how* to implement the role, though the pressure to maintain control is strong from other teachers.

On the theme of the sameness of classrooms, Lortie surmised that the classroom unit is maintained, with low interdependence of classrooms, because of the high turnover rate of teachers and the greater ease of adapting classroom units to local population changes. In our own view, the *moral* difficulties of rationalizing the teaching role contribute to the persistence of the autonomous classroom. About half the teachers interviewed in one of Lortie's surveys "emphasized moral outcomes that would result from their work."

Teachers are charged with maintaining good order and discipline in their classrooms. It is highly probable, in my view, that elaborations along moral lines, in addition to demonstrating continuities within teaching, give additional meaning to these disciplinary activities.[17]

The possibility of interpreting the conditions of schooling in a way congruent with one's own moral principles may be greatest in one's "own" classroom, whatever the teacher's stage of development, in Fuller's terms. The autonomy of the classroom also protects the teacher from being observed in moral compromises, be they screaming, favoring compliant children, or more subtle departures from an ideal. The mystique of teaching —the feeling of many that the problem of control defies pedagogy, the *sacrosanctum* of the classroom—seems to emanate from this personal moral factor.

The Problem of Control and the Conditions of Schooling

We alluded at the outset to three basic conditions of schooling: the expectation that teachers will accomplish learning in their pupils, the time frame of schooling, and the high ratio of pupils to teachers. We turn to these now to ask *why* discipline should be such a problem in the school and what further ramifications control has in the culture of classrooms.

[16] Dan C. Lortie, *School-teacher: A Sociological Study* (Chicago: University of Chicago Press, 1975).

[17] Ibid., p. 112-13.

Waller[18] anticipated much of what we understand today from a sociological point of view; Jackson[19] presents the most complete ecological analysis. Smith and Geoffrey[20] combine these perspectives. We shall take up the three basic conditions of schooling in the reverse order of their statement above.

The Ratio of Children to Adults

A far larger number of children or youths—simply in the aggregate, and in proportion to adults—is present in classrooms and schools than in any other setting of everyday life outside of school (or church school), except certain recreation settings. Jackson explores the implications of this crowding in detail. He attributes to it teachers' determining who will and will not speak, allocating supplies, granting special privileges, and serving as official timekeeper. The necessity of waiting, the denial of desire—for example, only some can answer a question or be granted a request—and the frequency of interruptions are shown to be further consequences of the crowding of children in classrooms. Most poignant of all is what Jackson summarizes as the requirement that children be "alone in the crowd," ignoring the potential distractions of peers with whom they are more intimately associated in school than they are likely to be, in such numbers, in settings outside of school. This last point is particularly crucial because it, especially, seems to arise out of the circumstances of the school situation itself, rather than obviously serve some socializing function for future life.

A further implication can be drawn, the underside of the points that Jackson has made. The crowding of children in classrooms makes it difficult for them to exercise the peer competencies, the skills of regulating their relationships to one another, that the children are already developing in settings outside the school. Younger children playing in unsupervised settings rarely interact in groups exceeding three or four individuals. Where larger numbers of young children (still rarely as large as in school) are coordinated, they tend to be organized by adults or by older youths in a game, a party, or an adventure. In any case, the activities are almost invariably related to physical things, the toys and found objects, spaces, and surfaces of children's play. Things mediate children's relationships to one another. This is the social order that kindergarten recognizes. It is thus quite understandable that young children might be "unruly" when they are congregated in large numbers and expected to orient almost exclusively to language encoded information, spoken or written. The children's already learned rules for regulating their interactions do not apply, but in fact they will resort to these rules—forming spontaneous groups and making play objects of whatever comes to hand—whenever the pressure to attend to

[18] Waller, *Sociology.*

[19] Jackson, *Life.*

[20] Smith and Geofrey, *Complexities.*

exclusively language encoded information is relaxed. "Socializing" young children to the standard classroom is thus not just a matter of teaching them the expected conduct once-and-for-all, but one of continual vigilance to maintain it.

As children grow older, the patterns of their interaction change, but the end result remains problematic for a classroom. The children's friendship bonds strengthen, not to the same degree for every child, but in networks wherein increasingly stable clusters of children are directly or indirectly connected to certain individuals who emerge as the centers of attraction. However, some children (Gronlund[21] estimated 11 to 22 percent of the children in all classes at all grade levels) are persistently excluded. Outside the classroom, in the extracurricular activities of schools and in the settings of the children's and youths' nonschool recreation—streets and fields, fast-food establishments, car parks, community dance centers, parties, and so on—the children interact, or watch the action, in increasingly larger numbers with minimum adult organization or surveillance, if any at all. The largest interactions, for example, sports contests and dances, continue to be organized around things; but language emerges as a sufficient medium for many social activities. Some interpretations of "adolescent society" argue that youths are exercising capacities that will be prized when they are adults: leading and following, self-assertion, and affiliation.[22] Youths eagerly take what part-time work is available to them, and in recent years some have been active in political causes—desegregation, antiwar activity, and ecology. One of every ten girls today becomes pregnant before age 18, and an increasing number of adolescents formally marry while still in high school. However, the limited opportunities for youths to participate in the economy and the political system, linked with the continuance of most in their childhood homes past the point when they are biologically capable of forming separate families, result in their capacities being, to say the least, out of phase with what adult society is prepared to accommodate.

It is the crowding of these youths into the secondary school that the Martin Report[23] emphasizes. The report argues that the sheer logistics of maintaining custody of youths in school for six or more hours a day, not just in classes, but in study halls, libraries, cafeterias, hallways, and so on, disperses the teachers allotted to a school in such a way that the average class has to be large. Of course, one must ask *why* a certain proportion of teachers to students, resulting in a relatively constant range of class sizes,

---

[21] Norman E. Gronlund, *Sociometry in the Classroom* (New York: Harper and Row, 1959).

[22] James S. Coleman, *The Adolescent Society* (Glencoe, Ill.: Free Press, 1961); cf. Jules Henry, *Culture Against Man* (New York: Vintage Books, 1965).

[23] Martin, *Report on High Schools and Education.*

has been allotted to schools in modern times. What society is willing to pay for teachers certainly figures in this somehow. Society's valuation of teachers, however, is based in part on some estimate of how many teachers are required to do the work of schooling. It might not be too outrageous to suppose that 20 to 40 students represents the comfortable and barely tolerable extremes to which a teacher's voice and vision can be adapted from the front of the room. In ways that we shall explore further below, the standard pupil-teacher ratio might thus tend to perpetuate the traditional modes of teaching with which it is consistent. Be this as it may, adolescents are bound to test themselves, to express their interests in one another, to pull out now one and now another stop in the exquisitely elaborated instruments of their social expression, in the most ordinary converse of the classroom. For the adolescent, more than for the younger child, a classroom is a potential forum. For the teacher of adolescents, as of younger children, it is necessary either to employ pupils' social competencies or to repress them.

The Time Frame of Schooling

The fact that children between the ages of six and sixteen are *required* to attend school for certain days and hours clearly relates to the youths we have just been discussing, as part of their exclusion from adult society. Stinchcombe[24] has demonstrated that those youths for whom the connection between schooling and subsequent employment is most tenuous are those most alienated from high school, particularly lower-class males. Drop-out statistics tell the same story. At the same time, exclusion from adult society affects all students in ways that the drop-out statistics do not begin to indicate.

What more general effect on school experience does the requirement to attend school have? Jackson[25] reviewed a variety of earlier and more recent studies of both younger and older children's feelings about school. These studies showed relatively small proportions of students with *strong* feelings of like or dislike after the earliest years of school. Most students' feelings toward school could be characterized as stereotyped acceptance or indifference. A provocative finding in two studies, however, was that students who indicated a liking for school most often selected negative adjectives from a checklist to describe their *typical* classroom feelings. Contrary to conventional school wisdom, the studies contained no evidence for a correlation between students' academic success and their liking of school. Jackson relates all of this to school's becoming "old hat," holding few surprises "after the first few thousand hours of attendance" (!). Jackson points also to the fact that children *must* attend school whether they want

[24] Arthur Stinchcombe, *Rebellion in a High School* (Chicago: Quadrangle, 1969).

[25] Jackson, *Life.*

to or not. To us this latter fact has the prior significance, linking first of all to the physical quality of school life, its peculiar mixture of passivity and many things happening that Jackson describes so effectively. School attendance is prescribed legally in terms of days and hours and a span of years. The law affects most directly the distribution of children's activities in time. School starts and ends at prescribed hours of the day. The tempo of activity from minute to minute speeds up and slows down in a regular rhythm punctuated by arrival, snack or recess, luncheon, the brief breaks at class or activity-changing time, and the approach of a day's, a week's, and a season's end. The tempo is lifted or depressed by less regular happenings: special assemblies, fire drills, jokes, things falling, working, failing, whatever events can occasion an outburst of appreciation or a groan of despair. Children's *energies* course through school like waters in a stream, moving faster or slower as the stream bed changes, and finding their way even under ice. Our analysis of crowding emphasizes the social dimension of schooling; the knowledge required in school directs us to its intellectual aspect. The fact of compulsory school *attendance* focuses us on the physical dimension of the school environment. Control of a physical aspect of children's lives, their time, is the point of departure for the law.

It remains to be said that the time frame of schooling does not entirely dictate how the children's energies are to be regulated. As the crowding of children *creates* the problem of control of their social propensities, children's restriction in time creates the problem of control of their activity. Teachers might attempt themselves to control children's energies entirely, or they might accommodate more to the children's own, individual and cultural, definitions of work-, play-, and rest-time.

The Expectation That Teachers Will Foster Literacy

The teaching of reading, writing, arithmetic, and knowledge articulated by these means—broadly speaking, the development of literacy—is very much a matter of control. First of all, just the fact that certain individuals, all of them adults, have been officially designated as teachers suggests that it is their knowledge which is to be definitive in the classroom. This does not simply mean that teachers' answers are correct answers. The very form in which knowledge is to be demonstrated—as answers to questions, storytelling, moves in a game, or actions of a craft—is itself a definition of knowledge. Thus the form that the teacher fosters conveys knowledge *about* knowledge. If a teacher is pressured by environmental circumstances into the enactment of one or another form, the teacher's role sanctions this as knowledge nonetheless.

For *anyone* to teach reading, writing, and arithmetic to *any* number of others would involve the exercise of control in some way. Consider simply the nature of the alphabet. Insofar as its letters stand for sounds that combine to form the words of spoken language, "decoding" and "encoding" might be thought to be purely rational processes. In certain respects, however, the alphabet is highly arbitrary: the shapes used to represent the sounds, the order *A* to *Z* in which the alphabet is transmitted, and, particularly in English, the inexact correspondence between the letters and sounds (a given letter may stand for more than one sound, and a given sound can be formed from more than one combination of letters). Learning reading and writing, and in partly similar ways learning arithmetic, thus entails accommodation to conventions as well as sheer perceptual discrimination and reasoning. What we mean by *control* in this case is linked to what Dawe[26] has called "the imposition of meaning." Spelling is a blatant example of this for virtually all school children, a paradigm for more subtle disciplines of knowledge to come. For children whose spoken language is not standard English, the imposition of meaning in learning to read and write is compounded.

Reading, writing, and at least advanced arithmetic are conducted exclusively through symbols. One gets virtually no information from *isolated* symbols directly. Information is extracted from their connection with other symbols of their system and from whatever associations they may have with sensory experience. This fact distinguishes symbols from concrete things and events, which contain relatively more information *within* their shapes or boundaries, information that, further, yields more directly to sensory actions.

That symbols can be used to represent objects and events one has not experienced constitutes their most immediate power and simultaneously presents a problem of access to their meaning. Progressive educators' criticism of exclusively verbal and numerical modes of conveying knowledge in classrooms concentrated on the superficiality and distortions of understanding that can result from having to employ concepts whose referents have not been directly experienced.[27] In characterizing this as "passive" learning, the progressives also anticipated the point of view which Piaget[28] especially has worked out: that thought must be developed through actions on concrete objects before it can be operationalized more formally. Piaget, however, leads us to the edge of a more profound level of the problem of meaning, let us say of the problem of control over meaning, one that the progressives slighted. This level is the capacity of symbolically represented knowledge to form and transform experience, to arrange the objects and events symbols refer to in relationships that are not simply induced from experience.

[26] Dawe quoted in Michael F. D. Young, *Knowledge and Control* (London: Collier-Macmillan, 1971).

[27] William A. Brownell, and Gordon Hendrickson. "How Children Learn Information Concepts and Generalizations," *49th Yearbook of the National Society for the Study of Education,* pt. 1 (Chicago: University of Chicago Press, 1950).

[28] Jean Piaget, *Science of Education and the Psychology of the Child* (New York: Orion Press, 1970).

Abstraction—the separation of properties from things and events in their contexts to define categories and relationships—is crucial to the regulation of experience in modern society. Modern science, industry, agriculture, commerce, administration, communication, and warfare (how can we leave this out?) all depend upon abstraction. That children and youths from different sectors of society have different degrees of access to this mode of thinking will be central to questions to be pursued later in this chapter. Here we can observe more simplistically that schools in our society are expected to foster abstract thought. Blum has speculated that "remoteness from everyday life . . . is an important element in legitimating academic knowledge in schools."[29] *Why* would this be so? The *capacity* of remoteness for legitimating academic knowledge derives in part from the role abstraction plays in the control of the systems of modern life. At least one intended or claimed function of academic knowledge is the transmission of this control to students.

Abstraction itself, however, is not the only source of the remoteness of academic knowledge. Another source is suggested more by the term academic. This is the fact that the disciplines of knowledge have been organized around bodies of information and conceptual frameworks that are conventional, the knowledge compacts of the academies. These conventions, more complex than those of the alphabet, link academics to one another in a common discourse that constitutes for them a different "reality" from the reality of nonparticipants. As a *discipline* becomes a *subject,* the conventions become submerged; yet they continue to control meaning. The difference is that the learner has less access to the rules of a subject than of a parent discipline, except the most primitive rule of all, which is to replicate the contents of the subject.

A final aspect of academic knowledge is somewhat paradoxical in relation to its basis in conventions. This is what Goody and Watt[30] have delineated as the solitary and individualistic nature of writing and reading as communication. Compared with talk, communication through writing is more solitary not just because it can be done alone, but because there is less opportunity for immediate adjustment of differences of interpretation between reader and writer than between speakers. These characteristics can cut two ways in a classroom. On the one hand, writing can be developed as a personal medium of expression, and the discussion of writing— or of reading done in common—can emphasize individual pupils' differences of interpretation. On the other hand, reading and writing can be used to isolate pupils from one another, however consciously or unconsciously this may happen. The process is most conspicuous in seatwork that is "busy

[29] Alan F. Blum, "The Corpus of Knowledge as a Normative Order," in *Knowledge and Control,* ed. Michael F. D. Young (London: Collier-Macmillan, 1971), p. 154.

[30] J. Goody and I. Watt, "The Consequences of Literacy" in *Comparative Studies in History and Sociology,* v. 3, 1962.

work." It also enters into the classic pattern of teacher question/pupil answer/teacher reaction followed by teacher question when the teacher takes the presumed standpoint of the author of a reading, especially a textbook, and monitors the pupil's interpretation of the reading. This second way to use reading and writing especially links the nature of them to the evaluation that Jackson underscores as another pervasive quality of classroom life. Reading and writing and discussion of them evoke evaluation. They can further be employed to occasion evaluation when it is central to the teacher's control of the pupils' social relationships and thus contributes to maintenance of the teacher's authority more generally.

What all this amounts to is that by its very nature the intellectual material of schooling requires the learner's acceptance of cultural conventions at various levels of abstractness. More often than not, however, the classroom teacher does not share with students the intellectual gains and trade-offs of these conventions, but requires instead the students' submission to a more personalistic authority, the teacher's own knowledge.

Much of what we have been saying here about academic knowledge and control can be illustrated by a discussion Hughes recorded in an intermediate grade classroom.

TEACHER: Incidentally, did the California Indians have a pretty easy life?

ARTHUR: No.

TEACHER: Yes, they did, Arthur. Don't you remember? Who can tell me about it? (Hands up) Eddie.

EDDIE: (Tells about Indians not having to work.)

TEACHER: Why didn't they have to work as hard as other Indians? Larry.

LARRY: They didn't have to fight.

TEACHER: They were peaceful Indians. But one fact. One word will answer it. Robert.

ROBERT: (Tells about freedom)

TEACHER: That's right. They had freedom. Rebecca.

REBECCA: Lots of food.

TEACHER: Yes, they had lots of food. Janice.

JANICE: (Says more about food)

TEACHER: All right, but why did they have lots of food?

CHILD: They had all the food they wanted.

TEACHER: All right, why?

CHILD: (Comments)

TEACHER: All right, but there is still one thing I wanted you to say.

CHILD: (Tries to tell about raising crops) I can't think of the word.

TEACHER: Fertile.

CHILD: Yes.

TEACHER: I'm going to tell you. I wanted you to think this out. One reason was because of the climate. Things grew the year around. The winters were not severe and there was always plenty of food.[31]

[31] Hughes, *Assessment of Quality*, pp. 105-106.

This discussion is a rather *haphazard* course of learning, for *any* child. The rules that govern meaning are opaque. To the extent that children have difficulty mastering these rules, communication is threatened, and the teacher's questioning must serve a more general strategy of holding the class together. The discussion above is skating on the brink of *the discipline problem*. Allow us to point to the deliberate pun.

The Congruence of Classroom Controls

Each of the three basic features of schooling discussed up to this point—the crowding of pupils, the compulsion of school attendance, and the expectation that teachers will foster literacy—entails a heavy exercise of control. Still we have recognized at each point that things could go more than one way. Teachers could employ or repress pupils' social competencies, could share more or less control over the course of activity, and could exclude or include pupils in the explicit construction of knowledge. These possibilities, together with the constraints in which they are couched, constitute the core problem of control inherent in schooling. They are problematic even before we raise the question of how social class and caste affect schooling. Before turning to this question, let us ask why, in the standard classroom, the set of the more restrictive of each of these alternatives emerges as the most common solution to the problem of control. The most encompassing explanation combines social ecology and developmental psychology. Space allows us only to suggest the argument here.

Recall that we have connected the three basic conditions of schooling to the social, the physical, and the intellectual aspects of the teaching-learning environment. The connections might have been drawn in other ways. For example, Foshay[32] adds to these three domains another three— the emotional, the aesthetic, and the spiritual realms of the curriculum and the learning environment. In our view, these are variations on the social, the physical, and the intellectual, emphasizing the affective aspects of judgments of the good, the beautiful, and the true. The idea we have attempted to set up is that the social, physical, and intellectual domains of environments, not just in schools but more generally, tend to be congruent with one another. Intuitively, this idea is conveyed by the image of the standard classroom quoted from Goodlad and Klein above. Operationally, it is best understood in terms of human judgments: an individual tends to orient consistently to one or another authority for all three kinds of judgments to be made in a given environment—intellectual, social, and physical, or matters of the true, the good, and the beautiful (pleasing or tolerable to the senses, etc.). Thus if a teacher sees himself or herself as the ultimate

[32] Arthur W. Foshay, "Toward a Humane Curriculum" in *Essays on Curriculum,* Arthur W. Foshay ed. (New York: Curriculum and Teaching Dept., Teachers College, Columbia University, 1975).

arbiter of what is true in the knowledge realm of the classroom, the teacher is likely also to assume the role of ultimate authority for social and physical questions as well. If a child perceives the teacher as the authority or not the authority in one of these realms, the child equally tends to see the teacher this way in the other realms. Varying the psychology of this argument now, let us say that in order for the teacher to accept the child as the authority, or as an authority to be negotiated with, in any one of these realms—again, matters of the true, the good, and the beautiful—the teacher *must* accept the child as an arbiter in the remaining realms. Now let us relate this discussion to Fuller's theory of teachers' development. If a teacher has, perhaps in education courses, been persuaded of the validity of the child's own intellectual construction of reality, the teacher cannot act effectively on this without corresponding views of the meaning of the child's social and physical activity.[33] The fact that teachers are probably not and children certainly not conscious of these distinctions in the everyday running course of classroom events does not contradict our basic supposition, but rather adds weight to it. In short, an individual tends to look to some source in an environment, be it self or other, to determine what's "right" in all matters.

Individuals' judgments are influenced by environments through both their pragmatic and their symbolic properties. Individual desks facilitate certain behaviors and impede others. They also *signify* that certain behaviors are expected and others not expected. Each of the three basic conditions of schooling conveys first—initially and most emphatically—the *message* that the teacher is supposed to be in control. The herding of children into social situations in which their rules do not apply, the external regulation of their energies, the conventions of knowledge to which they must submit—all these *signal* that the teacher is to exercise control. Pragmatically and symbolically, these conditions reinforce one another.[34] To be changed significantly, a classroom or school must be impacted physically, socially, *and* intellectually.[35]

Differences Between Classrooms

The differences in classroom culture that appear to be associated with differences among children are best understood as variations on the standard classroom. A gradual accumulation of studies, especially in the ethnographic mode, is filling in details of these variations.

[33] Cf. O. J. Harvey, Misha S. Prather, B. Jack White, and Richard D. Alter, "Teachers' Belief Systems and Preschool Atmospheres," *Journal of Educational Psychology* 57 (1966): 373-81.

[34] Jeremy D. Finn, "Expectations and the Educational Environment," *Review of Educational Research* 42 (1972): 387-410.

[35] Seymour B. Sarason, *The Culture of the School and the Problem of Change* (Boston: Allyn and Bacon, 1971).

Metz[36] observed classrooms in the upper and lower tracks of three junior high schools in a city where it was the policy that a given teacher be assigned to classes at both levels. The academic separation of the children was based on prior school achievement, which probably contributed to the fact that it was strongly associated with social class and ethnic separation—since previous school experience, not just ability, is reflected in achievement. The upper-track students expected school to influence their growth, and they expected to be treated as junior partners, i.e., to have their opinions taken seriously. The lower-track students did not see any justification for performing the tasks of school, except that, as in Herndon's classes, that was "the way it spozed to be"; and they did not have the upper-track students' sense of proprietorship in the school. Metz writes:

> For teachers one of the most important aspects of students' behavior is the challenges which all classes make as they get to know a teacher and attempt to establish patterns to their own liking in areas of disagreement. Teachers in Canton were systematically questioned about these challenges, and all agreed that they were a fundamental fact of classroom interaction.
>
> Most agreed that students in Tracks Three and Four posed theirs primarily through overt physical or verbal disorder, while those in Track One and Honors classes most often test the teacher's mastery of the subject and related intellectual matters.[37]

When the children engaged in explicitly proscribed behavior in class, it was more boisterous, expressive, and public in the lower tracks and more private or "sneaky" in the upper tracks.[38] Teachers, in turn, responded with different management and disciplinary techniques in the upper and lower tracks. The latter children were assigned more to independent routine written tasks, which cut down on the opportunity for collective interference. Metz speculates that this was also more comfortable for the children themselves because they were less exposed to public failure in independent work. The upper-track students were engaged in more class discussion. Teachers less often felt they had to countervene behavior in the upper-track classes; and when they did, an academic strategem—for example, a question aimed at a napping child—usually sufficed to restore the expected order. In the lower-track classes, teacher attempts to quell student misbehavior were harsher, more protracted, and further removed from the substance of the academic task concerned.

Metz's study strongly suggests an interpretation for the Goodlad and

---

[36] Mary Haywood Metz, "Teachers' Adjustments to Students' Behavior: Some Implications for the Process of Desegregation," paper presented at Annual Meeting of American Educational Research Association, Toronto, Ont., 1978.

[37] Ibid., pp. 4-5.

[38] See also Frances Schwartz, "Continuity and Change in Student Adaptation to One Alternative School: The Transformation of Academic Behavior" (Ph.D. dissertation, Teachers College, Columbia University, 1976).

Klein finding that, already in the primary grades, disadvantaged children were assigned more to seatwork. One could ask, however, whether this is not a constructive adaptation to the children's needs or learning styles. On the basis of still other studies, we would argue that in most cases it is not. The kind of "independent" activity that is involved here is typically associated with low percentages of time engaged in the presumed task. Grannis[39] made ecological observations of second grade classrooms recommended as exemplars of several different models in Project Follow Through (the primary grade sequel to Head Start). He found that, across the models, children tended to be *on task* only 64 percent of the time that they spent in those self-paced arithmetic and language arts activities which they had had no part in selecting, and the materials of which contained no explicit feedback to confirm the correctness of the children's operations (an answer card, answers in the margin, manipulative materials). Time on task *dropped* to 61 percent if one considered just those situations where, in addition, the children were discouraged from interacting with one another. In other words, the children interacted anyway, and the task materials, furniture arrangements, and teacher "desists"[40] conveyed mainly the message that interaction was not relevant to the task! Conversely, the same children—"disadvantaged," of course—were progressively more on task as they gained more control over self-paced activity, that is, as they could interact, were provided with materials that contained feedback, and had at least some choice of the specific task they pursued. However, these more consistently learner-controlled conditions were relatively scarce in the self-paced arithmetic and language arts activities— the seatwork—of most of these classrooms. A variety of other studies[41] suggests that inconsistent, let us say "low support," conditions predominate in classroom seatwork generally, with correspondingly low percentages of task engagement. Finally, there is mounting evidence that time engaged in academic tasks is associated with achievement in those tasks.[42] Thus low task engagement predicts low achievement, to which we must add that it is likely to generate, if indeed it does not represent, alienation.

Further aspects of recitation or discussion in classes with children from economic or ethnic minorities are important to note. A pattern re-

[39] Joseph C. Grannis, "Task Engagement and the Distribution of Pedagogical Controls: An Ecological Study of Differently Structured Classroom Settings," *Curriculum Inquiry* 8 (1978): 3-36.

[40] Cf. Jacob S. Kounin, *Discipline and Group Management in Classrooms* (New York: Holt, Rinehart & Winston, 1970).

[41] For example, Frederick J. McDonald, *Beginning Teacher Evaluation Study, Phase II, 1973-74: Executive Summary Report* (Princeton, N.J.: Educational Testing Service, 1976).

[42] For example, Charles W. Fisher and others. *Final Report of the Beginning Teacher Evaluation Study. Technical Report V-1* (San Francisco: Far West Laboratory for Education Research and Development, June, 1978).

ported in a variety of studies involves the teacher's asking more concrete questions of lower-income than of higher-income children. Leacock[43] observed this pattern in arithmetic, reading, and social studies instruction in contrasting inner-city elementary school classrooms. Leacock stresses the consequences of the pattern: the perpetuation of the categories of thought that control relationships in society and between society and nature.[44] Smith and Geoffrey show how Geoffrey shifted his level of questioning in a social studies lesson from more abstract to more concrete *in order to obtain* what he recognized as correct answers from his students.[45] Without our denying the socializing effect, this latter explanation, closer to the classroom, appears to be very important to attend to.[46] It is intriguing in this connection that Goodlad and Klein found that most of the children's answers to the questions teachers asked in primary grade classrooms were correct. Perhaps one could amend this statement to say the answers were *accepted* by the teachers, thereby including the device by which a teacher "accepts" an unwanted or divergent answer in the process of dismissing it, as in the California Indians discussion quoted above. Obtaining correct answers seems to be central to the use of recitation *to manage a class,* as much as to develop knowledge and understanding in their own right. Where children have less access to the knowledge in question ahead of time, or from their experience, the first tactic appears to be to obtain the answers from other children in the class, the second tactic to lower the level of the questioning, and the third to dissolve the discussion in favor of seatwork.

A number of sociolinguistic studies, especially Boggs,[47] Philips,[48] and Lein,[49] have called attention to the contrast between the individually oriented interactive style of the standard classroom and the collectively oriented interactions of minority children in their own subcultural settings. The children in the above-mentioned studies—native Hawaiian, American

[43] Eleanor B. Leacock, *Teaching and Learning in City Schools* (New York: Basic Books, 1969).

[44] Nell Keddie, "Classroom Knowledge" in *Knowledge and Control,* ed. Michael F. D. Young (London: Collier-Macmillan, 1971).

[45] Smith and Geoffrey, *Complexities.*

[46] See Jonathan H. Turner, *The Structure of Sociological Theory* (Homewood, Ill.: Dorsey Press, 1974), on the question of teleological explanation.

[47] Stephan T. Boggs, "The Meaning of Questions and Narratives to Hawaiian Children," in *Functions of Language,* eds. Courtney B. Cazden, Vera P. John, and Dell Hymes (New York: Teachers College Press, 1972).

[48] Susan U. Philips, "Participant Structures and Communicative Competence: Warm Springs Children in Community and Classroom," in *Functions of Language in the Classroom,* eds. Courtney B. Cazden, Vera P. John, and Dell Hymes (New York: Teachers College, 1972).

[49] Laura Lein, "You Were Talkin' Though, Oh Yes, You Was: Black Migrant Children, Their Speech at Home and School," *Council on Anthropology and Education Quarterly* 6 (1975): 1-11.

Indian, and migrant American Black—were found to be loathe to compete against one another in the presence of an adult authority, specifically in the language game of the standard classroom. Knowing that it is a few children who dominate the discussion in most classrooms, one might relate this observation to the collectivization of subordinate children in classrooms generally. Roberts[50] analyzed various manifestations of the problem of control in urban junior high school classrooms. Teachers tended to conduct question-and-answer sessions or individualized work, in neither case utilizing and developing the students' relationships to one another. Even the relatively rare "group work" observed was used as a device for funneling correct answers to a teacher or for pitting one group against another. Roberts interpreted the students' responses as group reactions nonetheless:

> Structurally, apathetic groups are fragmented assortments of persons united in one purpose: If we can't be trusted to relate to each other, we will not relate to the teacher. In contrast to the silence of this covert rejection, the overt reaction against authority produces a structure consisting of strong subgroups, each with one aim: Destroy authority and nullify the structure of one-to-one interaction with the teacher.[51]

In the light of the above discussion, it is interesting to examine the Oregon (Direct Instruction) Program of Bereiter, Engelmann, and Becker, which has produced the strongest academic achievement test gains of the various programs in Project Follow Through.[52] The Program infuses the traditional classroom recitation and seatwork settings with behavior modification practices. The seatwork assignments are called *take homes,* signifying that they will be taken home *after* they have been completed correctly—a switch on homework that is often the occasion for failure at home. The take homes are programmed. On a given day they can generally be done in whatever order each child determines, in between recitation periods. Otherwise, the take home setting resembles the conventional seatwork setting. The recitations, too, are programmed to produce high rates of correct responses to questions that are concept- and skill-patterned, but still single-answer. The recitations involve mass choral chanting. Children also recite individually on command, but there is no hand waving to be selected by the teacher. The behavior of the teacher is prescribed as closely as that of the pupils.

The fact that three-quarters of the day in these classrooms is allocated to language arts and arithmetic, coupled with the fact that much of this time is spent in the relatively on-task recitation settings, is the simplest

---

[50] Joan I. Roberts, *Scene of the Battle: Group Behavior in the Classroom* (New York: Doubleday, 1970).

[51] Ibid., p. 84.

[52] Mary M. Kennedy, "Findings from the Follow Through Planned Variation Study," *Educational Researcher* 7 (1978): 3-11.

explanation for the achievement results of the Oregon Program. Apart from the achievement question, the somewhat higher support conditions in the seatwork setting and the positive cast of the recitations, especially the collective responding, appear to reduce the disorder and alienation commonly found in classrooms with minority children. On the other hand, the Oregon Program's exclusively standard English orientation rejects the language of the children's cultures,[53] and its total programming allows for no differentiation among the children, except in the rate at which different groups in the classroom progress.

It is probably no accident that the highest achieving program in Follow Through most closely resembles, and builds upon, the traditional classroom.[54] Intriguingly, the teachers Stallings[55] had observed implementing the Oregon Program most in accordance with the model were the ones who expressed the most dissatisfaction with it! One might speculate that the model had enabled them to increase control of their classes and thus to resolve the major concerns of Fuller's initial teaching phase, and that the teachers then were ready to change toward a more differentiated, child-oriented classroom.

An example of the latter can be understood as a further variant of the standard classroom. Marshall[56] reports his struggle to establish a nonauthoritarian discipline in a sixth grade classroom in an inner-city, low-income black community. During a first, turbulent year, the classroom yawed back and forth between teacher control from the front of the room and peer control from the back. Slowly, in second and third years with new students, a learning stations approach evolved, shaped almost as much by the students as by the teacher. Marshall summarizes the major differences of the system from the conventional classroom as follows:

1. Kids sit in groups spread around the room rather than in rows.
2. Worksheets in seven subject areas (Math, English, Social Studies, Spelling, Creative Writing, General, and Reading) are put in pockets scattered around the outside of the room every morning Monday through Thursday.
3. On these station days, the students are free to move around the room and do the worksheets in any order they like as long as they finish all seven by the end of the day.
4. The teacher's role is not one of controlling the class or teaching seven subjects (or even one) at the front of the room, but rather: (a) writing work-

[53] Clifford A. Hill, "A Review of the Language Deficit Position: Some Sociolinguistic and Psycholinguistic Perspectives," *IRCD Bulletin* 12 (Fall 1977): 13.

[54] Cf. Jane Stallings, "An Implementation Study of Seven Follow Through Models for Education," paper presented at the American Educational Research Association Annual Meeting, Chicago, 1974.

[55] Ibid.

[56] Kim Marshall, *Law and Order in Grade 6-E*. (Boston: Little, Brown and Co., 1972).

sheets for seven subjects the night before and running off copies first thing in the morning; (b) moving around the room during the station time helping people with the work and any other problems; (c) planning other activities for the remaining part of the day after the stations are finished; (d) correcting the stations with the whole class in the last hour of the day; and (e) evaluating progress in the traditional subjects with tests every Friday.[57]

Marshall's documentation—students' writing, sample worksheets, and photographs of the classroom—shows a high level of adaptation between teacher and students, for example in the accommodation of concept and skill instruction to students' concerns (the reason for writing the worksheets the night before they were to be used). Marshall systematically linked everyday events to more general categories of thought. His students started out behaving no less obstreperously than Herndon's, but in the end their intelligence and sociability were directed more toward educational goals.

Open classrooms represent a still greater departure from the conventional classroom, particularly in the wider range of options for activity they generally give, their greater use of manipulative materials, and, more or less following from these conditions, the lesser time they allocate to academic instruction.[58] Since open classrooms tend to be concentrated in the primary grades, a comparison with Marshall's classroom might be inappropriate. Theoretically, however, open classrooms are an alternative at any grade level. What is important to notice here is, first, that they optimize the possibility of the pupils', especially younger children's, regulating their interactions through concrete activities. Ross, Zimiles, and Gerstein[59] observed much higher frequencies of interaction, especially initiated by children, in nine open classrooms than in four traditional classrooms, all of which classrooms were in public schools in lower-income, inner-city neighborhoods. Similar findings obtained for two "developmental" (Bank Street) and two traditional classrooms in middle-income schools.

. . . when the content of the interactions is more closely analyzed, important qualitative differences among the four groups are seen. In the classrooms of the traditional groups, for example, a much larger proportion of all *Gives Information* interactions was concerned with rote and routine behaviors compared to classrooms of the nontraditional groups. In both nontraditional groups, too, most of the cognitive statements were distributed among subcategories representing higher-level behaviors. The proportion of questioning behavior that dealt with routine inquiries was highest in the Traditional Lower group and lowest in the Developmental Middle group. The traditional groups' expressive interactions more often involved expressions of need (social, physical, and

[57] Ibid., pp. 158-59.

[58] Grannis, "Task Engagement."

[59] Sylvia Ross, Herbert Zimilies, and David Gerstein, *Children's Interactions in Traditional and Nontraditional Classrooms* (Grand Forks, North Dakota: University of North Dakota, 1976).

task-related), whereas the nontraditional groups had a greater proportion of expression of preferences, of feelings and attitudes, and of concern for others. The largest differences in subcategory patterns occurred in relation to the category concerned with representational and symbolic behavior. Virtually all of the interactions of the two traditional groups involved reading-drill activities, while the bulk of these behaviors in the Developmental Middle group and a sizable proportion of those of the Open Lower group included forms of dramatic and creative expression and a much wider variety of experiences involving symbolization.[60]

Using a questionnaire survey of children in two parochial middle schools in lower-income neighborhoods, one an open and one a traditional school, Franks, Wismer, and Dillon[61] found that the open-school children judged each other as good or bad students more on the basis of factors related to peer interaction, whereas traditional school children emphasized conformity to teacher authority and de-emphasized attributes important to peer endeavors. It was also found that the labeling process was relatively rigid in the traditional school, the labels good and bad being distributed among a smaller proportion of children than in the open school.

Our discussion of the culture of classrooms with minority students has led us into discussing alternatives to the standard classroom, in part to demonstrate that "the way it spozed to be" is not the way it has to be. However, it could be fateful to ignore students', and their parents', ideas of what school is supposed to be. Barth[62] has chronicled the failure of a rush into open education in one inner-city elementary school. Marshall took great care to arrive at a classroom system that was meaningful to his students and their parents. Bernstein,[63] particularly, has raised the question of whether the more "visible" pedagogy of the traditional classroom might not have more currency for lower-income children than the relatively "invisible" pedagogy of the open classroom—though Bernstein's analysis is oriented to British society and cannot easily be translated into American terms.

Much of what we have written here about, in effect, the classroom's stereotyping behavior patterns for majority and minority students, applies to the roles of boys and girls in classrooms. Lee and Kedar[64] have specifically argued that teachers favor docile behavior in their attempts to

---

[60] Ibid., pp. 47-48.

[61] David D. Franks, Susan L. Wismer, and Stephen V. Dillon. "Peer Labeling in Open and Traditional Schools," paper presented at Annual Meeting of the American Educational Research Association, New Orleans, 1974.

[62] Roland S. Barth, *Open Education and the American School* (New York: Shocken, 1972).

[63] Basil Bernstein. *Class, Codes and Control, Vol. III: Towards a Theory of Educational Transmissions* (London: Routledge & Kegan Paul, revised ed. 1977).

[64] Patrick C. Lee and Gita Kedar, "Sex Role and Pupil Role in Early Childhood Education," *Resources in Education* 10 (January-June 1975): 493.

cope with the crowding of children in the classroom and that this results in more positive sanctions for girls', and more negative for boys', traditional sex roles. Lightfoot[65] has called further attention to the double jeopardy of young black girls who may learn a more aggressive coping style outside of school and thus not conform to the norm of girls from the majority culture.

From Goodlad and Klein's study, summarized at the outset of our chapter, it would be surmised that alternatives to the standard classroom are very scarce, at least by behavioral standards. We have argued, indeed, that there are reasons to expect them to continue to be scarce. However, Epstein and McPartland,[66] using a questionnaire survey of 7,361 students in the elementary and secondary schools of a county public school system, did find substantial variation between schools on a measure of what they called "formal school structural properties of openness": individualization of instruction, control of student conversation and movement, control of student assignments, and frequency of supervision of student assignments. These properties were only slightly associated with the open plan architecture of some of the schools but might be attributed to the extensive developmental efforts of the school system in question. The schools did not differ significantly on what Epstein and McPartland called "informal openness"—for example, whether teachers expected originality and personal opinions in students' classwork, as opposed to close conformity to their own directions and ideas; and whether teachers reserved most of the decision-making prerogatives for themselves or extended decision-making opportunities informally to students. Still, while there was not *between*-school variation on informal openness, there was *within*-school variation on this measure. Furthermore, the informal properties were strongly associated with nonacademic student outcomes such as self-reliance and attitudes toward school, while the formal properties were found to have only a small effect on these outcomes. (Academic achievement was not affected by either set of properties.) The socioeconomic status of the students was controlled in these analyses.

Reasoning from the lack of differences in informal openness between the open and traditional schools, Epstein and McPartland suggest that teacher personality might have contributed to the within-school differences in informal openness. This would bring us back to Fuller's idea of teachers'

[65] Sara Lawrence Lightfoot, "Socialization and Education of Young Black Girls in School," *Teachers College Record* 78 (1976): 239-62.

[66] Joyce L. Epstein and James M. McPartland, "Family and School Interactions and Main Effects on Affective Outcomes, Report 235." (Baltimore: The Johns Hopkins University Center for Social Organization of Schools, 1971); and Idem., "Authority Structures and Student Development, Report 246." (Baltimore: The Johns Hopkins University Center for Social Organization of Schools, 1978).

developmental stages and to our realization of the fundamental constraints on teachers' yielding control over classroom events.

A recent study by Moos[67] differentiates secondary school classrooms more broadly than the Epstein and McPartland study and might be taken as a "state of the art" example of the measurement of classroom climate. Moos administered the Classroom Environment Scale (CES) to students in 200 classrooms from 36 schools. Included were public general high schools; vocational, private, and alternative high schools; and junior high schools. The schools were located in a variety of communities on the East and West coasts of the United States. The CES consists of 90 true-false items which fall into nine different subscales, each of which measures students' perceptions of the emphasis on one dimension of classroom climate. An analysis of the students' responses yielded five distinct clusters of classrooms: control oriented (47 classrooms), change oriented (44), affiliation oriented (26), task oriented (47), and competition oriented (32). Four classrooms could not be located in any cluster. One of the interesting details of these patterns is that within two of the clusters, affiliation oriented and task oriented, there were two subclusters, one with an above-average and the other with a below-average emphasis on teacher control; while within the competition-oriented cluster, there were three subclusters, one having an above-average, another an average, and the third a below-average emphasis on teacher control. Thus variations on control continue to be central in Moos' more fine-grained analysis. The competition-oriented subcluster with average teacher control was further distinguished from the other two competition subclusters by having a greater than average emphasis on "teacher support" or personal-affective teacher-student relationships. Moos labeled this a "supportive" competition-oriented type, as opposed to the "structured" and "unstructured" competition-oriented types of the other two of these subclusters.

Moos also administered a questionnaire asking the students how satisfied they were with their school, their class, the other students in the class, their teacher, and their learning in the class. Analyses of variance were conducted to ascertain the extent to which these five student satisfaction variables discriminated among both the five clusters and the nine subclusters. Satisfaction with school did not significantly differentiate in either analysis. However, each of the other satisfaction variables significantly differentiated among class types in both sets of analyses. We notice the parallel to Epstein and McPartland's findings. The parallel is seen more specifically in the discussion of what amounts to the within-school differences.

Students in control oriented classes were the least satisfied with the class, the teacher, and the amount of material they were learning. A similar pattern

---

[67] Rudolf H. Moos, "A Typology of Junior High and High School Classrooms," *American Educational Research Journal* 15 (1978): 53-66.

of results occurred in the structured task oriented classes and, to a somewhat lesser extent, in the unstructured competition oriented and affiliation oriented classes. Students were relatively highly satisfied with the class and the teacher in innovation oriented and supportive competition oriented classes. Surprisingly, students in task oriented classrooms felt they were not learning much actual material; however, the class milieu may have led to higher expectations about the amount they should be learning. Finally, students liked each other more in classes which emphasized student-student affiliation.[68]

Moos' discussion of these findings emphasizes the discovery of 47 classrooms "almost exclusively oriented toward teacher control of student behavior" and the finding that students—and teachers—were in general "more satisfied with innovation oriented than with control oriented classes."

Conclusion

We began this chapter with the observation that classrooms everywhere are different and the same. Our analysis attended first to the sameness of classrooms, but in these last pages it has recognized more the differences between classrooms. How can classrooms be both same and different? We suggest that this is largely a matter of point of view. When classrooms are compared with other settings, including the alternative educational settings that are the reference points for the Goodlad and Klein and the Martin Report judgments, they appear to be more same than different. When classrooms are compared with themselves, the judgments implicitly accept the constraints of the classroom situation, and differences stemming more from the students' and the teachers' styles become more prominent. Moos, in his use of the term "relative" to characterize different levels of student satisfaction and in his discussion of the importance of structure in the classroom, recognizes the boundaries of the classroom situation.

The finding of differences does not diminish the need to explore alternatives to the classroom. Our analysis of the classroom situation has made us more aware of how far-reaching alternatives to the classroom might have to be in order to develop fundamentally different educational possibilities. It may be that the most significant changes in classrooms would be possible only if the basic conditions of schooling—again we mean the pupil-teacher ratio, the fixed time frame, and academic testing— *were so altered that the standard classroom simply would not work.* This is a different way of rendering the conclusions reached by Goodlad and Klein and the Martin Report. One wonders what effect a new understanding of these things will have upon education.

---

[68] Ibid., p. 60.

Section Two.
Some Aspects of
Curriculum Theory

THE NEXT FOUR CHAPTERS deal with curriculum theory. Our purpose in including this section is to indicate that considered action must be based on theory. If the difference between professional teachers and amateur teachers is, as is said in one of the chapters, that professional teachers have not only a theory of subject matter but also a theory about the student, then the difference between professional and amateur curriculum workers is that the professionals have some theories about the work they do, the way they talk, and the basic concepts they employ.

First we consider how curriculum is written and talked about. Walker looks at the forms the writing takes. In a somewhat wry statement, he distinguishes between the popular and the serious writing and offers readers ways of making the distinctions for themselves. Foshay deals with metaphors that control curriculum thought and action. Offering several metaphors for students (some unpleasant) and some metaphors for schools, he argues that in the degree that we are in control of the metaphors we unconsciously use, we may penetrate the language of our field.

In chapter 6 Connelly and Elbaz take us through a somewhat informal account of what they have learned about the curriculum in the course of years of reading, writing, acting, and thinking. Theirs is an attempt to rise above the usual curriculum theorizing to a human level that allows for uncertainties, acknowledges inconsistencies and weaknesses, and offers hope.

Geneva Gay presents a definitive account of the conceptual models of the curriculum-planning process. If one will but recognize that curriculum workers are in the business of modifying, or changing, the functioning of the curriculum, then the available models for this process are basic to a theory of curriculum action.

4 A Barnstorming Tour of Writing on Curriculum
Decker F. Walker

THERE ARE the curriculum materials themselves, of course. Teachers' guides, textbooks, syllabi, courses of study, scope and sequence charts, and the like.

And then there are books and articles about the curriculum. Textbooks for curriculum courses, like Tyler;[1] Taba;[2] Smith, Stanley and Shores;[3] or Saylor and Alexander;[4] and so on. Books on this or that innovation— the nongraded-school, individualized instruction, inquiry approaches to the social studies, multicultural education, and the like. Articles urging us to adopt this or that new or old practice. Articles analyzing this or that development.

And, finally, there is writing about the writing about curriculum. Most of what is called curriculum theory is writing about writing about curriculum. So are most histories of the curriculum field or of curriculum thought. Philosophical analyses of key terms used in curriculum writing fall into this category. And reviews of research. In fact, most of the writing for academic presses and journals on curriculum is writing about writing about curriculum. You are reading an example now.

There's another helpful distinction. Writing of the types just described is about *the* (or *a*) curriculum, about the actual program of studies or plans for it. Other writing is about related processes—curriculum development, organization, management, evaluation, the policies of curriculum making, and so on.

[1] Ralph W. Tyler, *Basic Principles of Curriculum and Instruction* (Chicago: University of Chicago Press, 1950).

[2] Hilda Taba, *Curriculum Development: Theory and Practice* (New York: Harcourt, Brace, and World, 1962).

[3] B. Othanel Smith, William O. Stanley, and J. Harlen Shores, *Fundamentals of Curriculum Development* (New York: Harcourt, Brace, and World, 1950).

[4] J. Galen Saylor and William M. Alexander, *Curriculum Planning* (New York: Rinehart and Company, 1954).

71

Once again, we can distinguish writing that is part and parcel of these processes—such as tests, policy statements, management plans, and so on—from writing about the processes and from writing about this writing.

We have just completed a lightning, jet-speed tour of writing on curriculum. You now have a rough idea of the main features of the existing literature. What follows is a more leisurely, up-close tour. If our super-quick tour has given a view from a jet, the upcoming one gives the view from an open-cockpit two-seater hopping from field to field—a barnstorming tour.

Curriculum Documents

Curriculum documents are the writings teachers and students use. Included are schoolbooks, workbooks, teaching aids of various kinds, tests, teachers' guides and teachers' editions of textbooks, courses of study, syllabi, district or state curriculum guides, and the what-do-I-do-Monday? writing in publications for teachers. The associated processes include those in which these materials are created; selected for use; used, not used, or misused; as well as the processes by which the materials have their effects on teachers and students. Various documents are also produced during these processes: agenda and working papers of writing teams; guidelines and criteria for materials selection; memoranda, guidelines, and plans for use and adaptation of the materials selected; the written materials teachers distribute to students to explain how the published material should be used; and even evaluation reports.

All these types of documents are an integral part of the curriculum as it is realized in practice, or of the processes leading to its realization, or both. They *are,* in some sense, the curriculum; part of it, at any rate. The writing of these documents *is* the writing of curriculum.

Curriculum documents such as these are written artifacts, tangible traces of the otherwise evanescent thoughts and actions that constitute the curriculum in practice. They are produced by specialists in education, in writing, in test construction, and the like—by professionals rather than by laypeople. They are also normally read and used by professionals; laypeople (other than students) seldom are an intended audience. The materials are produced in publishing houses, in district offices, and in the teacher's classroom or study.

Documents produced for a mass audience, such as textbooks and tests, are generally labored over for years by a large staff of writers and specialists. Documents produced locally are, by contrast, usually products of a few weeks or months of part-time work by teachers and school administrators; they are documents produced in a great hurry, almost off-the-cuff in some cases. (This is not to say that the mass-produced materials are necessarily better. A single teacher with a good idea may produce documents worth many months of labor by specialists working on faulty assumptions.)

The problems faced by writers of curriculum documents include:

1. How to attain sufficient clarity and specificity so that those who are supposed to be instructed by the document know exactly what they are being advised to do;

2. How to make the document easy to consult, attractive, and helpful so that it will be used;

3. How to allow for the variety of settings, personalities, and circumstances for which the document is intended;

4. How to maintain the widest possible acceptability so that the document's guidelines will be followed in the school or community.

These problems make the writing of curriculum documents a special and difficult craft. To do it well requires a high level of writing skill in addition to a thorough familiarity with the content to be presented and the educative processes associated with it. Some curriculum textbooks have chapters devoted to preparing courses of study. But the amount written about the craft of writing curriculum documents is quite small compared, say, with what has been written about the more specific art of stating behavioral objectives. Here, perhaps, is an opportunity for professional improvement in the coming years.

The general or casual reader of educational literature would have to make a special effort to come in contact with curriculum documents. Textbooks and other privately published documents are freely available, of course. However, they are not normally sold to individuals, libraries almost never stock them, and so someone not closely connected with schools may have difficulty obtaining them. But documents produced by schools and school districts are unmanageably difficult for a layperson to obtain and to interpret. There are so many of them. They are so varied in title, format, content, and quality. They originate in so many ways, and their true origin is often unknown because they are routinely attributed to the superintendent in many cases! Even when these local documents are available, it would be difficult for any person outside the local situation to judge their serviceability because they are intended for use in a particular context and must be judged for their usefulness in that context.

In short, for anyone except those (professionals, usually) directly concerned with them, curriculum documents—especially locally produced ones—resist casual inspection and informal assessment. Nevertheless, in one sense, at least, locally produced curriculum documents are more important than any other sort of writing about the curriculum. They are more closely bound up with the actual people and events that constitute the curriculum in practice, that produce whatever tangible effects a curriculum has on students and, through them, on civilization.

Simply to summarize the current state of local publications would require a research study, with a scientific sampling design and formal methods of interpretation. Most persons interested in curriculum, however, would not be so much concerned with typical practice as with the best or most innovative practice. It is precisely here that the difficulties of a scattered and largely fugitive literature become most frustrating. How are we to know what is most interesting unless we are monitoring the complete body of such writing? And who can manage this?

The result of this frustrating situation is the formation of informal networks among educators. Word gets around that this district has done a fantastic job with K–12 language arts sequencing, that that one has an excellent set of behavioral objectives for elementary mathematics instruction, and that over there they have a beautifully crafted poetry teaching guide.

Some modest attempts are being made to sift through the mass of local publications and bring some of them to wider attention. ASCD has a large display of such items at each annual conference and publishes a directory which can be purchased separately.[5] A more ambitious venture has been undertaken by Fearon-Pitman Publishers. They produce the Curriculum Development Library,[6] which consists of hundreds of curriculum guides on microfiche plus a seven-volume index.

Individuals and organizations will continue to want to sift through locally produced documents for specific purposes of research or practical inquiry, and some of these results will and should be published to a wider audience.

Writing About Curriculum: Primary Literature of Curriculum

The literature of widest interest and greatest appeal, the writing most widely published, the writing on curriculum that the layperson is most likely to run across is writing *about* it or the processes associated with it.

First and foremost, this type of writing is about what is wrong with the curriculum and what we should do about it. "The curriculum is deficient in *this* way; therefore we should make *that* change." "If we are to fulfill *this* part of the American dream, we must have that curriculum change." "*Here's* what's happening in education today; get on the bandwagon." Or, more subtly: "Since education is a matter of ———, the curriculum should be like *that*." "Students learn *this* way; therefore the curriculum should look *that* way." "Modern life is like *this*; the curriculum, therefore, should be like *that*." Both writing intended for professionals and writing intended for laypeople take these forms.

Essentially these writings are calls to action, exhortations, urgings, imperatives—justified and unjustified, basic and refined, rational and emo-

---

[5] For example, *Curriculum Materials 1979*, Exhibit of Curriculum Materials at the 34th ASCD Annual Conference, Detroit, Michigan, March 3-7, 1979. $2.00 prepaid from Association for Supervision and Curriculum Development, 225 N. Washington St., Alexandria, Va. 22314.

[6] *Curriculum Development Library*. Fearon-Pitman Publishers, 6 Davis Drive, Belmont, Calif. 94002. New materials are added annually.

tional. The problem to which most literature about the curriculum is addressed is how to improve or reform curriculum. Writing which fails to address this problem seems somehow unsatisfying, perhaps even irrelevant. We read it and wonder what we are supposed to *do* about these things we've read.

The ultimate measure of the success of this sort of writing, I suppose, is the magnitude of its effect on the actual curricula offered in schools. But this indicator is not available; we do not know what changes are taking place in school curricula—except in a vague, general sense—and so we are hardly able to tell what has produced those changes.

One proximate indicator of success is the popularity of the writing— sales of books, numbers of articles published in professional journals or magazines of general circulation, and so on. By this measure, the most successful writing about curriculum treats popular innovations. In some cases these are primarily professional enthusiasms—individualization, competency-based education, behavioral objectives, for example. In other cases the reform's main impetus comes from the lay community—career education, basic education/three Rs/back to basics, and accountability are recent examples. Sometimes the innovation is a specific practice or program; but more usually the really hot and long-lasting reform movements center on a broad, vaguely delineated philosophy, point of view, or orientation, such as open education, bilingual education, career education, basic education, or community-based education.

From an academic or intellectual point of view, this literature is a very mixed bag. Although some of the seminal writing on any of these reforms is thoughtful, well considered, well argued, and based upon an explicit, worked-out set of ideas, much of the great flood of writing on any popular reform is just bad rhetoric. It is one-sided, superficial, long on enthusiasm but short on thought. It cannot be taken seriously as professional inquiry, as a contribution to knowledge or understanding of education. But it nevertheless serves a vital professional function: it helps to shape the beliefs and opinions of those who determine the curriculum. And since in our schools the curriculum is shaped by both professional and lay opinion, the most successful reform literature is directed at both audiences.

If we choose a different proximate indicator of the impact of writing about the curriculum, different writing emerges as successful. Suppose, for example, we assume that the influence of a work over a long time period is a good indicator of its ultimate impact. Then works by more serious writers rise to the top of the list, and the wave of writing on once-popular innovations sinks near the level of yesterday's news. The works of Plato, Aristotle, Locke, Rousseau, and Dewey continue to be read and to influence thought and action in innumerable, barely perceptible ways hundreds of years after their publication. On a less grand scale, works by Montessori,

Thorndike, Kilpatrick, Rugg, Counts, and Taba continue to be read and used by professional educators, even though they may have been largely forgotten by the general public. And among writers still active, some continue to make important contributions year after year regardless of the bandwagon currently attracting most attention. (Any mention of persons still active is sure to be controversial, but any such list would surely include such distinguished senior figures as Tyler, Bloom, Foshay, B. O. Smith, Broudy, and Schwab.)

This literature is more systematic, more acceptable in scholarly terms, more penetrating, and often more original than all but the very best of the literature devoted to any specific reform. It, too, is directed toward the question of what to do, but in very different ways. Instead of exhortations, one finds reasoned argument appealing to evidence; one finds counterarguments and claims against the proposed innovation considered seriously; one finds strenuous efforts to discover fundamental considerations of great weight that would, properly applied, help decide the merits of the proposed innovation.

But this type of writing, as distinguished as it is, is not without its shortcomings. Its rigor and thoroughness make it unsuitable as a steady diet for the millions of teachers who must be reached in some way by writing about the curriculum. More popular treatments are essential, even if rigor must sometimes be sacrificed. Scholarly writings may set forth a basic line of approach by means of which day-to-day practical problems of educating may be addressed and solved, but many pressing problems will necessarily not be treated. So more detailed treatments, elaborations, extensions to other problems, and examples of putting these ideas into practice will always be necessary. The task of persuasion will also always be necessary. For all these reasons, purely scholarly works are never sufficient treatments of curriculum problems.

Furthermore, scholarly writing has a tendency to wander from the practical point at issue, never to return. The best educational scholarship stretches far from the terms of the practical problem into various fields of knowledge—philosophy, psychology, social sciences, and content fields. It returns to the problem with some terms or ideas that advance our thinking on the original issue, even if the advance is to question the importance of the issue, how it was posed, or whether it is really an issue at all. If only all scholarly writing made the return trip safely, all would be well. The return trip is difficult though, especially for scholars not familiar with the traditions and current practices of education. The world of pure knowledge is lovely to a scholar. It is tempting to tarry there. Meanwhile, those concerned about what to do are frustrated by discussions that lead them to scholarly ideas which are relevant to the resolution of some issues, but which do not discuss concrete resolutions. Even worse, these readers may be misled by a specialized scholarly discussion that makes recommendations based soundly on good scholarship in one discipline but all too often reflects superficial comprehension of practical realities. And so scholars need help from those they serve, especially from informed practitioners and policymakers.

Both popular and scholarly writing are necessary and potentially mutually corrective in writing about curriculum. What we need from the entire corpus of work is a thorough consideration of possible courses of action. Writing about the curriculum should help us act better, more wisely, more in tune with our highest values. The *us* to be helped includes a wide variety of persons who play many roles and who take part in curriculum decisions and shape the climate of opinion that influences these decisions. So different types of writing will be needed for the different audiences. We must also expect the writing to reflect a variety of opinions and points of view.

What we need, in fact, is a dialogue, a communal discussion, deliberation extended in space and time to include the many writers and readers who participate in realizing the curriculum. Joseph Schwab has articulated this view in his "practical papers." [7] His ideas suggest that the major need is for a closer relation between language and action. Action is being taken on curriculum matters nearly every day in localities around the country—in state capitols and in many regional and national agencies. For the most part, this action is accompanied by some sort of discussion of what should be done. But this discussion is more often than not desultory, abbreviated, superficial. It includes an extremely restricted set of considerations. These inadequacies stem from structural characteristics of the discussions more than from the abilities and inclinations of the people involved. Ways must be found to make a time and place on a regular basis for searching examination of the merits of actions. Incentives must be built in to reward thorough, careful, good deliberation. These structural innovations will have to be substituted for current procedures or built into revised versions. Perhaps the paradigm case of generally inadequate deliberation is the selection of textbooks.

Meantime, in scholarly journals, the ideas that need to be brought to bear on the practical decisions and actions may be found expressed in an abstract form by scholars who rarely, if ever, become involved in the action they claim their ideas should guide. Perhaps a series of critical reviews could be arranged so that scholars and concerned knowledgeable experts of various kinds could have the chance to assess the various proposed alternatives. This process could be supplemented by trials in classrooms and critical reviews by teachers, possibly teachers elected by their peers. Certainly, parents and the public's representatives, the board of education, should be involved. Some persons might even be commissioned to represent the students' point of view. Then the curriculum committee could draft a public statement of the pros and cons of each alternative, as the committee saw them in light of input from the various sources, to accompany the committee's recommended decision.

What is described above is only one hypothetical example. There are many other important curriculum decisions, and no one all-purpose procedure can be found. Consideration of various institutional mechanisms for improving the discourse that accompanies curricular action should be a high priority for our professional associations in the coming years.

In addition, the universities and the scholars have an obligation to bring their work into closer relation to the realities of schooling. The scholarly books and articles need to show continuous evidence of attention to real school problems. The implications of ideas for practice need to be prominently featured, not just appended. The research needs to be better attuned to the needs of those who must make decisions.

James Hessler,[8] in a recent dissertation at Stanford, studied the literature on individualization of education in journals over the past 50 years. He found that in some 252 articles, the average percentage of citations of empirical evidence (other than logic or the author's personal experience or opinion) was 32 percent, compared with nearly 80 percent in a comparison group of articles from the field of medicine. Arguments given for individualization outnumbered arguments against it by nine to one. Among the articles published in this period, he found a few that seemed to be quite thorough, careful, considered treatments of the pros and cons of individualization; but these few articles were not more cited or used than the mass of others that were more superficial. This situation contrasted rather sharply with the body of professional literature that he used as a comparison: the medical literature on the heart bypass operation, a controversial surgical procedure for severe heart disease. He also found onesidedness and superficiality in much of the medical literature, but not nearly to the same degree.

If education aspires to the status of a profession, it must adopt the procedure of a profession.[9] Careful, unbiased consideration of alternative courses of action with a full comprehension of both the pros and the inevitable cons of all actions is characteristic of good professional practice. Wild, bandwagon enthusiasm and unquestioned reliance on global models instead of treatment of each case are not. The next decade could well be critical in determining whether curriculum moves further toward professionalism, or . . . what?

Writing About Curriculum Writing: Metatheory and Criticism

When writers write for themselves, they often write about writing. What others have written, as much as what others have done, calls out for

---

[8] James Hessler, "The Content of Arguments in Individualization of Instruction" (Ph.D. dissertation, Stanford University, September, 1977).

[9] Arthur W. Foshay, *The Professional as Educator* (New York: Teachers College Press, 1973).

response. It is only actions described or interpreted in some way that are accessible to language and discursive thought. Views must be expressed before they can be considered and discussed.

When a writer comments on specifics of another's writing, the result is criticism. When a writer builds a more abstract set of ideas that logically encompasses the ideas in another's work, the result is metatheory. Both criticism and metatheory are essential to an informed and sophisticated body of discourse about any subject. Both are in part a matter of attending to one's tools of thought. They are also in part a matter of testing through argument the relative adequacy of contending views. And they are forms of persuasion, means of attacking and defending competing value positions or even competing ideologies. Both criticism and metatheory can disclose implications and assumptions that would otherwise remain tacit in the ways we talk about and interpret curriculum matters to one another and to ourselves.

The most direct form of writing about writing gives attention to the message itself, to what the writing says, to the substantial claims and assertions made. This type of writing ranges from letters to the editor to scholarly reviews of literature. Obviously we are here concerned more with serious responses which often take the form of books or articles whose writing was stimulated by other books or articles. In this sense, any writing with a bibliography is to some extent a response to others' writing. The most direct responses—reviews of research, integrative scholarship, reflective essays or "think pieces"—are vital links in a chain of dialogue that is self-critical and self-improving. For example, the detailed, in-depth criticism of concepts and ideas found in *Psychological Concepts in Education*[10] can be a vital help in strengthening the foundations which most practitioners (and, for that matter, scholars addressing other curriculum questions) are much too busy to examine at all thoroughly. The debate that appears in professional journals, written by practicing curriculum people, is also essential to informed practice. It is a form of putting our professional heads together—obviously a central professional task.

More generally, but less directly, writing about curriculum writing may attend to assumptions and implications of what was explicitly stated. Often this means attention to the social and political values implicit in the writing. The writing of Michael Apple[11] and of the authors represented in M. F. D. Young's *Knowledge and Control*[12] illustrates the outstanding recent work that has been done in this vein. In the domain of personal values, the volume edited by William Pinar, *Curriculum Theorizing: The*

[10] Paul B. Komisar and C. J. B. Macmillan, eds., *Psychological Concepts in Education* (Chicago: Rand-McNally & Co., 1967).

[11] Michael W. Apple, "The Hidden Curriculum and the Nature of Conflict," *Interchange* 2 (1971): 27-40.

[12] Michael F. D. Young, ed., *Knowledge and Control* (London: Collier-Macmillan, 1971).

Reconceptualists,[13] illustrates the flood of recent work, much of it extremely thoughtful and thought-provoking.

Attending to assumptions of what was explicitly stated can also mean identifying basic, underlying orientations. The conflicting conceptions of curriculum identified by Eisner and Vallance[14] in their book of that name illustrate this type of work, an important staple of writing about curriculum writing. And this kind of writing can mean analysis of the language used in the writing, as in the volume *Psychological Concepts in Education.*

Finally, some writing about writing in curriculum is devoted to reflexive inquiry into the field itself. Such writing asks questions like: What should curriculum specialists study and write about? Is a science of curriculum making possible? What is the role of the arts in curriculum thought? Is curriculum planning inherently a moral activity or can it sometimes be strictly technical? On what ideas or what disciplines should the curriculum field be based? What is the present condition of the curriculum field and where is it heading? Examples are: Eisner,[15] Goodlad,[16] Huebner,[17] Schwab.[18]

Writing logical and critical analyses of the work of those who identify themselves with a field is an important function. It is a vital part of healthy self-examination. Without it, fields would not adapt and develop with changing conditions. The danger of preciousness—of in-groupness and of flight from the primary problems of the field—is always present, however. The audience for this type of writing is, after all, small. And members of the audience are also contributors to the writing, so the potential for domestic squabbles is great. When such writing is carried to excess so that the primary problems are lost sight of and writing becomes excessively and obsessively self-conscious, something is wrong with the field and corrective action is called for. But too often the attempt to determine what corrective action is needed draws still further energy into writing about writing. If such a vicious circle closes, a field may find itself moribund, as Schwab[19] has argued in the case of the curriculum field. But the circle can always be broken by creative attention to the primary problems.

---

[13] William Pinar, ed., *Curriculum Theorizing: The Reconceptualists* (Berkeley, Calif.: McCutchan Publishing Corp., 1975).

[14] Elliot Eisner and Elizabeth Vallance, *Conflicting Conceptions of Curriculum* (Berkeley, Calif.: McCutchan Publishing Corp., 1974).

[15] Elliot W. Eisner, "Sources for a Foundation for the Field," in *Confronting Curriculum Reform* (Boston: Little, Brown and Company, 1970).

[16] J. I. Goodlad, "The Curriculum: A Janus Look," *The Record* 70 (1968): 95-107.

[17] Dwayne Huebner, "Curriculum as a Field of Study," in *Precedents and Promise in the Curriculum Field,* ed. Helen M. Robison (New York: Teachers College Press, 1966), pp. 94-112.

[18] Schwab, "The Practical."

[19] Ibid.

Conclusion

Our barnstorming tour of curriculum writing has revealed an extremely varied pattern. Curriculum is clearly an iffy subject. It belongs to Aristotle's "region of the many and the variable" where certain knowledge is not possible, only opinion—multiple and various, more or less considered, more or less adequate, but never clearly true or false. The overall picture of curriculum writing today looks much like Nietzsche's characterization of his own field, philology: "mixed together like a magic potion from the most outlandish liquors, ores, and bones." Technical pieces, scholarship, rhetoric, news, comment, exposes, editorials, ideological diatribes, political broadsides, sales pitches—virtually every form of discourse imaginable—circulate among the most diverse audiences for the greatest imaginable variety of purposes and on practically any occasion.

The overall impression is certainly not of a disciplined body of knowledge or of a profession based upon such a body of knowledge. If the curriculum field is a field, it is a field of problems, problems so divergent that no coherent body of knowledge can be singled out as uniquely appropriate to their resolution. Practically everything known to humanity is relevant, importantly so, to the resolution of some curriculum problem. The activity of those who work on curriculum problems is not and could not be dominated by a tightly knit body of experts in some foundational study or discipline. The nature of the problems does not permit a hierarchical organization of the knowledge bearing upon them.

For me, the field resembles a gigantic marketplace of ideas and proposals. I see workshops where specialized craftspeople are quietly turning out useful (they hope, anyway) gadgets and modestly putting them on display. I see bookstalls where scholarly types are intently discussing the contents of books they almost don't want to sell. I hear vendors hawking their wares and vans with loudspeakers calling people to rallies. I see dimly lit cabarets where plots are being secretly made to overthrow the dominant powers as well as sumptuous clubs where the powerful casually discuss how they should exercise their obviously justly endowed powers.

Curriculum writing seems to me to be a slice of public life itself. It is as rich and varied as that life, and as confused and confusing. It can be described, its pulse can be taken, its course can be predicted with more or less accuracy; but it resists our efforts to reduce it to an orderly, stable pattern. After years of near-despair, I am now content with this state of affairs. Robert Frost expresses my own attitude far better than I could:

> Earth's the right place for love,
> I don't know where it's likely to go better.

A rich confusion is the right state for curriculum writing. I don't know how it could do better.

5 Curriculum Talk
Arthur W. Foshay

IT IS SCARCELY RECOGNIZED that the way we talk and think has a controlling effect on our action. Behind our manifest language is metaphor, which carries latent meanings to events. Behind our action is also theory about the domain of action. The difference between professional teachers and amateur teachers, for example, is that professional teachers act on a theory (however incomplete) of the learner in interaction with subject matter, but amateur teachers have only a theory of the subject matter. One difference between thoughtful curriculum people and those who are superficially controlled by the popular press is that the thoughtful ones use language with care for its latent meanings.

Here, we shall examine a number of metaphors that appear commonly in talk about the curriculum. We shall try to show that each of them is true in some sense, but that none of them is sufficiently true to guide us—nor are all of them, collectively, adequate to our tasks. We shall also consider some things curriculum people *don't* talk about much, but ought to.

First let us explore, briefly, the way metaphors work. Behind every word we use is a history that continues to influence its meaning, at one level or another. The word *curfew,* for example, once meant that it was time to cover the fire for the night. It is still associated with the night, and it continues to mean that the day's activity shall come to an end. A *kindergarten* was a garden where children grew. The idea that children grow and develop like flowers is deeply buried in today's kindergarten. It was not always thus. These unrecognized latent meanings are what we shall explore here, for it is the substratum of meaning that leads to whatever style a curriculum worker creates as he or she speaks and writes. Much of the ridicule directed at educational writing arises justly from ridiculous latent meanings.

We say that professional teachers have a theory of the learner. Let us remember that the hundred-year-old systematic study of children has not yet fully revealed them to us; in so remembering, let us acknowledge that we fill in the gaps in our knowledge with metaphors about children.

82

Metaphors About Children

The Child as Flower

The most popular metaphor among current elementary teachers is that the child is a flower, to be nurtured so that its potentialities may blossom. This metaphor, most would say, has its origin in Rousseau's *Émile*. Rousseau believed that everything a child could become was present in childhood and that, like a growing plant, all the child needed was nourishment. Like others during his century, Rousseau believed that if we would only stop interfering with the state of nature, things would be ideal. Wordsworth, following Rousseau, thought of little children "trailing clouds of glory"—i.e., that they came from heaven and were potentially angelic. The direct implication of the child as flower is that teachers should guide them as little as possible—that left to themselves children would develop ideally, that the natural wisdom of childhood is a sufficient guide for education. Hence deschooling, child-centered school, and in certain respects both Summerhill and the open school came to be.

The difficulty with this metaphor is that it does not allow either for guidance from elders (hence it denies the validity of adult experience) or for deliberation by growing children. An impulse is as valuable as a thought, as the appropriately named "flower children" of the sixties seemed to believe. The hazard is that education would be governed by the whims of children, and everyone knows that a child has a whim of iron.

The advantage of the metaphor is that it encourages whatever potential strengths children have to show themselves. There is such a thing as natural development, of course; it includes much that no one understands.

The Child as Nigger

This metaphor is as harsh as one can imagine. A nigger is one without rights, without status as a fellow human being. To be a nigger is to be cruelly stereotyped; ultimately, to be treated as property—as a slave. Are children ever viewed this way?

The old *tabula rasa* notion is such a view. Teachers who think that a child knows only what the teacher has taught conform to this cruel view. Old-fashioned military training acted on this metaphor. In many schools, children are disciplined without appeal; they have no rights, nor is there any appeal to their reason since the metaphor denies that they have reason.

One interpretation of conditioning theory proceeds from this ugly metaphor. Those teaching methods that proceed on a strict, rather brutal reward-punishment basis arise from the idea that the child is more like a pigeon than a human being. Ultimately, the child is a nigger.

The metaphor is violent, and it breeds violence. Children accept the implications of the metaphors they are subjected to. Children as niggers are treated violently, and they come to believe that violence is the name of the game. Hence the brutality of the social relationships of such children; hence their slavish dependence on the teacher for approval and legitimacy; hence their unchallenged belief, in later years, that at root we are more like animals than like human beings.

The Child as Enemy

We have spoken of metaphors that carry latent meanings. One of those most thoroughly concealed from the general consciousness is that the child is an enemy to be overcome. The metaphor is concealed in the military lingo that has become common recently: "objectives," "strategies," "target populations," "maneuvers," and the others; we "attack problems." In war, the intent is to overcome the enemy. Without an enemy, there is no action. The latent view of children in this language is that they are an enemy to be overcome. It is presumed that they will fight back as best they can, and the teacher's "strategies" are intended to defeat them so that their inherent resistance will come to an end. Like an infantry team, everyone is to obey the demands of the "objectives," totally rejecting all distractions.

On the other hand, the military metaphor reminds us of the desirability of clean organization to achieve whatever purposes are intended and especially of the need for clear-cut purposes. The teacher who takes a pleasing classroom process as sufficient runs the risk of "building a superhighway to nowhere," in Kurt Lewin's phrase. While purposes will emerge out of activity, and some consequences of rich learning activity cannot be anticipated, the current vogue of "objectives" has the desirable effect of leading people to plan as much as they can.

The Child as Cog

If one takes a school to be a smooth-running machine, then the various parts must perform their separate functions efficiently, dependably, and accurately. Each part derives its meaning from its relations with the other parts. No cog has meaning of itself, but the whole machine stops if any of the cogs malfunction.

The hierarchical school structure encourages this metaphor, a metaphor buried deep in the system and rarely if ever used overtly. It comes closest to the surface in a sort of teamwork view: you do your part, and I'll do mine. The idea of independent development is lost in such a view, which has its greatest effect, perhaps, on one's view of the teacher's task. If both child and teacher are cogs, then neither is responsible for the other. The teacher lays out the subject matter, and the child works with it. The possibility of personal relationships as a part of the educative process is ignored. The teacher is best thought of as one "bureaucratic functionary," as Sloan Wayland pointed out years ago, and the child as another.

It is true that in an important sense children are dependent on one another and their teacher. Social development arises from such interdependence, and so does morality. The child as cog has to learn the virtues of cooperation. However, it is obvious that a child is much more than a cog, even if the child is willing to act like one in the interest of playing the game by the apparent rules.

The Child as Machine

When a machine is running properly, it is completely predictable. There are those who yearn for a completely predictable child. Much educational research arises from this metaphor: one seeks that which is "lawful" and predictable about learning behavior. Machines, of course, are run by operators. They are constructed by people—they do not construct themselves, science fiction to the contrary. The metaphor of the child as machine, like some others rather deeply buried in our assumptions, conjures up a child who is nothing of himself or herself, but exists only to fulfill the wishes of others. The child is manipulated for the purposes of these others. If the child will respond predictably (and he/she will) to a combination of negative and positive reinforcement, then that is what is used—some variation of the carrot and stick.

There is truth in the metaphor. People are somewhat predictable. People can indeed be manipulated, often to their benefit. What is required when one manipulates children is that the action be carried on within strict ethical standards, on the one hand, and that the manipulation be carried on only within the limits necessary, lest the children come to expect manipulation and give up on their own abilities to run their lives satisfactorily. Children will submit to manipulation easily in many areas, since it relieves them of the responsibility for thinking and making decisions. Thinking and decision making are hard work, and children will avoid them if they can.

The Child as Chameleon

A chameleon has the astonishing ability to take on the color of its immediate environment. The child as chameleon is under the control of his/her environment, and teachers who work within this ancient metaphor are forever trying to arrange the surroundings so that the child will react appropriately. This view of the child, like some of the others discussed here, does not take into account the child's independence as a person.

The metaphor was first used by Pico Della Mirandola during the Renaissance: "man the chameleon." It was true then, though an incomplete account of what a human being is, and it is true in the same way now. A child is highly responsive to his/her environment—the physical environment, the aesthetic environment, the social environment (or classroom climate). It follows that these environments must be appropriate to the tasks at hand in school and that attention to them is important.

The Child as Miniature Adult

This metaphor was common during the eighteenth century. However, since in education we never seem to wholly abandon ideas or beliefs, and the school system as a whole is something of an attic where all that has ever happened is present somewhere, one can still find schools where the child is viewed as a miniature adult. It is less common now than it was a generation or so ago to tell little boys to "be men!" or little girls to "be ladies," but it is by no means unknown.

Now, old ideas like this one had some truth to them. It is true, for example, that children are forever anticipating adult roles, that they have "a lust for growth." It is true, too, that adults owe children the skills, attitudes, and knowledge that constitute their introduction to an increasingly adult life. Children can, indeed, act somewhat like miniature adults, thus winning praise from the adults. As Ariès points out, during the eighteenth century and earlier, adults did not even see children as such: they were portrayed as having adult proportions, though smaller, or they were portrayed as *putti,* the chubby little cherubs of the painting of the period. Only later did adults see children in their actual proportions. And, we must emphasize, the children would try to act the part.

The Freudian Child

The Freudian account of childhood portrays the growing child as one who (more or less successfully) overcomes a series of conflicts that arise from deep inner drives. The child is a mystery, even to herself or himself; the child lives in a delicate balance among the inner forces that control him/her. All interpersonal relationships reflect this series of conflicts; everything is symbolic of what goes on unconsciously in the child's life. Even the child's reading of such nursery tales as *Little Red Riding Hood* contributes to the resolution of these conflicts, as Bettelheim has pointed out recently.

Such beliefs seem verifiable, though beyond the knowledge of those not psychoanalytically trained. The risk of this metaphor (for the Freudian view is best understood as an array of metaphors) is that the rest of us, lacking such training, can do harm by meddling with forces we don't understand. The practical implication of the Freudian view, in real schools, is not unlike the practical implication of the child as flower: the thing to do, in the face of mysterious powerful forces, is to let them have their way. It is not surprising that both at Summerhill and in the early work of Susan Isaacs one finds the school rooted in a Freudian view of childhood. Basically, the view denies to ordinary teachers the possibility of guidance.

The Child as Gentleman

In the days of Tom Brown, Rugby was an institution devoted to whipping the devil out of boys while at the same time training them to be English gentlemen. To be a gentleman meant that one had a strong conviction of the importance of class distinctions and of the superiority of the gentry. The tradition is very old, going all the way back to medieval times and the training for knighthood. It had its roots, as do so many of our traditions, with the Greeks; the tradition of *areté* (honor, virtue, bravery, excellence) is at the bottom of our tradition of gentility.

What is left of this tradition is the elitism associated with the liberal arts at the college level and the tradition of mannerliness in the lower schools. Like many of the educational traditions associated with the rise of the middle class, this one suffers from superficiality. Just as grammar is no substitute for fluency in writing or gracefulness in expressing oneself, so manners do not a gentleman make.

It's still an attractive ideal, provided it is pursued as it actually is. There is every reason for individuals to behave with grace, generosity, and dignity; to seem to do the difficult without effort; to be modest about accomplishments; yet to accomplish greatly; and so on.

However, the associations that have accumulated around *gentleman* are in general unpleasant. Over the centuries, the principal association with the term is elitism. To be genteel, to act with gentility, means principally to act as if one were a member of the upper class. For an ordinary American to act like a gentleman means, ultimately, for him to put on airs. However, to be a gentleman means, most of the time, no more than to be polite.

It is well to remember the original meaning of the term. While the centuries have betrayed the meaning, it has noble origins.

The Child as Reasoner

For a long time, it was believed that since human reason is not shared with the animals, it was the only virtue worth cultivating. Everything else about human beings was to be subordinate to reason. If something was not obviously reasonable, it was to be suppressed. Hence the suppression of emotion, of the aesthetic, even of the spiritual qualities of what it is to be human. To this day, the education of the reason is thought by most people to be the chief purpose of schooling and by some to be its sole purpose. The development of cognition dominates research on instruction at the expense of research on the other human qualities, and the prestige system reinforces this imbalance.

Teachers act on this metaphor when they try to reason with a distraught child. They act on it when they proclaim that highly charged public problems, such as those that arise from racism, ought not to be highly charged, but rather should be amenable to problem solving. Carried to its extreme, as this metaphor sometimes is, it reduces human beings to computing machines. The famous *New Yorker* cartoon that has the computer printing out "I think, therefore I am" was, like all great humor, closer to the mark than it appeared to be.

We have considered ten metaphors that often govern the way we think about children. Others might be thought of: the child as animal, the child as art object, the child as empty vessel, for example.

The important thing about these metaphors is their widespread influence. Much of the quarreling among educationists arises from them. The quarrel just now, for example, between those who emphasize the importance of objectives and those who see the school as primarily a nurturing institution derives some of its bitterness from the unacknowledged metaphors that underly these positions: the child as enemy and the child as flower. The scorn that the famous prep schools teach their students to show toward the public schools does not arise from an examination of either the prep schools or the public schools. It arises ultimately from the conflict of two metaphors: the gentleman and the commoner.

Each of the ten metaphors contains some truth. Children are indeed, in some sense, flowers, machines, enemies, niggers, chameleons, cogs, miniature adults, Freudian beings, reasoners, and gentlemen. The difficulty with the metaphors, aside from the fact that they do their work undetected, is twofold: they are often carried to harmful extremes; and they are, each of them, inadequate pictures of what a child is.

Not only are they individually inadequate, they are inadequate collectively. All of them together do not describe a child. The fact is, we do not yet have an adequate theory of childhood, though much knowledge and insight have accumulated. Childhood is still, in large measure, a mystery. Every time we try to legislate development, we collide with the fact of individual differences. Not only that, but we collide with the fact that children have minds of their own, about which next to nothing is known.

What follows from the above discussion is that curriculum workers will do well to be pragmatic about where they get their information. The research on child development continues to be a primary source for them, of course, but the research is far from being explanatory of the reality teachers face. Other sources exist: one's considered experience, the experience of teachers and parents one hears about and thinks over, observation of children, and literature. This last, literature, is usually overlooked. Given the present inadequate systematic knowledge we have to work with, we would do well to consider seriously the insights of the great literary figures; for it is precisely their insightfulness that makes them valuable to us. Is a child something like Tom Sawyer or Huckleberry Finn? Tom Brown? Penrod? The young Eleanor Roosevelt? Anne Frank? *Little Women?* Yes, of course; a child is something like all of these and others at one time or another, and in every case the writer has described aspects of childhood not included in our systematic knowledge.

Metaphors About Schools

We turn from metaphors about children to metaphors about schools. Since organized education is an old institution, and since in our time it has become a socially expensive one, it is not surprising that metaphors about schools have accumulated.

The School as Factory

Ever since the rise of factories, people have wanted so to view the school. The earliest factory-form school most of us have heard about was the Lancastrian school of the early nineteenth century, but more recent expressions of the metaphor have also appeared.

A factory is a highly productive, essential, single-purpose organization intended to produce products. Ideally, there is nothing in a factory that does not contribute to its production. Factories are centrally managed, and the work is laid out and supervised by the manager or his surrogates. The workers are organized hierarchically, and there is a distinct division of responsibility between management and labor. Modern factories are organized into systems and subsystems, with the input, process, and output carefully monitored.

A considerable number of schools are put together according to this metaphor, and some educational research also proceeds from it. As originally proposed, team teaching was based on the factory metaphor, for its most striking (and to some, attractive) feature was the hierarchical organization, with team leaders, assistant team leaders, and so on. As in a factory, the work of the team was supposed to be subdivided, specialized, and delegated.

Educational research that is organized on an input-process-output basis also presumes that the school is a factory. One serious drawback to this research is that at present the process is not adequately understood or described, yet some researchers seem to think that an input-output model is sufficient.

There are advantages and disadvantages to the metaphor. Its main advantage seems to be that many public schools, being large, benefit from large-scale management techniques. Such techniques make it possible for the manager of such a school to be readily accountable to the public that pays for the schools and "consumes" the "products." Such techniques offer the promise of increased efficiency both in the use of people and the care of the expensive physical plant. While some criticize the factory model for its impersonality, it is evident that the factory-school need not be impersonal, any more than an actual factory need be. This is a matter of managerial style.

The principal disadvantage of the factory model is that it offers an illusion of certainty in an area dominated by uncertainty and ambiguity. The many serious gaps in educational knowledge require that teachers improvise constantly. To act as if jobs could be described adequately and then distributed according to a table of organization or to act as if the "product" could be monitored satisfactorily is to deceive oneself.

The School as Clinic

One alternative metaphor to the school as factory is the school as clinic. A clinic has an intake procedure, a referral procedure, and specialists who work with individuals according to their needs. Some schools act on this metaphor, though rarely completely. In such schools, one hears a great deal about "individualization," "diagnosis," and "special needs"; one does not hear nearly as much about "evaluation of the output."

Indeed, evaluation appears to be very difficult for such schools. The teachers are preoccupied with the differences and complexities children bring with them and also with that unknown entity, the whole child.

If the school were to respond wholly to the metaphor of the clinic, it would replace the input-throughput-output metaphor of the factory with a diagnosis-referral-specialized treatment metaphor. Typically, this is not done, even in schools dominated by the metaphor of the clinic. Instead, everything is done by one generalist, and the "clinic" suffers accordingly.

The School as Bureaucracy

A bureaucracy is an organization of nonelected government officials, governed by rules and arranged in a hierarchy. Within a bureaucracy, there is a constant struggle to increase the scope of one's authority and, at the same time, to avoid responsibility for anything that goes awry. The much-criticized Senate Office Building in Washington is an excellent example of bureaucratic maneuvering. Designed during one national administration, it was funded during another and built during yet another. Each administration made changes. The beauty of the building, from a bureaucratic point of view, is that its many faults are not ascribable to anyone in particular.

So it often is with the schools. The personnel in the schools are, indeed, nonelected government officials. To the extent possible, they do their work according to sets of rules which are above reason, and they certainly try to avoid responsibility for things that go wrong.

To leave it at that would be unjust. There are, of course, excellent school systems, or school bureaucracies, just as there are excellent government agencies, or government bureaucracies. They rise above the stereotype of the bureaucracy because they have managed to achieve good morale. There is a generalization here: the lower the morale in an organization, the more the individuals in it will behave like the stereotype of the bureaucrat.

Good morale is made of many things, of course. Chiefly, it appears to consist of very frequent recognition of good performance. The people in an organization with good morale take an informed pride in one another. It follows that the curriculum worker can contribute to good morale by seeing to it that excellent teachers are recognized and their advice is sought out.

Consequences of the Metaphors

We have urged here that metaphors function, usually unconsciously, as controls over the kind of approach taken to children and the operating policies of schools. They also influence the way curriculum people talk to each other. Most of the talk is concerned with group management, content management, teaching styles, and politics and power. Let us examine these briefly and then consider what curriculum people *don't* talk about.

Group Management

Since numbers of children arrive at school to be educated, it is not surprising that the management of groups of children occupies much of the attention of school people. The basic fact appears to be that while children arrive in groups, they are all different from one another. What makes individuals a group is what they have in common, not what distinguishes them from each other. So children are grouped according to some commonalty—age, reading ability, sex, or apparent abilities, such as academic proficiency. Of course, every one of these commonalties is a stereotype ignoring most of what a student is. Our tendency to create stable groups on bases such as these arises from the apparent ease of administration of the factory metaphor. When we group children according to some single criterion, then seek to teach them as individuals, the factory metaphor and the clinic metaphor are in conflict. Confusion results.

Such confusion is very widespread in the schools. The grouping that results from the factory metaphor implies that the children are to be taught as a unit—"whole class instruction." The grouping that results from the clinic metaphor would be temporary and transient, according to the shifting needs of the students. Many teachers try to achieve such temporary groupings within a class organized according to the factory metaphor. The frequent (not universal) confusion that results could be reduced if the whole school were to follow the clinic metaphor; as things stand, teachers are left dealing with classes too small to allow the clinic metaphor to operate fully, and they lack the specialized knowledge or assistance that would make the metaphor complete.

An NEA publication of the fifties was called *Labels and Fingerprints*. The point it made was that we tend to deal with children by labels, but that they are as different as their fingerprints. The tension between the two points of view continues to plague us. Perhaps, if we would be consistent with the metaphor we act on, the tension would be reduced.

Content Management

There is a difference between managing content that has been chosen and deciding what to teach. Curriculum people spend more effort on managing than on selecting.

Here, again, the factory metaphor, together with the child as cog or as machine, is found in operation. In a factory, one places manufacturing machines on a production line. The processing of selected inputs is what factories do.

Pursuant to the metaphors, it was almost inevitable that we would adopt a special submetaphor to describe the management of content: the "learning package." Now, a package is a complete entity. It is bounded; it is self-contained; it requires no further attention. A "learning package," to be true to itself, would be a self-monitoring throughput system. It would function most efficiently where no original thinking was required—indeed, no thinking at all. It is not surprising, therefore, that "learning packages" chiefly seek to train students in skills and that the metaphor tempts the curriculum designer to reduce all knowledge to skills, especially those skills that make no demands on the imagination.

The other aspect of managing content that preoccupies the curriculum person is the ancient matter of scope and sequence. Since it appears to be the case that in almost all fields there is no best sequence, much of this concern has little to do with the quality of the offering, only its tidiness. The child is viewed as a self-governing machine in the process of being assembled.

It is interesting that the question of scope, or depth, is not discussed very much in the real school world. A little thought suggests that scope is the only aspect of managing content that has to do with the quality of the offering. Shall we "cover the ground" or, as Earl Kelley used to say, "uncover" it? Shall we seek breadth or depth? Shall we integrate the various subjects or teach them separately? If integrate, how to do it without risking superficiality? If separate, how to avoid overcompartmentalizing the curriculum? This mixture of questions, some very old, seems to occupy little of the curriculum worker's attention. Instead, following the factory metaphor, the tendency is to "plug in" prepackaged content.

Teaching Styles

A significant but lesser amount of the curriculum worker's attention is devoted to teaching styles. Since so little is known about the effectiveness of teaching, and since all kinds of methods and styles seem to work, talk about teaching styles would seem to be for the amateurs. Yet we carry it on.

Perhaps the matter of style arises from the attractiveness of the metaphor of the child as flower. If the child is a flower, we need only tend it; we cannot manufacture it. A teaching style that is gentle, nurturing, respectful, and sensitive to the beauty of the growing child is therefore desirable. Of course, the actual style a teacher adopts is a function of the teacher's view of himself/herself in the role. The gentle, nurturing style is characteristic of the teacher who takes a growing, flower-like view of himself/herself. The contrasting authoritarian style is most commonly found among those who consider themselves gentlemen and ladies and who view the student as a potential member of the gentility. A teaching style arises from a view of how life ought to be lived. To have an effect on style, therefore, curriculum workers would be required to indicate how they think teachers should live their lives—what view they should take of themselves, what basic metaphors they should act on personally, and the like.

Such talk probably would not be permissible. Teachers would tend to think it was presumptuous, and possibly an invasion of privacy.

Politics and Power

A great deal of the talk that goes on among curriculum workers has to do with who's in charge. With the recent resurgence of mandated curriculum by state legislatures and the accompanying demands for accountability in rather narrow ways, the school is being treated like a bureaucracy and the curriculum workers like bureaucrats. The orders are issued, the responsibility is fixed, and in true bureaucratic fashion, everyone tries to place the responsibility elsewhere in the structure.

To prevent this trend toward the bureaucratization of the schools from leading to widespread irresponsibility and rule making, it is necessary for the people in the schools to *take* responsibility. Since it is in the nature of bureaucracies to avoid responsibility, anyone who will take it stands out at once; such a person will find that others will grant it, willingly.

For example, one of the widespread current weaknesses in education is the failure to carry on well-designed local evaluation. Here is a field that cries out for local leadership, a field in which much excellent technique and knowledge have been developed over the years. Anyone in a local school who becomes informed about evaluation can take the responsibility for leading in its development and thus counteract the trend in the public mind to make a mindless bureaucracy out of the schools. The answer to the question "Who's in charge?" would be found; the professionals would be in charge, as they ought to be.

What Curriculum People Don't Talk About, but Should

We have considered what curriculum people talk about in the main. We turn now to look at several topics one rarely hears discussed. In our failure to talk about them, we risk leaving them to be determined by others.

Purposes

We are paying the piper for our failure to take the formulation of purposes seriously. The last widely recognized statements of the purposes of American education were *Education for ALL American Children* and *Education for ALL American Youth,* now nearly two generations behind us. Our failure to devote sustained attention to the formulation of purposes has resulted in the fragmentation of the high school curriculum and the re-emergence of the basics movement. If we won't tell the people what we are trying to accomplish, they will tell us—and they have. They are amateurs at this task, of course, and their efforts are full of mistakes. So far, however, we have not even tried to talk back. The price for our neglect is very high.

Cost

A curriculum decision has seven parts: the *student* (his nature and needs), the *content* (in relation with the student), the *learning method* (in relation with the student and the content), the *purposes* (in relation with the preceding components), the *context* (including instructional materials and the social and physical environment), the *governance* (who makes the decisions and how are they made), and the *cost* (in time, talent, and money). Leave one of these elements out of a curriculum decision, and it will erode or collapse.

Of these, the element least discussed by curriculum people is the cost. We resist the efforts of others to help. Notice how we successfully avoided PPBS (Planning-Programming-Budgeting System) and other attempts at cost-benefit analysis. We make grievous mistakes in this field constantly. For example, school after school has adopted programs from elsewhere without providing adequate staff training. Talent is a part of cost. If you can't staff a program, you can't have it. New programs, such as the excellent ones in geography, have languished because nobody faced squarely the question of time for the new material. Schools have bought portions of expensive curriculum programs because they didn't want to spend the money for the entire program, thus in many cases aborting the program. Some programs cannot be cannibalized.

We are naive about cost, and most of us find the problem distasteful to deal with. We could use expert help in this field. Major economists, such as Fritz Machlup, have given educational cost their serious attention. We would do well to study such books as his *(The Production and Distribution of Knowledge)* and in general to seek to bring to bear on curriculum problems the skills of economists.

What we are talking about is entirely different from what is studied in school finance, and the local assistant superintendent for business is not the consultant suggested here. There is a crucial difference between managing cost and merely holding it down.

Summary

In these pages we have attempted to acquaint the new curriculum worker with the kind of language he is likely to come across in his field and to remind the experienced curriculum worker of some aspects of his work he may have overlooked. If this statement does its work, we will all speak with our minds on the basic metaphors we are using; we will attend to the fundamental assumptions we are expressing about children and schools; we will seek to expand the professional talk we carry on; and we will attend to some unfinished business.

6

Conceptual Bases for Curriculum Thought: A Teacher's Perspective

F. Michael Connelly and Freema Elbaz

OUR ASSIGNED TASK in this chapter was to develop conceptual bases for curriculum thought. Our ponderings on the problem drifted into a world of theories, concepts, and conceptual schemes for organizing our thinking *about* curriculum. We saw ourselves in a land of Tabas, Stratemeyers, Foshays, Beauchamps, and Ruggs; and we imagined that this yearbook challenge might permit still another theoretical addition to the land. But the land is already densely populated. New additions are common. We decided that one more theoretical view, however sound, would be of little benefit to teachers.

Indeed, we thought that there were so many concepts and theories, each of them useful in their own way, that it would be better for us to offer a conceptual criticism of them. In this way teachers could stand on top of all the concepts and theories, classify them, examine their assumptions, and compare their strengths and weakness. But, again, we realized that others had gone before us, for example, Pinar, Eisner and Vallance, Schwab, and Hyman. There are important teacher uses of criticism, and these will be discussed later in this chapter. However, we realized that it was, in principle, possible to construct as many critical theories as there were theories to which the criticisms apply. Again, we could not imagine how we could usefully add to the collection. Besides, our passage from curriculum to theories of curriculum, to critical theories of theories reminded us of Dr. Seuss's Yertle the Turtle who, in his attempt to reach the moon by standing on top of a pole composed of turtles standing on each other's back, fell back into the pond.

Yertle the Turtle's story highlights the problem that finally altered the direction of our ponderings. In the story, the higher the turtle pole grew, the more difficult became the life of the bottom turtle who lived in the pond. Our reflections on curriculum reform over the past 20 years suggested that the teacher's plight in that period was not unlike that of the bottom turtle in Yertle's pole. The prescriptions derived from theories, theories of theories, and corresponding curriculum developments all weigh on the teacher and add complexity to the naturally complex practical world of the teacher. Indeed, theory appears to have done the exact opposite of what is normally claimed for it, namely, to simplify and order a complex world. With these considerations in mind we decided to orient our thoughts directly to the bottom turtle's thinking. Instead of proposing a way of viewing the curriculum, we determined to understand how teachers view the curriculum. What, we asked, is the character of their curriculum thought? How can it be conceptualized?

But if that was our target, how should we proceed? One methodology, borrowed from the traditions of the theoretical world noted above, would be to adopt a theoretical starting point. Thus, for example, we might begin with a set of statements about human nature, learning, and the teacher's place in curriculum. We might show that we view human beings as individuals whose freedom is an important quality which conditions their learning; this view might then be joined with a compatible theory of learning, for example, a Piagetian view of the learner as structuring his own learning; or we might link our notions to a humanistic view or to some other. From this starting point we would go on to make statements about the nature of students, the learning process, and the teacher, thus linking up our theoretical starting point with the experience of the reader and thereby demonstrating the appropriateness of the proposed conceptual basis.

Such a methodology resembles a pattern of curriculum development which will be discussed later in this chapter in the section on methods of curriculum reform. Borrowing a conclusion from that section, we can now assert that this methodology is inadequate to our purpose since it "exhibits a deductive, applied relationship between research and curriculum practice."[1] Accordingly, we not only turned away from the development of a theory about curriculum, we also turned away from the accepted theoretical method. Instead we begin our discussion with our own experience of developments in the curriculum field over the past 20 years. This experience has led us from a starting point in theory, identified below as the Sputnik-Skylab era, through an exploration of the notion of the practical and an appreciation of the centrality of the practical for curriculum, to a new understanding of the need for integration of theory and practice in our view of the teacher.

We invite the reader to follow our account of the notions of theory and practice as they have developed and have been used in the field of curriculum in recent years and to share the understandings we have gained from this view of the field. This account gives rise to a view of the teacher as an agent deploying practical knowledge in the work of teaching and planning for teaching. The centrality of the teacher in this account of curriculum emerges as a necessary feature of our understanding of the nature of curriculum over the past 20 years viewed through the lens of theory and practice.

[1] F. Michael Connelly, "The Functions of Curriculum Development," *Interchange* 3 (1972): 161-77.

Finally, it is this view of the teacher, grounded in our experience of the curriculum field, which will be used at the end of this chapter to generate a conceptual basis for curriculum thought. Readers will then be able to evaluate these notions, not according to whether they accept our theoretical starting point and the line of argument leading out from it, but according to whether they share, retrospectively, our experience and can participate in the process we undertake of giving meaning and order to this experience.

What We Have Learned in 20 Years of Curriculum

The past 20 years have been extraordinary ones for curriculum. It remains for the historians to name and explain the era. Those of us who worked at the time have marked its origin in the Sputnik blast-off and its grounding with Skylab. During that time much was done and much was thought about curriculum.

There were numerous new curricula developed in North America, Europe, and elsewhere. Many were under the sponsorship of governments and foundations and may be traced in yearbooks, handbooks, libraries, and curriculum centers. Myriad others were developed by local teams of teachers. There were new instructional plans, organizational plans, facilities plans, and management plans.

At the same time as these things were done, there was a great deal of thought about the curriculum. Curriculum research, which had only a small place in educational research, virtually developed new subfields of study, for example, curriculum development, curriculum implementation, curriculum evaluation, and curriculum decision making. The curriculum and instruction departments of some universities were upgraded with the addition of research-oriented staff; and in other places new organizations such as laboratories, centers, and institutes were formed with a strong curriculum emphasis. Three new journals started publication: *Curriculum Inquiry, Journal of Curriculum Studies,* and *Curriculum Theorizing.*

Now that we have had such an intense experience with curriculum and now that we are reasonably geared up to think about the curriculum, what have we learned? Five points stand out. The five provide a context for making the case that we must look to the teacher for a conceptual basis of curriculum thought.

Learning No. 1: To Return to Practical Ground

The first thing we have learned is that Skylab brought us back to earth at Sputnik's point of departure. This point is a practical one, a feature that has always characterized curriculum. Traditionally curriculum was concerned with the nuts and bolts of schools and of teacher education programs. People who worked in C and I departments were normally ex-teachers, chosen for their practical success in schools. Commonly these C and I teachers of teachers held the same formal education as did their student teachers. Practical wisdom, not theoretical competence, marked the separation of the two teaching levels.

Sputnik took us on a theoretical ride. For one thing, many of the heavily funded centralized projects were dominated by philosophers, psychologists, sociologists, and subject matter experts. Moreover, the process of materials development relied heavily on scientific procedures for field testing with user opinion and student-effects data helping shape the final product. Many programs were introduced in a rhetoric of theoretical and public debate on purposes of schooling, nature of knowledge, concepts of the learner, role of the teacher, and social need. Theoretical writings proliferated on the development and implementation of curriculum and on the various conceptions upon which these practices rested. The various theoretical arguments and positions came into a semblance of order by a brand of curriculum theory which might be called curriculum criticism. Here, authors, frequently plumping for their own view, wrote *about* the various theoretical views by identifying underlying assumptions and by developing classification schemes.

The return to practical ground from our theoretical ride was directed by Schwab.[2] Schwab's curriculum-as-practical theme was echoed throughout the educational literature. For example, the 1972 National Society for the Study of Education Yearbook, *Philosophical Redirection of Educational Research,*[3] contained practical themes. In the field of educational administration and organizational theory, Greenfield[4] has been arguing for more practical and less theoretical and rationalistic views of organizational development.

These writings on curriculum-as-practical have led to an expanded and more useful notion of what it means to be practical than that with which Sputnik began. As Schwab reminds us, his is no mere "curbstone" notion of the practical. It is a notion lodged in the Aristotelian distinction between practical and theoretical pursuits of men. Using this distinction, we may say that the practical is a very different source for conceptual basis of curriculum thought than is the theoretical; and if we follow Schwab and others, we might even say that the theoretical is inappropriate to our task. The distinction commits us to the view that people have theoretical interests which lead them to pursue the knowing and understanding of things, and they have practical interests which direct them to pursue the doing and

[2] Joseph J. Schwab, "The Practical: A Language for Curriculum," *School Review* 78 (1969): 1-23; Idem., "The Practical: Arts of Eclectic," *School Review* 79 (1971): 493-592; Idem., The Practical: Translation into Curriculum, *School Review* 81 (1973): 501-22.

[3] Harold B. Dunkel, D. Bob Gowin, and Lawrence G. Thomas, eds., *Philosophical Redirection of Educational Research,* in 71st Yearbook of the National Society for the Study of Education, pt. 1. (Chicago: NSSE, 1972).

[4] Thomas B. Greenfield, "Organization Theory as Ideology," *Curriculum Inquiry* 9 (1979): 97-112.

making of things. Science, psychology, and curriculum theory are theoretical pursuits; painting, acting morally, teaching, and doing curriculum are practical pursuits.

The distinction further commits us to the view that the proper study and thought about these pursuits must reflect the nature of their subject matter. Thus, if our subject matter is that of science or psychology, we will properly adopt a theoretical stance as our conceptual basis for understanding events in those fields. And if our subject matter is art or education, we should adopt a practical stance as a conceptual basis for doing better in those fields. To apply a theoretical stance to a practical field is to commit a conceptual fallacy. Following this distinction it is clear, then, that the proper purpose of curriculum thought is not understanding, although this may play a role, but is the improvement of the practice of curriculum. As Dunkel, Gowin, and Thomas state, "The improvement of all of the various activities that make up educational practice . . . is the hope of both empirical researchers and educational philosophers."[5] Thus, the practical ground on which we stand is one in which the conceptual basis of our thought must serve the improvement of curriculum practice, not simply the understanding of it.

Now that we know that our primary source for a conceptual basis of curriculum thought is practice and that the study of practice properly conforms to characteristics of the practical and is governed by the intention to improve practice, we may ask: What are the marks of practice that are of interest to a conceptual basis for curriculum thought? Interested readers would do well to begin with Schwab's essays on the practical and then, depending on their predilections, move backwards in time to Schwab's Aristotelian underpinnings or forward in time to works such as Reid's *Thinking About the Curriculum*,[6] Westbury's *Science, Curriculum, and Liberal Education*,[7] Reid and Walker's *Case Studies in Curriculum Change*,[8] or Connelly's "The Functions of Curriculum Development."[9] It will suffice at this point to note that whatever conceptual bases of curriculum thought are developed out of the practical will be marked by limited applicability. This statement follows from the fact that actions, and the decisions that lead to them, are extremely varied and complex; they do not take necessary paths or use necessary strategies. The paths and strategies could be otherwise, depending on the mix of personnel and environmental factors. Fur-

[5] Dunkel, Gowin, and Thomas, *Philosophical Redirection*, intro., p. 5.

[6] William A. Reid. *Thinking About the Curriculum: The Nature and Treatment of Curriculum Problems* (London: Routledge and Kegan Paul, 1978).

[7] Ian Westbury and Neil J. Wilkof, eds., *Science, Curriculum, and Liberal Education* (Chicago: University of Chicago Press, 1978).

[8] William A. Reid and Decker F. Walker, eds., *Case Studies in Curriculum Change: Great Britain and the United States* (London: Routledge and Kegan Paul, 1975).

[9] Connelly, "Functions."

thermore, since the practical purpose of a conceptual basis for curriculum thought is to improve curriculum, and since curriculum is characterized by various kinds of actions, the scope of application can only be to certain types of actions. Indeed, it is possible to argue that every action is unique and that, at most, we can conduct detailed case studies to aid the formation of conceptual bases of curriculum thought. According to this view, each incident is unique; and while it may be studied in depth, the researcher cannot offer generalizations. Generalizations, according to this extreme view, cannot be constructed from the case by the researcher, only by another practitioner in a situation that he/she deems like that described in the case study. Our own view is that we need not go this far.[10] Later, we will argue that it is possible to construct practical rules, practical principles, and images, each of which is marked by the power of limited generalization.

Learning No. 2: To Use Curriculum Theory for Finding Curriculum Assumptions

The various curriculum theories to which we referred earler are useful to a teacher to the extent that he/she can identify theories which have perspectives coinciding with his/her own. A teacher sympathetic to a given theory may use it as a conceptual basis for thinking more deeply about whatever aspect of curriculum the theory treats. But how does a teacher know which of the theories coincides with his/her own perspective? Indeed, we may ask, is compatability between teacher and theory an adequate view of the possible uses to which a teacher might put theory? We, along with others, think not. The literature which we identified above as curriculum criticism, while primarily intended for other theoreticians, is useful to teachers in revealing theoretical assumptions and in permitting the classification of theories. The following examples from works by Pinar,[11] Eisner and Vallance,[12] Schwab,[13] and Hyman[14] illustrate our point.

In his book *Curriculum Theorizing,* Pinar introduces a classification of theorists according to *function*: "traditionalists," who he claims are atheoretical since their function is to guide practitioners; "conceptual empiricists," who investigate phenomena and whose function is to predict and control practice; and the "reconceptualists," whose function is to under-

---

[10] Idem., "How Shall We Publish Case Studies of Curriculum Development? An Essay Review of Reid and Walker's Case Studies in Curriculum Change," *Curriculum Inquiry* 8 (1978).

[11] William Pinar, ed., *Curriculum Theorizing: The Reconceptualists* (Berkeley, Calif.: McCutchan Publishing Corp., 1975).

[12] Elliot W. Eisner and Elizabeth Vallance, eds., *Conflicting Conceptions of Curriculum* (Berkeley, Calif.: McCutchan Publishing Corp., 1974).

[13] Schwab, "The Practical: A Language."

[14] Ronald T. Hyman, *Approaches in Curriculum* (Englewood Cliffs, N.J.: Prentice-Hall, 1973).

stand the nature of educational experience. The "reconceptualists" further divide into the "critics," who study other theories, and the "post-critical," who are concerned to create their own theory. The marks of enthusiasm for Pinar's own preference, "reconceptualists," are found in such comments as: "They represent an avant-garde" and "Their importance to the field far exceeds their number."

Another widely used critique is Eisner and Vallance's *Conflicting Conceptions of Curriculum*. Their key critical term is not function but *conception*. They are interested in the ways people conceptualize the curriculum for purposes of curriculum development. Five conceptions are presented: the development of "cognitive processes," which is oriented to intellectual operations and stresses the learning processes as a basis for curriculum development; "curriculum-as-technology," which is oriented to strategies of developing curriculum and focuses on the technology of the development process; "self-actualization," which is oriented to the learner's personal growth and stresses curriculum content for this purpose; "social reconstruction," which is oriented to the role of education in society and focuses on curriculum for social adaptation and change; and "academic rationalism," which is oriented to the intellectual tools of culture and stresses disciplined modes of knowing. The Eisner and Vallance criticism is offered without an indication of their own preference.

Schwab presents still another classification to which, with a touch of whimsy, he refers as "flights" from the field. Schwab's key terms are *theory* and *practice,* and he is concerned to identify the various theoretical movements relative to the practice of curriculum. There are six such "flights": a "flight of the field," in which the problems of the field are redefined in terms of some other field; a "flight upward," to theories about theories; a "flight downward," which consists of the stripping away of theory entirely; a "flight sideways," to the role of critic of which his own set of "flights" is an example; "perseveration," which consists of repeated statements of well-known positions, for example, the Tyler Rationale; and a "flight to contentiousness and ad hominem debate." Schwab's preferences are seen in his metaphor of a field dying from an overdose of theory. His own proposal is for the replacement of these theoretical "flights" with a language for talking about curriculum based on the nature of curriculum as practiced.

Hyman's critique uses *focus* as the key term to generate eleven theoretical views on what ought to be done in curriculum. The eleven, he says, are an extension of two identified earlier by Dewey, namely, writers who fix their attention on subject matter and those who attend to the child. The eleven, in which the focus is named in the title, are: "continuing reconstruction of experience"; "activities"; "persistent life situations"; "common learnings"; "structure of the disciplines"; "broad fields"; "existential integration"; "youth views"; "student protest"; "communications"; and "hu-

manistic processes." Hyman, like Eisner and Vallance, is more concerned
to classify than to present his own views.

Consider the fact that each of our critics bases his criticism on different terms: function, conception, theory-practice, and focus. Consequently,
each identifies different assumptions and constructs different classifications
of the *same* literature. This situation points up the fact that the literature of
both theory and critical theory is diverse. Undoubtedly, with some exercise
of the imagination, we might imagine other ways of organizing this literature as, indeed, an inspection of the theoretical literature of curriculum will
reveal. For example, this yearbook presents Geneva Gay's critique.

In summary, our position is that the theoretical literature of curriculum
is an important source for understanding the conceptual basis of curriculum. Probing more deeply into the criticisms of this literature, we are able
to identify some of the assumptions, functions, conceptions, "flights," and
foci that sweep through this literature, thereby obtaining an even deeper
and more theoretical conceptual basis for curriculum. But for the purpose
of understanding and improving the curriculum-as-practiced, these theoretical sources seem somehow removed. Most are curriculum sources for
theoreticians. They are sources primarily aimed at facilitating further
theoretical thoughts about curriculum. In so directing their attentions,
critical authors move apart from the conceptual underpinnings of the practice of curriculum. In short, as Pinar notes, the "reconceptualists'" purpose is "not to guide practitioners" but, rather, "to understand the nature
of educational experience." Their purpose, in other words, is governed by
the traditional intellectual state of mind for theoretical inquiry, crucial for
facilitating debate among theoreticians, but of questionable relevance for
promoting the affairs of practice.

But the fact that the critical literature is designed to be irrelevant to
the improvement of practice does not mean that it is practically useless. We
have already noted that practical benefits accrue to the identification of
assumptions and to the classifications permitted by the critical literature.
The following strategy is suggested as a teacher tool for reading and
pondering usefully the two kinds of theoretical literature.

Let us begin by recognizing that the difference among the various
critics permits us to ask a number of questions of any one theory, thereby
sizing it up from different sides. For example, we might read an Illich proposal by first asking Pinar's question, "What is its function?" Then we would
decide whether the article was directly aimed at the improvement of practical work, was concerned with an empirical basis for curriculum thinking,
or was intended to reconceptualize our thoughts about curriculum. Upon
satisfying ourselves about the theory's function, we might ask Eisner and
Vallance's question, "What is the paper's guiding conception?" Then we
would determine whether the conceptual orientation of the paper was
primarily the technology of developing curriculum, the cognitive processes
of children, children's personal growth, the social growth of individuals

and/or society, or the disciplined modes of knowing. Upon settling the function and guiding conception of the paper we might ask Schwab's question, "What is its movement relative to practice?" Then we would determine whether the author was proposing to solve curriculum problems from the point of view of another field, to offer abstract theoretical accounts, to move laterally to criticism of theoretical writing, and so on through Schwab's six categories. Upon settling the matter of the paper's function, guiding conception, and theory-practice movement, we might then ask Hyman's question, "What is its focus?" Then we would determine whether it was primarily focused on the child or on the subject matter, and we would explore each of the 11 Hyman foci. These questions generate a rich view of the Illich proposal with which we began. The proposal might, for example, turn out to be seen as a "reconceptualist's" "flight" from the field which was focused on the learner with a "social reconstruction" orientation.

One difficulty with the criticisms and the theories of theories is that as yet we have no clear idea of where they are likely to stop. We noted that we might easily have imagined more; and we observed that there were, in fact, more in the literature. What are the limits? In response to just this kind of concern, Schwab and Dunkel, building on the back of Tyler[15] and ultimately grounding their notion in the Aristotelian Topics, proposed the notion of the *commonplaces:* the learner, the teacher, the subject matter, the milieu. As with our critics' questions above, the commonplaces are a practitioner tool. They comprehensively bound the field of curriculum. This fact implies that any fully adequate statement of curriculum will deal with each of these matters in one way or another. The terms themselves are as free from specific meaning as possible. They are merely the corners of the box or, as Herron[16] has described them in his notion of commonplaces of scientific inquiry, the mosaic tiles which may be put together in various ways. If we grant, for example, that even the most abstract and theoretical curriculum argument will somehow deal with the learner, then we are able to ask, What does the theory make of the learner? The same is true for each of the other commonplaces. Their function for us as practitioners in trying to use the theoretical literature as a source for curriculum thought is precisely the same as the set of questions derived from the critics. But now, the commonplaces are both simpler and more comprehensive. For our purposes they are more useful.

Now if we as practitioners are to deal with theory as a conceptual basis of curriculum, then the principle function of our various questions is to determine the compatability between the actual or the imagined practical intentions of the work and our own predilections. When everything theoretical is said, it still remains to be done; and it is done by practitioners

---

[15] Ralph Tyler, *Basic Principles of Curriculum and Instruction* (Chicago: University of Chicago Press, 1970).

[16] M. D. Herron, "The Nature of Scientific Enquiry," *School Review* 79 (1971): 171-212.

with their own beliefs and assumptions and with their own notions of what is worth doing. Thus, for meaningful dialogue with the theoretical world, the practitioner must reach outside the theory to its intentions; and he/she must conduct his/her personal deliberations at this level. There is little point, for example, in laboring through a sophisticated behaviorist's account of learning if one is not willing to entertain the possibility of support for or modification of one's own views on how to teach. Similarly, if one is not prepared to consider radical social reform, he/she may, after asking of Illich the various questions, decide not to read Illich in depth. Thus, our critic-inspired questions are important first and foremost because they permit us to determine *what the author is doing,* thereby allowing us to assess whether the author has any interest for what *we as practitioners want to do.* When that issue is settled, we may then decide to find out *what the theoretician has to say.*

Learning No. 3: To Tolerate Diversity

The third thing we have learned from the recent period of curriculum reform is a tolerance for diversity. Walker, for example, terminates his chapter in this Yearbook with what appears to be almost a sigh of relief that he can now view the many curriculum policies, beliefs, proposals, and theories as proper and according to nature. For many of us the acceptance of diversity represents a kind of personal psychological maturity. Tolerance is a virtue associated with the old and the wise. Our curriculum wisdom is conceptually grounded in an experience which has taught us to think of curriculum as practical. Practical matters are, of course, diverse. To acknowledge this state of affairs is not a consequence of immature theoretical thinking but of taking curriculum for what it is. Curriculum situations and circumstances vary, as do policies and public debates on the curriculum. Furthermore, since, as noted above, our conceptual understanding of curriculum has limited applicability, our concepts will be close to experience. The closer to experience and the narrower their range of application, the more concepts there are. In addition, we have already seen that a further retreat to theory as a source for a conceptual basis of curriculum thought leads also to diversity both in the theoretical views themselves and in the products of critical thought about them. Accordingly, we are led to the view that the diversity of curriculum policies and thought is part of the nature of our beast, curriculum.

There are those, of course, who still believe that it is possible to reduce curriculum diversity. Indeed, comprehensive curriculum orderings such as open classrooms, inquiry teaching, the new math, and Piagetian psychology undoubtedly gain popularity, in part, because they promise order and simplicity. But our experience with bandwagons suggests more than a little caution in this regard. The orderings soon begin to falter as legitimate diversity asserts both its theoretical voice and its practical effect. First one, then another idea is offered as an alternative to the plan. At the same time teachers appear who function poorly according to the plan; some students succeed while others have difficulty; and so on. The comprehensive ordering which was designed for all turns out to be good only for a few. Thus, what at first appears to be a wholistic account is eventually seen as a conceptual reduction.

Easley's[17] review of Gelman and Galistell's *The Child's Understanding of Number* is illustrative. The book is on the cognitive psychology of children's arithmetic and, as Easley points out, presents a view very different from the behavioristic studies popular in the sixties and the even more popular epistemological studies of Piaget which followed. Most of us are aware that Piaget's many theoretical writings found their way into curriculum-oriented journals such as *Science Education,* into the curriculum policy documents of ministries of education, and into preservice and in-service teacher education programs. We might well have thought for a time that Piaget, along with his epistemological orientation, was all that was needed by curriculum planners concerned with the development of basic concepts. But, says Easley—clearly uncomfortable with both the Piagetian and, before it, the behavioristic reduction—Gelman and Galistell have written a "landmark book, because it is part of the reawakening of the cognitive psychology of children's arithmetic." For those of us who have learned our curriculum lessons well, we might have predicted that such a book would be written and that someone would refer to it as a landmark book. Piaget has things of importance to say, but he does not say it all. Children are more diverse than Piaget's view suggests; and other views—behavioristic, cognitive, and others—also have things of importance to say. When one of the views passes for the whole, we may recognize it for the reduction it is.

Learning No. 4: To Evaluate Methods of Curriculum Reform

The 20 years of curriculum activity marked by Sputnik and Skylab were fueled by a drive to improve schooling through curriculum reform. Thus, the theoretical "flight" of this period contains the notion that theory would improve practice. But did it? Undoubtedly, more is now known about curriculum, and there are better curriculum materials available. This outcome can only have beneficial results in the long run. But there is almost unequivocal evidence that the improvements did not come about as intended. There are numerous research studies, reviews, and evaluation reports to support this point.[18] One of our favorites in this regard is Gal-

---

[17] U. A. Easley, Jr., "Review of R. Gelman and C. H. Galistell, *The Child's Understanding of Number,*" *Educational Researcher* 8 (1979).

[18] Some examples are: a) Mary E. Diederich, "Physical Sciences and Processes of Inquiry—A Critique of Chem-Study, CBA, PSSC," *Journal of Research in Science Teaching* 6 (1969): 309-315; b) Michael Fullen and Alan Pomfret, "Research on Curriculum and Instruction Implementation," *Review of Educational Research* 47 (1977): 335-97; c) Joseph B. Giacquinta, "The Process of Educational Change in Schools," *Review of Research in Education* 1 (1973): 178.

lagher's study[19] of the Biological Sciences Curriculum Study classrooms; he reports that it is not possible for a visitor to determine whether he/she is in a BSCS classroom or a traditional classroom without noticing the text used. The curricular field of study known as curriculum implementation is a response to the fact that research, theory, and new programs are not used by schools as intended. Implementation research is designed to discover factors inhibiting implementation and to develop successful implementation strategies.

From the point of view of the relationship of theory and practice, the putting of research, theory, and curriculum programs into practice requires application. Theory is applied to practice. Just as physics studies physical events and applies its theory to engineering practices, so—according to the applied view—social science theories study social events and apply their theory to the practice of education. Thus, the commitment to theory brought with it a methodology of school reform which denigrated practice in the interests of applied theory. In the next section of this paper we exhibit the various theoretical responses that have been made to the inadequacies of this methodology. For now it suffices for us us to point out that we have learned that the application of theory, research findings, and well-researched curriculum developments is an inadequate methodology for the improvement of schools. The corollary to this learning is that practice is most appropriately viewed as an independent starting point for the construction of methodologies aimed at the improvement of practice. We cannot satisfactorily proceed by continually adjusting the application methodology as resistance develops during implementation. Rather, methodologies localized in the nature of practice itself are required.

Learning No. 5: To See the Teacher Role in Curriculum Reform

The impediments to curriculum reform through the application of theory to practice are commonly viewed in implementation studies as originating in either of two sources: the teacher or the organization of schooling. According to research lore, teachers actively resist change, and organizations prevent it by the weight of inertia. There is a rich, relatively independent literature on both of these matters. Space permitting, we might profitably pursue each. However, the pursuit of organizational theory would bring us back to practice and practitioners—hence, the teacher. Organizational theorists tend to view organizations in terms of the arrangement of goals and personnel. Thus, the investigation of an organization is the investigation of the mutual and interactive actions of the people who make up the organization. From the point of view of the curriculum, the key practitioner is the teacher. He/she is the curriculum agent who acts as an intermediary between learners, theoretical knowledge, and the world to

[19] J. T. Gallagher, "Teacher Variation in Concept Presentation in Biological Science Curriculum Study Curriculum Program," (Urbana: Institute for Research Exceptional Children, University of Illinois, 1966).

which knowledge refers. Accordingly, we shall pursue only that line of implementation work which views the teacher as an impediment. The reader should recognize this simplification while granting us our view that other practitioner agents are best seen according to an understanding of the teacher. Our account closely follows a review of this matter by Connelly and Ben-Peretz in a paper titled "Teachers' Roles in the Using and Doing of Research and Curriculum Developments." [20] The various developments are summarized in Table 1.

Table 1. Teachers, Curricula, and Curriculum Theory

A. TEACHER-PROOF CURRICULA	B. TEACHERS AS ACTIVE IMPLEMENTERS	C. TEACHERS AS PARTNERS IN DEVELOPMENT
x ↓ x' ↓ Materials designed to minimize teacher influence on programs. ↓ x"	x ↓ x' ↓ Teachers assumed to have impact on implementation of curricular ideas. Action research and implementation-oriented strategies aimed at helping teachers understand curricular innovations. ↓ x"	x ↓ x' ↓ Teachers assumed to be full partners in development as user-developers. Teacher inquiry oriented toward: discovery of curriculum potential; change and transformation of materials; formation of new alternatives and decisions. y x" z

Legend: x—developers' curricular ideas; x'—translation of ideas into curricular materials; x"—implementation versions of curricular ideas in classroom; y, z—alternative versions of curricular ideas in classroom

Early in the Sputnik-Skylab period, the curious phrase "teacher-proof materials" was popular; journals actually published articles on whether such materials were possible. (See Table 1, A.) This attempt to bypass the teacher's influence altogether is the most visible expression of the applied theory methodology of school reform. Now, however, few researchers write about such notions. Largely due to the implementation-evaluation efforts of large-scale curriculum projects, it is generally recognized that teachers do *not* neutrally implement theories and programs; they develop programs of study for their classrooms by adaptation, translation, and modification of given programs and research findings; they may even occasionally develop their own curriculum materials.

As a result of this reawakened awareness of the teacher's function in curriculum development, somewhat more sophisticated notions of the teacher's relationship to theory and proposed curriculum programs were

[20] F. Michael Connelly and Miram Ben-Peretz, "Teachers' Roles in the Using and Doing of Research and Curriculum Development," *Journal of Curriculum Studies,* forthcoming.

developed. (See Table 1, B.) These ideas respect the influence of teachers on programs and encompass the combined concepts of *implementation* and *action research*. For instance, McNamara,[21] in an article entitled "Teachers and Students Combine Efforts in Action Research," writes that the objective of his article "is to analyze and suggest some supporting roles that teachers and students can assume" in regard to system planning within a school district. Although McNamara refers to the active involvement of both teachers and students in school planning, he points out that this might be an answer to the recognized difficulties in implementing external innovative projects in schools. Likewise, in an article called "Action Research in the School: Involving Students and Teachers in Classroom Change," Fullen[22] describes a project which is concerned with factors that take into account the difficulties of unlearning old roles and learning new roles in ongoing social systems. For Fullen, school change would be facilitated by an understanding of role changes.

The joining of action research with implementation represents an approach to school change which focuses on the implementation process with the assumption that if enough were known about teacher involvement in curriculum implementation, theoretical findings and program developments would find their way more directly into the classroom. Admittedly, this approach is more realistic in its recognition of the teacher's influence and more responsive to the teacher's need to feel involved and effective. Yet the approach retains the same basic stance on the teacher's role that characterized the research and development efforts of the 1960s.

At first, action research-implementation strategies might appear to be courteous and respectful of teachers and ideologically on the right side of school change since they recognize the influence of teachers over the actual uses of research and program materials. But closer inspection suggests that such programs depend upon an unnecessarily restricted view of teacher inquiry. They hold that teachers should limit their investigation to strategies for adopting an idea and should not do an investigation of the relative merits of the idea itself. If idea x is to be implemented, teachers, however humanely, are to be converted to a belief in x and to a deeper understanding of x. Believing in x and knowing what is intended by x, they will, according to action research-implementation strategy, teach x in a less modified, purer, and therefore more effective form. The principal fault in this orientation is the notion that teachers play mere supporting roles in the educative process and are unable to act as critics at the level of ideas. With such a notion it makes sense to be offended when teachers do not imple-

[21] James F. McNamara, "Teachers and Students Combine Efforts in Action Research," *Clearing House* 47 (December 1972): 242-248.

[22] Michael Fullen and others, "Action Research in the School: Involving Students and Teachers in Classroom Change," *Educational Change and Society: A Sociology of Canadian Education,* ed. R. A. Carlton and others (Toronto: Gage, 1976).

ment as prescribed, and it makes sense to construct sophisticated, humane methods to modify teachers' role behavior in the direction of minimizing their influence as adapters of the "good" new educational strategies.

The various efforts to retain the theory application methodology (Table 1, A and B) through accommodations to teacher impediments were the joint products of theoreticians, policy makers, and high-level practitioners. It was not merely the theoreticians who worried that their theory was not appropriately applied and who therefore undertook evaluation and implementation research. Policy makers who had a stake in demonstrating their accountability to public wishes were equally committed to applied theory as were administrative personnel who often saw their job in school boards as the application of local, provincial, and national policies to their situation. No doubt even teachers, educated as they are in the tradition of practice-as-applied-theory, aided and abetted the applied methodology. There was not, then, a mere theoretically abstract test of the application methodology for school reform, but a very concrete and concerted one as well. There can be little doubt that the application methodology is inadequate because teachers are autonomous curriculum agents.

We may summarize our point by noting that when the teacher's role as a thinking, deliberating agent oriented toward action is adopted, the picture changes. (See Table 1, C.) With such a view the teacher assumes a position of autonomy over instructional acts and, thereby, over theories and curriculum developments applied to instruction. In an earlier paper[23] it was argued that researcher-developers and teachers may best be seen as supporting each other in curriculum development by virtue of their different, but obviously related, functions. This relationship decisively shifts the teacher's function from implementer to decision maker and independent developer.

Consistent with this notion of an effective teacher is the concept of "curriculum potential." [24] For Ben-Peretz the potential of any given set of curriculum materials encompasses developer interpretations as well as possible uses that might be revealed by external analysts or implementers. We agree with her when she writes:

> Curricular materials are more complex and richer in educational possibilities than any list of goals or objectives, whether general or specific, and contain more than an expression of the intentions of the writers. If we look upon materials as the end product of a creative process, then any single interpretation yields only a partial picture of the whole.[25]

The analysis of "curriculum potential" for a particular classroom situation offers wide scope for the teacher's exercise of a reflective investigative spirit. Teachers try out various ways of using theory and curriculum materials in

---

[23] Connelly, "Functions".

[24] Miriam Ben-Peretz, "The Concept of Curriculum Potential," *Curriculum Theory Network* 5 (1975): 151-59.

[25] Ibid.

concrete classroom situations as they function in their particular, practical situation.

In short, the appropriate knowledge and experience held by theoreticians and by practitioners cannot easily be exchanged. Theoreticians, in their various guises as theoreticians, researchers, external developers, and policy makers cannot adequately plan for particular circumstances when they have no experience of them. Likewise, of course, practitioners cannot adequately plan for generalizable knowledge and generalizable materials development. Neither can the knowledge of the experts pass for the wisdom of the teacher, nor can the teacher's wisdom pass for theoretical knowledge of what is to be thought or developed.

We do not propose, therefore, that theoretical work be abandoned, but merely that our key practitioner, the teacher, be treated on his/her own terms and not as a derivative of the theoretical. Each has a role to play. Our problem is that the 20-year theoretical "flight" adopted a methodology which implied that the teacher's function could be subordinated to the theoretical function in the improvement of schooling.

Thus, our essential problem for this chapter is set. Theoretical knowledge has its place; and we have considerable insight into it, both from its own publication and from theoretical criticism of it. We believe that theory has a role to play in the improvement of schools. But we do not believe that improvement can come about by any mere application of theory. And, if we are *not* to think of the teacher as an adjudicator, adjuster, and adapter of knowledge, thereby retaining the application methodology, then we are committed to thinking of the teacher as a knower of the practical. We believe that this constitutes our rock bottom conceptual basis of curriculum thought when our concern is with curriculum as practiced.

There is very little direct research on the problem at hand. Certain notions based on our own studies are described below for purposes of better understanding this practical basis of curriculum thought. But we also recognize that what we have to say at this point constitutes a mere nibbling at the edges. The field of curriculum has been so devoted to its theoretical fancy and to the retention of its application methodology that little thought has been given to the nature of teachers' practical thought. As that work is undertaken, we may expect more satisfying practical conceptions of curriculum thought.

Intellectual Milieu for Teacher's Curriculum Thought

The intellectual milieu for teacher's thought is prescriptive in character. This characteristic derives, in part, from the fact that there are numerous stakeholders to the ground on which the teacher works.[26] They each

    [26] F. Michael Connelly, Robin J. Enns, and Florence Irvine, "Stakeholders in Curriculum," in *Curriculum Planning for the Classroom*, ed. F. Michael Connelly, Albert S. Dukacz, and Frank Quinlan (Toronto: OISE Press, forthcoming).

want something. More than that, they have a right to something. Parents, business people, principals, superintendents, and so on come to mind. It may be thought that students are the ultimate stakeholders, and so they are. However, they have a special role in that they constitute the primary subject matter of teacher's thinking; we will, therefore, postpone discussion of them until later. Policy makers also have a special role in that they carry legal authority for their expression of what should be done in the schools. It is, of course, the case that policy is often divisible into statements of must and statements of should where only the must statements have legal authority. Researchers and theoreticians have the least direct stake in schooling, although one might imagine differently upon witnessing the 20-year Sputnik-Skylab "flight." Nevertheless, while theoreticians are paid to understand practice and to think up ways of improving practice, they have no specific stake in any particular situation except insofar as they may privately represent a business interest, their own children, and so forth. Yet they too have operated prescriptively. It is clear that the intellectual stance behind the applied theory methodology of school reform is prescriptive in character. Thus, on all sides, the teacher is *not* in a knowing environment but, rather, in a prescriptive, doing environment of other stakeholders. Teachers are exhorted, expected, and required to do this, that, and the other thing, and to do it better. While the theortician does his/her work in a "what is" environment, the teacher does his/her work in a "what ought to be done" environment.

Furthermore, the teacher's own thinking is constrained by a need to do something educational which, by any account, is necessarily marked by the growth of children. Thus teachers' thinking is characterized by questions of what ought to be done to encourage the growth that is the purpose of their work, and their thinking takes into account the prescriptive wishes of stakeholders in their intellectual environment. A research-oriented professor reading this chapter will quickly grasp our meaning. His/her thinking is very different when he/she is pondering research problems than when he/she is planning for his/her own class instruction. Academics, in fact, think of these two functions as very different parts of their lives. Some think of research and teaching as mutually beneficial; others grudgingly do one at the expense of the other; and still others do only one or the other, either in university settings or in pure teaching or pure research institutions. But however they think of the relationship, few would hold that thinking about research and about teaching are the same.[27]

How does one function in this prescriptive teaching environment? Schwab [28] and others have named the method *deliberation*. People meet in

---

[27] There are exceptions, of course, for example, professors who teach as if teaching were merely an applied branch of their own theoretical work. Their counterpart in the schools are those few dry-as-dust subject matter secondary school teachers who are occasionally found.

[28] Schwab, "The Practical: A Language."

groups to discuss and debate ends and means; through this process decisions on what to do are made. A number of studies have been done on this deliberative method. Schwab [29] referred to deliberative methods as "arts" in the last of his three papers on the practical. Walker [30] studied the deliberative methods of a curriculum planning team. One of us has undertaken a study of teacher thinking relative to theory. And in Reid and Walker's [31] book of case studies of curriculum development, the notion of strategy is used to refer to the deliberative methods employed by the subjects in the case study. But these studies, important as they are to our understanding of the teacher's method of practical thinking, do not reveal the practical knowledge with which the teacher does his/her thinking.

In short, we have been taught that teacher thinking occurs in a prescriptive intellectual milieu. Furthermore, we recognize that teacher thought is, itself, prescriptive in character and proceeds by the method of deliberation on which there has been some research. But there is little research on the nature of the practical knowledge with which the teacher does his/her thinking. It is to this matter that we now turn our attention.

The Teacher's Practical Knowledge

Substantively, the content of the teacher's practical knowledge is easily cataloged. There is knowledge of subject matter, students, milieu of schooling, development and organization of curriculum materials, instructional procedures, and self. The latter is often overlooked when one's perspective is not practical. But when the teacher's point of view is adopted, personal goals, values, beliefs, talents, and shortcomings come to the fore. These matters affect the teacher's curriculum planning and teaching.

We might imagine that the above catalog of knowledge areas was merely filled with chunks of content knowledge drawn from the subject matter disciplines; bits of theoretical knowledge drawn from various social science disciplines; pieces of accumulated wisdom of the field; recipes drawn from the tradition of schooling in a given culture, school system, or school; and acknowledged items from the personal teaching habits of the individual. Indeed, to note these is almost to assert the commonplace. Teacher education programs, for example, are commonly organized according to the areas noted in the catalog. Program content is normally drawn from the subject matter disciplines, for example, the requirement of the equivalent of a B.A.; from the social science disciplines, for example, courses in psychology; from accumulated wisdom of the field, for example, methods courses and the use of associate teachers as "professors"; from

[29] Schwab, "The Practical: Translation."

[30] Decker F. Walker, "A Naturalistic Model For Curriculum Development," *School Review* 80 (1971): 151-65.

[31] Reid and Walker, *Case Studies.*

traditions of schooling, for example, special state or provincial certification requirements; and from local mores and personal traits, for example, practice teaching. This program, and the catalog on which it is based, appears to be a realistic account of the teacher's knowledge in which the practical and ad hoc character of that knowledge is recognized. But if no more than this can be said for the teacher's knowledge, the reader would be justified in wondering whether it warrants being called knowledge at all. We suggest that the teacher's practical knowledge is not simply a collection of random theoretical statements combined with handy hints for the care and feeding of students and leavened by personal idiosyncrasy. Rather, we suggest that the teacher's knowledge can most usefully be viewed as a body of knowledge, not a totally comprehensive or consistent one to be sure, but nonetheless a body of knowledge held in a uniquely practical way and structured in terms of the teacher's practical purposes.

Customarily, knowledge is thought to be structured in such a way that the parts form a coherent whole. This is recognized in our metaphor of a "body" of knowledge. Knowledge, moreover, is thought to stand in relation to further knowledge and to the phenomenal world. Its relationship to further knowledge permits its growth and development; and its relationship to the phenomenal world is one of order, simplicity, and generalizability. It is true, of course, that different thinkers on the notion of knowledge conceive of its structure, growth, and relationship to the world in a variety of different ways. But the problems set by these three features are common to all and recognized in branches of thought known as epistemology and ontology. We have, therefore, conceptualized the teacher's practical knowledge along the same dimensions: orientations of teacher's knowledge and organization of teacher's knowledge. Our notions of the orientation and organization of teacher's knowledge permit us to construct a view of the teacher's knowledge which allows for growth along the various orientation directions and according to its various levels of organization.

In what follows we outline the notion of the teacher's practical knowledge, using categories developed in a recent case study of a teacher's knowledge.[32] Illustrations presented here are drawn from that study. The teacher referred to is Sarah, a teacher of English and reading in a large suburban high school. We present five orientations: to situations, to theory, to others (social), to self (personal), and to experience; and we present three levels of organization: rules of practice, practical principles, and images.

Orientations of Teacher's Knowledge

To Situations. It is evident that the teacher works within the context of specific situations. His/her use of knowledge in these situations is *not* like the theoretican's application of a general statement to a particular

---

[32] Freema Elbaz, "A Case Study of a Teacher's Practical Knowledge" (Ph.D. dissertation, Ontario Institute for Studies in Education, forthcoming).

instance to determine whether the instance fits the theory. Nor is the teacher's use of knowledge akin to the lawyer's use of a body of legal precedents, subsuming the details of a case to the general features of the precedent which applies. For the teacher the instance, his/her case, comes first. The situation determines what aspects of his/her knowledge (theoretical view, classroom methods, procedural rules, habits, and so forth) will be selected as relevant and subsequently made use of. The teacher's orientation to situations implies that we cannot speak of the teacher's knowledge as fixed. In each case the teacher will bring to bear a different range or selection from his/her knowledge, chosen with a view to helping him/her deal with the situation at hand.

For instance, Sarah, the teacher in our case study, had extensive knowledge of communications and group dynamics which she used in developing one unit of a course on learning. She was well aware that this knowledge was equally relevant to the work of the group of teachers involved in developing the learning course. But in the latter context this knowledge was not brought to bear because it did not serve the group's task of preparing for instruction. As Sarah put it:

> Everything in the human side of me said, I should show him that I can risk expressing my own doubts . . . but I didn't, because it was only ten minutes till the class, and I couldn't allow myself that luxury, because we still had to get over a few points.

However, to think of situations as a sequence or series of unique events, each of which calls forth a different use of the teacher's knowledge, is to oversimplify. Teachers, we believe, perceive situations in their totality; and they cope with this perception by using knowledge to reduce complexity. For example, Sarah's perception of her situation was rich and complex. But, partly as a result of the perceived complexity, she found the classroom a stressful place in which she must "constantly be tuned in to so many things." One way Sarah oriented her knowledge to this situation was by developing and using materials with a relatively narrow focus in the area of learning skills. Structuring class work around specific techniques of reading, for example, enabled Sarah to better cope with her perception of a chaotic classroom situation.

To Theory. As someone who works with intellectual materials, the teacher must necessarily shape his/her work by some view of theory. This view may range from outright rejection—for example, the teacher who sees himself/herself as a pragmatist working by trial and error in the classroom—to deliberate, single-minded application of a particular theory—for example, the teacher who is inspired by Piaget. In between, the teacher may feel that theory is relevant but remote, or difficult to use; such a teacher may draw on theories of practice rather than on clearly theoretical formulations. Whatever the teacher's position, his/her stance with respect to theory determines what kinds of theoretical knowledge he/she will draw upon and how he/she will use it in a particular situation. Thus, the teacher's theoretical orientation shapes his/her practical knowledge in an important way.

Sarah's work with a learning course for secondary school students is illustrative. Her stance toward theory was a very respectful one. She saw theory as a body of knowledge standing above practice and "affording a broader view." But because of this respect, she was sometimes inhibited in making use of theory. The learning course, developed cooperatively with other teachers, began with the intention of preparing materials on thinking. But gradually the focus shifted to learning defined in terms of tasks such as essay writing, which students were asked to complete in school. The shift did not reflect a change in what the teachers wanted but, rather, in what they considered themselves knowledgeably capable of doing. They came, quite correctly, to believe that thinking was a very theoretical field, one in which they had little education. Consequently they shifted to learning, an area in which they thought they were better prepared by both training and experience. Thus, it is clear that the redirection of their work was directly influenced by their respectful view of theory. Since one way of proceeding did not satisfy their notion of the proper use of theory, they chose another way that did.

To Others. Inevitably, the teacher's knowledge is shaped by social conditions and constraints. Examples of the social shaping of teacher's knowledge have been provided in recent years by writers in books such as *Knowledge and Control*.[33] On the other hand, teachers also use their knowledge quite purposefully to structure their social situations by organizing classes to bring about particular teacher-student relations, by involving themselves in the development of curricula as a group effort, and by promoting particular notions of teaching and learning within the community of their colleagues. This active aspect of the social orientation of teacher's knowledge is of particular importance in our view because it supports the picture we are drawing of the teacher as an agent within the curriculum process.

The case study provides a striking example of the teacher's socially oriented use of knowledge. Sarah was a teacher who strongly disliked being in a position of power in her relations with students. She wanted to avoid the "phoney structure" in which she was "perceived as the one who judges, the one who passes and the one who gets the other person into university." In her work she gradually shifted her teaching focus from English literature to reading. In doing so she developed a subject matter and a style of work which allowed her to relate to students on the basis of skills she could share with them rather than on the basis of some intellectual property to be transferred to them. She also found a new context

[33] Michael F. D. Young, ed., *Knowledge and Control: New Directions for the Sociology of Education* (London: Collier-Macmillan, 1971).

for her work in the school's reading center. The center constituted a smaller social framework which was more congenial for Sarah than the school as a whole for the sharing of skills with students.

To Self. Every encounter between teacher and student reveals their divergent perceptions of their common situation, their attention to different aspects of the situation, and their different interpretations of the situation. These points of view, and the interpretations which they produce, reflect a personal need to integrate, order, and render meaningful one's experience. The teacher's personal orientation rests not only on intellectual belief but also on perception, feeling, values, purposes, and commitment. These are reflected in the example just cited: Sarah's development of subject matter in the area of learning skills enabled her to meet the goal of helping students to acquire skills and also allowed her to meet a personal need to be in a position of service to students and other teachers.

To Experience. Implicit in the situational and personal orieintations of the teacher's knowledge is its experiential base. The teacher's knowledge is drawn ultimately from his/her experience, gives shape to his/her world, and allows him/her to function in it. There are many ways of characterizing the teacher's experiential orientation. Schutz and Luckmann,[34] for example, suggest that we look at the form and degree of spontaneity the teacher manifests in teaching, at the level of attentiveness he/she brings, at the number of different features of his/her experience to which the teacher attends, and at the time perspective the teacher has on his/her work. Terms such as these allow us to focus on the quality of the teacher's experience and on the style of teaching and of thought. With respect to Sarah, these terms allow us to attend, for example, to a conflict between the spontaneity of her teaching and her wish to be in control of the direction taken by student learning. This focus of attention further enables us to discover that when the subject matter she was teaching had been fully worked out, Sarah was better able to mediate between spontaneity and control in her teaching.

In summary, Sarah's practical knowledge was composed of theoretical, practical, and personal fragments. These fragments were welded into an organized whole by virtue of the fact that Sarah was in an active exchange with her curriculum situation. Her knowledge was practical because it functioned to orient Sarah in a way that permitted her to act in the situation. Welding, of course, is a poor metaphor to label the forces which bonded her knowledge fragments into a functional whole. As the various orientations shifted in emphasis according to the task and the moment, the particular shape of her practical knowledge adjusted. Indeed, rather than welding, we would do better to adopt a biological metaphor

---

[34] A. Schutz and Thomas Luckmann, *The Structures of the Life-World* (Evanston, Ill.: Northwestern University Press, 1973).

and use the notion of regulatory adjustment to environment. With this notion in mind, we can say, in the case of Sarah and in general, internal readjustments continually occur as the organism (teacher) interacts with its environment. The adjustments change the shape and expression of the organism in the interest of maintaining its ability to cope with the environment.

Organization and Structure of Practical Knowledge

One consequence of adopting the notion of a fluidly structured personal knowledge composed of many fragments and oriented situationally, theoretically, personally, socially, and experientially is that, once again, we confront our old friend diversity. But now we are firmly on curriculum ground. Here, at least, is a conceptual basis for curriculum thought.

But have we created nothing more than a chimera in which flickering situational events call forth flickering conceptual responses in practical knowledge? This is one way of reading Schwab, who, it will be recalled, piloted the theoretical "flight" back to practice. Schwab noted that the bringing to bear of practical knowledge on a problematic situation results in a decision; and decisions, he holds, are always particular and non-generalizable. A distressing implication of this reading of Schwab, for Schwab as surely as for others, is that one cannot learn from one's experience. But surely teachers can and do profit from experience. Indeed, practical knowledge as described above comes *from* practice. It is constructed through time by the actions taken. Some recognize this learning with the phrase *the experienced teacher;* others, with the word *wisdom.* But whatever we call it, we are compelled to think of it as learned through practice. The reader is reminded that an orientation to theory is part of practical knowledge and that the teacher's study of research and theory in university courses will constitute a practical orientation. The teacher will study theory qua practice, unlike the inexperienced or the research oriented. Thus, when we talk of learning from practical experience, we include the study of theory by experienced teachers.

To account for this learning, and for the commonsense observation that teachers act "in general" to some recognizable degree, we have adopted three terms: *rules of practice, practical principles,* and *images.* The three terms reflect varying degrees or levels of generality in the teacher's organization of knowledge and embody his/her purposes in varying ways. Rules of practice are statements, sometimes highly descriptive, of what the teacher does. The use of rules of practice is a methodical carrying out of the teacher's purposes, which may or may not be articulated. The practical principle is a broader, more inclusive, statement than the rule. Practical principles embody purpose in a deliberate and reflective way; the statement of a principle enunciates, or at least implies, the rationale which emerges at the end of a process of deliberation on a problem. Finally, the image is a brief, descriptive, and sometimes metaphoric statement which captures some essential feature of the teacher's perception of himself/herself, his/her teaching, his/her situation in the classroom, or his/her subject matter. Images serve to guide the teacher's thinking and to organize knowledge in the relevant area. The image is generally imbued with a judgment of value and constitutes a guide to the intuitive realization of the teacher's purposes.

Sarah's knowledge of communication was expressed on all three levels. Some of the rules of practice she followed are expressed in this statement: "I certainly try very hard to listen very actively to the kids, to paraphrase, to encourage them to paraphrase, and at most times to allow them to express their concerns without judging them." The principle which orders Sarah's rules is that students should be provided with a class atmosphere in which they are able to take risks and thereby come to communicate more openly. The image which captures in a metaphoric way the purpose toward which Sarah worked is found in her statement that she wanted to have "a window onto the kids and what they're thinking." Equally, Sarah wanted her own window to be more open.

Conclusion

We have sketched a view of the teacher's knowledge as practical, illustrated with reference to the practical knowledge of one teacher. In doing so with Sarah we have shown how the world of practice continually shaped that teacher's knowledge and, conversely, how the teacher herself structured the practical situation in accordance with her knowledge and purposes.

The reader may be wondering, however, what substantive guidelines, if any, can be drawn from this analysis. Situations differ; teachers differ. What knowledge, what views are likely to serve teachers best? What sorts of training and professional development will provide the most appropriate practical knowledge and help teachers use their knowledge effectively? We can best answer these questions by summarizing what we have done here and giving our recommendations.

We begin by considering, and rejecting, a number of theoretical starting points for tackling the job of developing conceptual bases for curriculum thought. So we have not offered conceptual bases for the teacher's thought in the sense of substantive content taken as valid for all practitioners—conceptual "furniture" with which to fill the teacher's mind. Instead, we chose to share with the reader our own experience of events in the curriculum field and to show how this experience led us to see the teacher with his/her own knowledge and ways of using it as central to curriculum. We went on to describe in detail one research experience—a case study of a teacher viewed as a holder of practical knowledge—and to articulate the conception of practical knowledge to which this experience gave rise. In so doing, we have elaborated a process which teachers may follow to arrive at their own conceptual bases. We have argued that the teacher's curriculum thought is practical and that it arises from experience in a unique, personal—though not unprincipled—way.

Our view of teacher's knowledge as practical and as central to curriculum thought rests on assumptions about knowledge, about teaching and learning, about the social milieu; our assumptions grew out of our experience with curriculum and with the work of teachers. Here we can only suggest some of our assumptions. Following Dewey, we take a view of knowledge as a process of inquiry, emphasizing the act of creating knowledge through inquiry rather than the work of acquiring the fixed products of previous inquiry. Thus, we assume that the subject matter of instruction should be presented, at least at times, as a process of inquiry. We stress the active, constructive, and purposive nature of mind and of learning. We believe the teacher learns from the act of teaching.

Our purpose is not to argue that the reader adopt our point of view but to illustrate a process and recommend that teachers adopt a personal version of that process in their own work. That is, we are suggesting that teachers begin with their own experience and work to understand and articulate it. The concepts that will be needed to give form and direction to a teacher's experience cannot be specified in advance; they are dependent on the teacher's situation, needs, purposes, predilections, training, and the like and should be closely tied to these practical considerations. At the very end of such a process, when the teacher has come to a clear understanding of his/her own experience and is aware of the knowledge he/she uses to deal with that experience, then and only then he/she may wish to begin to operate in a theoretical manner, spelling out his/her basic assumptions and clarifying these, but always with a view to further serving his/her own practical needs.

This process we have discussed is a new one for teachers who have not generally been trained to respect their own experience as evidence of knowledge and as a means of extending that knowledge. It is important that teachers be provided, in teacher training and in in-service workshops, with varied opportunities to become aware of their own knowledge and of how they are using it. Only then will they be able to structure their own teaching situations so as to improve practice and at the same time to increase the range of their experiences and thus to extend their own knowledge. We believe that teachers would profit greatly from making this process a conscious part of their work.

7

Conceptual Models of the Curriculum-Planning Process
Geneva Gay

> Curriculum construction in the United States is generally conducted in a shockingly piecemeal and superficial fashion. "Reforms" are implemented in response to popular clamor and perceived social crisis; "innovations" are often little more than jargon; and the whole process is influenced mainly by mere educational vogue. The results, of couse, are school programs characterized by fragmentation, imbalance, transience, caprice, and at times, incoherence.[1]
>
> Robert Zais

SOME CURRICULUM WORKERS would argue vehemently with Robert Zais' assessment of curriculum planning in American education. Others would applaud his perceptiveness. Whether one agrees or disagrees with Zais' description of curriculum practice in the United States, most would agree that curriculum planning is an extremely difficult task. And, it is one that occurs without a single set of concise, prescriptive guidelines. Curriculum development is far from being a purely objective or scientific enterprise that follows a universal, predetermined planning process; curriculum development is more of an "artistic" endeavor that is often chaotic, political, and emergent. It embodies a combination of intuition, individual initiative and creativity, trial-and-error experimentation, social politics, and educated guesses.

While no one set of prescriptive guidelines is acceptable to all curriculum specialists, some consensus exists concerning the generic components of curriculum construction. Curriculum theorists and practitioners agree that, in one form or another, curriculum development includes: identification of educational goals and objectives; selection and organization of content, learning activities, and teaching processes; and evaluation of student outcomes and the effectiveness of the design process. However, what approach should be taken in trying to accomplish these tasks so that the process of curriculum planning is systematic, coherent, and effective

---

[1] Robert S. Zais, preface to *Curriculum: Principles and Foundations* (New York: Thomas Y. Crowell Company, 1976), p. xi.

is problematic. Some theorists and practitioners recommend the use of academic rationalism as the most feasible approach to the planning process; others appeal to the psychological order and experiential interactions of the individuals in the teaching-learning process; others endorse scientific technology; and still others recommend the political realities of given school situations.

In actuality curriculum practitioners usually do what the particular situations and circumstances prompting instructional development demand at a given point in time. Rarely, if ever, is a single conceptual model of curriculum planning used to guide curriculum practice. Rather, practitioners are more likely to use an eclectic approach. In the act of creating curriculum, they combine bits and pieces of content and processes from different theoretical models to make their actions coherent or to develop a workable format that can turn the potential chaos of conflicting demands, needs, and interests of different constituent groups into reasonable, manageable instructional plans.

Despite this "reality," there is a place for theory in curriculum practice. According to Ronald Hyman, a particular focus in the curriculum-planning process is necessary "to give coherence and rationality to the decisions made concerning the curriculum."[2] Louise Berman contends that "the curriculum must establish its points of emphasis or priority. Without such emphases the curriculum becomes bland and does not provide the means of dealing with problems of conflicting interests."[3] Robert Zais suggests that a "theoretical framework, judiciously conceived and utilized, is just as essential for the rational, orderly, and productive conduct of the curriculum enterprise"[4] as historical perspective. Hilda Taba declares that "any enterprise as complex as curriculum development requires some kind of theoretical or conceptual framework of thinking to guide it."[5] Curriculum theory can either guide practice or can be used as a perceptual screen through which practice is interpreted and ordered.

Four discernible models for conceptualizing the curriculum-planning process exist. For purposes of this chapter they are identified as the *academic model,* the *experiential model,* the *technical model,* and the *pragmatic model.* These models are not pure: they do not constitute mutually exclusive categories. None is functionally operational: curriculum practitioners will not implement the model in its idealized or theoretical form or employ one model to the total exclusion of all others. Rather, curriculum workers are likely to use segments of one or another of the models,

[2] Ronald T. Hyman, ed., "The Curriculum Issue," in *Approaches in Curriculum* (Englewood Cliffs: Prentice-Hall, 1973), p. 3.

[3] Louise Berman, *New Priorities in the Curriculum* (Columbus, Ohio: Charles E. Merrill Publishing Company, 1968), p. 2.

[4] Zais, *Curriculum,* p. 75.

[5] Hilda Taba, *Curriculum Development: Theory and Practice* (New York: Harcourt, Brace and World, 1962), p. 413.

depending upon the specific characteristics of the school's sociopolitical environment, constituent interests, needs and demands and upon general educational trends and priorities. There is some overlap among the models; however, each has a particular point of departure, a core of emphasis, a primary focus that is unique. Each of these models is discussed in detail.

The Academic Model

Some curriculum specialists contend that curriculum development is a systematic process governed by academic rationality and theoretical logic. This approach to the curriculum-planning process is an academic one in that it is based upon the use of scholarly logic in educational decision making. It praises the wisdom of intellectual maturity and academic rationality. The curriculum specialist is thus placed in the position of making most curriculum decisions unilaterally. This conception of curriculum planning appears more often in the literature of curriculum theorizing than in the field of actual curriculum practice.

The academic model of curriculum development, for which the Tyler Rationale provides the theoretical and ideological contours, suggests that there is a quality of curriculum planning which transcends idiosyncrasies of particular school situations. The process begins with the identification of objectives and continues through the selection of content, learning activities, teaching techniques, and evaluation procedures. As Taba suggests, "no matter what its nature, the statement of desired outcomes sets the scope and the limits of what is to be taught and learned." [6] The priority item, then, in the academic approach to curriculum planning is identifying objectives, using intellectual rationality to accomplish this task.

Curriculum workers who perceive instructional planning from an academic framework rely upon five foundational sources for determining desired learning outcomes. These are the learner, society, subject matter disciplines, philosophy, and the psychology of learning. "No single source of information is adequate to provide a basis for wise and comprehensive decisions about the objectives of the school. . . . Each source should be given some consideration in planning any comprehensive curriculum program." [7] Therefore, concerted efforts are undertaken to compile a *balanced* list of objectives which is consistent with all five of the major foundational sources of desired learning outcomes.

The academically oriented curriculum developer tries to get as much valid information as possible from as many reliable sources as possible to determine what kind of changes in student behavior (e.g., learning) is most desirable. Learners' needs and characteristics are examined in terms

[6] Ibid., p. 197.

[7] Ralph W. Tyler, *Basic Principles of Curriculum and Instruction* (Chicago: University of Chicago Press, 1949), p. 5.

of physical, psychosocial, intellectual, and moral development. The research and theories of such developmental psychologists and learning theorists as Piaget, Dewey, Maslow, Prescott, Kohlberg, Tanner, and Havighurst are used conjunctively to develop composite, general profiles of learners. Anything less than this comprehensive analysis is considered insufficient, in view of the fact that human growth is developmental, organismic, differential, asynchronistic, and cyclical.

Formulating a generalized profile of learners' characteristics is a necessary function of curriculum planning, but that profile is not sufficient to determine desired learning outcomes for individual students. The curriculum worker must also obtain data specific to individual students. The list of objectives must include "some needs that are common to most American children, other needs that are common to almost all children in the given school, and still other needs that are common to certain groups within the school but not common to a majority of the children in the school." [8]

Another source of objectives in the academic curriculum-planning model is societal needs and characteristics. The historical patterns of goal identification in American education provide some insights and directions into what might be plausible objectives. Knowing this, the academic curriculum worker consults Committee of Ten reports, "Seven Cardinal Principles of Secondary Education," Education Policies Commission reports, "Ten Imperative Needs of All American Youth," and more recent (1972-1973) reports by several commissions on the reform of secondary education. Also available are data from sociological surveys, technological advancements, employment studies, political action and public opinion polls, and marriage and family life studies. Economic crises, value conflicts, mass media, environmental pollution, racial disharmony, and personal alienation and isolation in a technological society may also be taken into account in determining instructional objectives.

Subject matter disciplines constitute a third data base for the identification of educational goals and objectives. Discipline specialists assist the curriculum worker in formulating objectives by providing both substantive content and syntactical processes for intellectual skill development. Philip Phenix has identified content as the greatest contribution disciplines have to offer to curriculum development. He argues that "*all* curriculum content should be drawn from the disciplines, or, to put it another way, that *only* knowledge contained in the disciplines is appropriate to the curriculum." [9] According to Cecil Parker and Louis Rubin, "The predominant value of a subject lies not so much in its accumulated information or in its intellectual artifacts, but in its special way of looking at phenomena,

---

[8] Ibid., p. 10.

[9] Philip H. Phenix, "The Uses of Disciplines as Curriculum Content," *The Education Forum* 26 (March 1962): 273.

in its methods of inquiry, its procedures for utilizing research and its models for systematic thought." [10]

The logical, rational, and systematic investigation of learners, society, and the disciplines produces far too many objectives to be manageable in an effective instructional program. The psychology of learning and philosophy of education, the two other sources for formulating desired learning outcomes, serve as screens for selecting the most significant objectives from among those already tentatively identified.

When using learning theories to select curriculum objectives, content, and learning activities, academically oriented curriculum workers consult experimental and developmental psychology, as well as anthropological, sociological, and sociopsychological studies. They investigate cognitive, behavioral, gestalt, moral, and sociocultural (or environmental) theories of human growth and development to derive comprehensive and prescriptive principles of learning. The resulting data enable them to identify desired learning outcomes that are developmental in nature, to determine the most appropriate sequence of objectives, and to ascertain the conditions requisite for learning certain types of objectives. These investigations also help curriculum planners to understand that consistency and integration among different learning activities produce multiple outcomes and are, thus, desirable guidelines for instructional planning.

The particular educational philosophy adopted by a curriculum planner implies major values and beliefs held about what is the nature of the good life, what is the role of education in its realization, what knowledge is worth knowing, whether schools should teach youth to fit into the existing social order or to reconstruct society, and whether the same educational experiences should (or can) serve equally well all classes and ethnic groups in society. In the academic process of curriculum planning, it is more important for these philosophical questions to be asked and carefully considered than for a particular set of responses to be endorsed. However, some schools of thought appear to be more compatible than others with the overall character of academic rationality in curriculum development. The more compatible include those philosophies which view the fundamental purposes of education as the preservation and transmission of the cultural heritage and cumulative knowledge of humankind, and the development of the intellect. Traditionally, these philosophies have dominated secondary curriculum relative to priority of objectives, disciplinary-based sources of content, and the structural scope and sequence of junior and senior high school learning experiences.

Since the Woods Hole Conference in 1958, the publication of Jerome Bruner's *Process of Education* in 1960, and the national curriculum reform movement of the 1960s, academic rationalism in curriculum planning

---

[10] J. Cecil Parker and Louis Rubin, *Process as Content: Curriculum Design and the Application of Knowledge* (Chicago: Rand McNally and Company, 1966), p. 22.

has broadened its conception of desirable content to include methods of disciplined inquiry, the development of cognitive processes or intellectual skills, and the structure of the disciplines. The change in Philip Phenix's conception of what constitutes legitimate curriculum content typifies this modification. He says:

> It is more important for the student to learn to become skillful in the ways of knowing than to learn about any particular product of investigation. Knowledge of methods makes it possible for a person to continue learning and to undertake inquiries of his own. Furthermore, the modes of thought are far less transient than are the products of inquiry.[11]

Parker and Rubin corroborate Phenix's arguments and extend them somewhat when they remind curriculum planners:

> It is through exposing the learner to those processes which accompany man's manufacture and utilization of knowledge that knowledge itself and its functional worth can best be clarified. Also, it is through exposing the learner to these processes that the unique characteristics of his personal learning aptitudes may be utilized effectively.[12]

Given the rapid obsolescence of factual information and the incredible rate of knowledge production, it seems useless for school curriculum to place too much emphasis on knowledge acquisition per se. Rather, it is more plausible to concentrate on those generic intellectual skills that are enduring and applicable in any learning context. These skills—decision making, problem solving, reflective and critical thinking, valuing, concept forming, data processing, etc.—have their own internal logical order which is conducive to systematic analysis and comprehension. As a result, curriculum workers using academic rationality in program planning view

> subject matter as . . . instrumental to the development of intellectual abilities that can be used in areas other than those in which the processes were originally defined. For example, content in history or biology is considered less important than the development of the student's ability to infer, to speculate, to deduce, or to analyze. These abilities . . . will endure long after the particular content or knowledge is forgotten or rendered obsolete by new knowledge.[13]

In order to assess the extent and kinds of changes in student behavior that result from planned learning activities, the academic curriculum planner designs evaluation procedures that will provide opportunities for students to demonstrate learning, will be multidimensional, and will occur at different intervals in the instructional process. The goal is to acquire information on both student academic achievement and the effectiveness of the curriculum-planning and implementation processes.

[11] Philip H. Phenix, *Realms of Meaning* (New York: McGraw-Hill, 1964), p. 11.

[12] Parker and Rubin, *Process as Content*, p. 29.

[13] Elliot W. Eisner and Elizabeth Vallance, eds., *Conflicting Conceptions of Curriculum* (Berkeley, Calif.: McCutchan Publishing Corporation, 1974), p. 19.

Numerous curriculum designs which are the products of the academic approach to curriculum development exist. The most familiar of these are the discipline-centered or separate-subject designs. Their focus and sequence are determined by the logic of academic rationality, by "expanding horizons" and "spiral" organizational patterns, and by the inherent structure of disciplinary content. The knowledge explosion, the proliferation of subjects, and an increasing emphasis on concept mastery in instruction have necessitated other curriculum organizational patterns. Noticeable among these are core programs (e.g., broad fields, problems approaches, correlated and fused designs); combinations of separate subjects to form single courses (e.g., sociolinguistics, ethnomusicology, social psychology, etc.); interdisciplinary studies; inquiry into the structure of the disciplines; and functional literacy skill development (e.g., teaching reading in the content areas).

The Experiential Model

Unlike the academic model of curriculum planning, which claims a high degree of objectivity and universality and tends to cumulate in discipline- or subject-centered instructional designs, the experiential model is subjective, personalistic, heuristic, and transactional. It is a learner-centered, activity-oriented approach to teaching and learning. It emphasizes such educational principles as teachers and learners working cooperatively to make curriculum decisions. It utilizes self-directed, self-paced, unstructured, and personalized instructional programs. It theorizes that personal feelings, attitudes, values, and experiences are critical curriculum content, that active involvement of students in planning learning activities is essential to maximizing learning outcomes, that people create their own phenomenal worlds through selective perception, and that people learn only that which has personal meaning to them. By extension, then, the most viable and valid curriculum is one that results from a planning process involving those most directly affected by it and one that is based upon open inquiry, is always evolving, is strongly rooted in interpersonal relations, and is sensitive to situational relativism.[14]

The distinguishing characteristics of the experiential curriculum-planning process are its emphases on child-centeredness, interpersonal relations, the syntactical flexibility of the development process, the existential order of the individuals involved in learning activities, and the primacy of affective content in instruction. It considers psychological and cultural characteristics and needs of learners (as seen from the perspective of their own perceptual reality) to be the major sources of instructional objectives and the substantive content of the curriculum. Particular attention is given

[14] Louise Berman and Jessie A. Roderick, eds., *Feeling, Valuing and the Art of Growing: Insights into the Affective* (Washington, D.C.: Association for Supervision and Curriculum Development, 1977).

to reinforcing and developing the human qualities of learners (both as individuals and as members of a social order), as well as to maximizing growth toward psychological integration or self-actualization of the whole person. Arthur Foshay's conception of a "humane curriculum" is consistent with the view of curriculum development as an experiential planning process. He suggests that the function of education is to celebate the human condition. To achieve this goal curriculum content and experiences must be responsive to all those qualities of individuals which are essential to the preservation of their humanity. These qualities include the intellectual, the emotional, the social, the physical, the aesthetic, and the spiritual.[15] Therefore, the learner as a being in a perpetual state of becoming more humane provides the directional focus for curriculum designing, and process skills and affective experiences constitute the content of the curriculum.

Self-control of one's educational experiences is a critical concern in experiential curriculum development. This conception of instructional planning accepts the argument that an individual's evaluation of self and sense of personal efficacy are, in part, a consequence of feeling in control of one's own destiny and of believing that one's opinions, ideas, values, and decisions are important. Students are likely to feel better about themselves and the validity of their educational experiences and to be more academically productive when they execute some power, authority, and control over their own learning.

An experientially oriented curriculum worker also believes that individuals know themselves better than anyone else knows them and are therefore capable of identifying and selecting learning experiences that will facilitate their own growth and development. Carl Rogers, an advocate of experiential learning, observes that "man's behavior is exquisitively rational, moving with subtle and ordered complexity toward the goals his organism is endeavoring to achieve." [16] William Kilpatrick argues similarly in his observations that "the very essence of life is the effort of the organism . . . to deal successfully with its confronting situation. The situation, external or internal, stirs the organism to action. The organism prefers one outcome rather than another, and it makes efforts accordingly. At the heart of this behavior process lies the fact of preference." [17] Thus, to the experiential curriculum planner, individuals' self-perceptions and

[15] Arthur Wells Foshay, "Toward a Humane Curriculum," in *Essays on Curriculum* (New York: Teachers College, Curriculum and Teaching Department, 1975), pp. 155-71.

[16] Carl A. Rogers, "Toward Becoming a Fully Functioning Person," in *Perceiving, Behaving, Becoming: A New Focus for Education,* ed. Arthur W. Combs (Washington, D.C.: Association for Supervision and Curriculum Development, 1962), p. 31.

[17] William H. Kilpatrick, "The Essentials of the Activity Movement," *Progressive Education* 11 (October 1934): 347.

personal preferences, their assessments of self-needs, and their progressions toward self-integration are essential formative data in the curriculum decision-making process.

Curriculum workers who operate experientially in designing instructional plans believe that since people are the products of their experiences, acquiring comprehensive perspectives of these experiences is central to the development process. A significant portion of learners' experiential realities emanates from their social/cultural backgrounds and frames of reference. Social experiences, ethnic identities, and cultural heritages and conditioning are as much a part of an individual's personal endowments and learning potentialities, and are as significant in curriculum planning, as intellectual abilities and psychological characteristics are.[18] Since learning results from the selection and modification of perceptions, and since cultural conditioning serves as a filter through which experiences are screened and assigned meaning, understanding the cultural life styles and heritages of learners is imperative for designing effective instructional plans. Therefore, educators should systematically investigate the cultural background of students "in order to comprehend the impact such a background has on the way in which the child perceives the world and is accustomed to learning and being taught. On the basis of such investigations the school and the teacher can promote continuity for the child." [19]

How students from various social, ethnic, and cultural backgrounds respond to school instructional plans and processes is partly a result of the degree of congruency between their culturally determined perceptions of teaching and learning and the characteristics of school curriculum content and learning activities. As A. I. Hallowell points out:

> What is learned and the content of acquired experiences in one society compared with another constitute important variables with reference to the full understanding, explanation, and prediction of behavior of individuals . . . personal adjustment in a behavioral environment with culturally constituted properties produce variability in the phenomena of set and expectancy so that in any given perceptual situation such factors take on differential directive importance.[20]

These differential perceptions are particularly apparent in learning styles, communication behaviors, value systems, and motivational patterns—categories of critical variables for planning and executing instructional programs of maximum utility to ethnically and socially diverse pupil populations.

---

[18] Cole S. Brembeck and Walter H. Hill, eds., *Cultural Challenges to Education* (Lexington, Mass.: Lexington Books, 1973).

[19] Thomas J. LaBelle, "An Anthropological Framework for Studying Education," in *Educational Patterns and Cultural Configurations*, eds., Joan I. Roberts and Sherrie K. Akinsanya (New York: David McKay Company, 1976), p. 81.

[20] A. I. Hallowell, "Cultural Factors in the Structuralization of Perception," in *Intercultural Communication: A Reader*, eds., Larry A. Samovar and Richard E. Porter (Belmont, Calif.: Wadsworth Publishing Company, 1972), pp. 50-51.

The experiential curriculum model places high priority on educational objectives that are person- and process-oriented and that contribute to the personal integration of learners as individuals and members of a social order. These objectives include: learning how to learn and how to think critically and autonomously, valuing, developing positive self-concepts, taking social perspectives, participating in democracy, developing individual creativity and social efficacy. Identifying these outcomes as "education for life," Louis Rubin explains that people should learn to think, to feel, to love, to value, to live, to act, and to find personal meaning in daily activities.[21] Bruno Bettelheim argues that because our technological society causes psychological problems and disintegrating behaviors in individuals, the curriculum should help individuals learn to relate to others, to analyze past experiences and make inferences from them for future behavior, to understand self well enough to maintain personal identity and respond reasonably and meaningfully to life's situations according to personal interests, values, and beliefs.[22] These emphases on process skill development are not intended to imply that knowledge, content, intellectuality, and cultural heritage have no place in the educational process. Rather, they merely suggest that "it is the 'doing acts' of schooling which produce the greatest good." [23]

Activity and experience create the primary syntactical contexts for the realization of social, interpersonal, and intellectual process skill development. John Dewey expressed these sentiments in 1897 in Article III of his Pedagogic Creed. This creed said, in part:

> The social life of the child is the basis of concentration, or correlation, in all his training and growth. The social life gives the unconscious unity and the background of all his efforts and of all his attainments . . . the true center of correlation on the school subjects is not science, not literature, nor history, nor geography, but the child's own social activities . . . education must be conceived as a continuing reconstruction of experience, that the process and the goal of education are one and the same thing.[24]

Educating the "whole" child through the use of experiential content and processes led William Kilpatrick to advise curriculum planners:

> Experience in which we interact meaningfully with situations is thus the essence of human life. Being what we are, a situation stirs us chiefly by the

---

[21] Louis J. Rubin, "The Object of Schooling: An Evolutionary View," in *Life Skills in School and Society* (Washington, D.C.: Association for Supervision and Curriculum Development, 1969), pp. 15-34.

[22] Bruno Bettelheim, "Autonomy and Inner Freedom: Skills of Emotional Management," in *Life Skills for Schools and Society,* ed., Louis J. Rubin (Washington, D.C.: Association for Supervision and Curriculum Development, 1969), pp. 73-94.

[23] Rubin, "The Object of Schooling," p. 31.

[24] John Dewey, "The Subject-Matter of Education," in *Approaches in Curriculum,* ed., Ronald T. Hyman (Englewood Cliffs: Prentice-Hall, 1973), pp. 25-27.

meanings it arouses. We then react with efforts at controlling the situation according to our preferences. In these efforts we are progressively changed (i.e., we undergo learning effects) and we also change the situation.[25]

Hilda Taba has applauded the cruciality of activity and experience in curriculum development. She says:

> People learn only what they experience. Only that learning which is related to active purposes and is rooted in experience translates itself into behavior change. Learning in its true sense is an active transaction. . . . To pursue active learning the learner needs to engage in activities which are vital to him, in which he can pursue personal goals and satisfy personal needs.[26]

Curriculum workers operating from an experiential framework may employ the methodology suggested by Florence Stratemeyer and associates for the selection and organization of curriculum content. According to them the most significant learning activities for students are determined by the persistent life situations that recur throughout a person's life. These persistent life situations fall into the categories of individual capabilities, social abilities, and abilities to deal wth environmental forces. This strategy for selecting and organizing instructional content is consistent with the experiential model of curriculum planning in that it recognizes the uniqueness and the similarities of individuals, helps learners face the world at their own levels of readiness, uses personal meaning and individual experiences as legitimate curriculum content, and values the daily life of learners as important to education. The planning process suggested by Stratemeyer and associates is also characterized by emergence, flexibility, environmentalism, involvement learning, and differentiation in learning activities. These authors remind curriculum workers:

> Since it grows out of the experiences of learners, the curriculum will always be developing and flexible. Persistent life situations recur in many combinations in the learners' daily life. Exact predictions as to how or when a given group of learners will face a particular problem or as to which persistent life situations may be interwoven in an immediate concern are not possible. To differences occasioned by variations in individual maturation rates must be added those resulting from the experiences learners have had and from the homes and communities in which they are growing up. The choice, organization, and guidance of the experiences for any group, therefore, will grow out of the situations of home, school, and community the particular group faces.[27]

In actualizing important experiential content and learning activities, the curriculum-planning process must make provisions for students to develop their individual differences, to develop self-knowledge and per-

---

[25] Kilpatrick, "The Essentials of the Activity Movement," p. 349.

[26] Taba, *Curriculum Development,* p. 401.

[27] Florence Stratemeyer and others, *Developing a Curriculum for Modern Living,* 2nd ed. rev. (New York: Bureau of Publications, Teachers College, 1957), p. 117.

ceptions, to experience relating to others, and to understand themselves as social beings operating in a multitude of social systems. These goals can be attained by using such content and methodologies as laboratory learning, aesthetics, values analysis, experimentation, role reversals and social perspective-taking, moral dilemma discussions, critical thinking and problem solving, inquiry and discovery, multicultural education, and introspective self-analysis.

Experiential curriculum planning encompasses and encourages human growth within particular sociocultural systems and/or contexts. It recognizes the importance and resilience of ethnic, environmental, and cultural backgrounds in assigning meaning, value, and priority to human experiences. It contends that education is of greatest worth to culturally different students when the curriculum content and learning activities complement their ethnic identities, culturally determined learning styles, and perceptual frames of reference. The experiential curriculum worker is thus compelled to understand different ethnic groups' cultural characteristics, value systems, communication styles, historical experiences, and interactional patterns and to create learning opportunities that interface with these particular perceptual sets. Recent curriculum innovations which embody some of these components and aspire to broaden an individual's sense of humanity within the context of cultural differences are ethnic studies, multicultural education, women's studies, parenting courses, death education, and programs for understanding the aged.

Many other curriculum designs claim to embody experiential planning principles in one form or another. These include Montessori methods, open education, learning centers and stations, independent study, mini-courses and phase electives, schools without walls, and humanities and fine arts programs. To some degree all of these claims are legitimate, especially since the experiential process of curriculum planning does not specify a narrowly defined set of assumptions and priorities that are translatable into a few design possibilities. This fact is both its major strength and weakness. Its broad-based assumptions, emergent nature, and eclectic characteristics, along with its affective and activity content emphases, make it more susceptible to a wide range of interpretations and to greater difficulties in practical field-based implementation than some other models of curriculum development.

The Technical Model

Curriculum development, like all other aspects of education, has been influenced significantly by the massive technological advancements occurring in America and in the world during the last 50 years. Philosophies, ideologies, and techniques prevalent in industrial planning and production are frequently borrowed by educators as guidelines for curriculum planning, implementation, and evaluation.

The technical model of curriculum development is essentially an analytical approach which perceives instructional planning in terms of "systems," "management," and "production." It seeks to maximize educational program proficiency and performance through applying the same principles of scientific management and production operating in industry. The concept of curriculum development as a technical process first appeared in 1918 in Franklin Bobbitt's references to instructional planning as "educational engineering" and "scientific curriculum-making." [28] Its greatest momentum and most definitive articulation, however, have emerged out of more recent trends toward behaviorism, accountability, competency-based performance, and cost-effective analyses of educational programming.

The technical curriculum-planning process is similar to the academic model in that it uses a means-ends paradigm and is based upon the Tyler Rationale. The specification of educational ends, or desired terminal learning behaviors, is the first order of business in both the academic and technical planning processes. Differences occur between the two models in the perceived relationship between means and ends, the methodologies used to identify objectives, the structural form the objectives take, and the evaluative criteria used to assess student achievement. Both the academic and technical models claim to be systematic, logical, and rational approaches to curriculum planning. However, the foundations on which these claims are made are quite different. While the academic model appeals to theoretical logic and academic rationality as the bases for sound decision making, the technical model uses the logic of "systems analysis," empiricism, scientific objectivity, and managerial efficiency.

The stimulus-response and operant conditioning theories of behavioristic psychology comprise the epistemological foundations of technical approaches to curriculum development. Their ontology is fundamentally scientific realism or logical empiricism. This instructional planning model ascribes to the belief that nothing is real or meaningful unless it is observable and is susceptible to objective analysis, using publicly verifiable data. It presupposes, further, that knowledge worth knowing is "preparation for life's functions"; that life's tasks are reducible to their constituent parts; that learning represents a change in behavior and since behavior is demonstrative, learning is observable and measurable in quantifiable terms. Robert Gagne explains these ideas accordingly: "A learning occurrence . . . takes place when the stimulus situation together with the content of memory affect the learner in such a way that his performance changes from a time before being in that situation to a time after being in it. The change in performance is what leads to the conclusion that learning has occurred." [29] To insure that learning will occur most expeditiously, the instructional

[28] Franklin Bobbitt, *The Curriculum* (Boston: Houghton Mifflin Company, 1918).

[29] Robert M. Gagne, *The Conditions of Learning,* 3rd ed. (New York: Holt, Rinehart & Winston, 1977), p. 5.

plan must observe the laws of contiguity, repetition, reinforcement, and preconditioning.[30]

Technical curriculum development perceives learning as a "system." This "system" can be reduced to its constituent parts; it occurs in certain systematic and predictable ways; and its efficiency and effectiveness can be improved through good control or "management" principles. This conception of learning and curriculum places "more stress upon reliably measurable and clearly communicable behavioral objectives than it does upon any other dimension or element of the entire system."[31] The priority given to scientifically determined behavioral objectives and quantifiable performance-based data to verify the occurrence of learning are two major factors which distinguish the technical curriculum-planning process from the academic model discussed earlier.

An analytical approach to decision making is basic to the technical model of curriculum development. It emphasizes exact formulations and rigorous procedures in instructional planning. It is also based upon the beliefs that "objectives should be stated in precise behavioral terms, that teaching proceeds most efficiently when what is to be learned is arranged hierarchically, that students should be taught what they do not know and not what they already know, and that the goal of instruction is mastery."[32] This highly ordered process is designed to minimize subjective and intuitive decision making and to maximize scientific objectivity in both curriculum planning and the assessment of student performance. Several new "management" tools are available to curriculum technicians to assist them in the effective execution of a "systems" approach in instructional planning. Among these are needs assessment and discrepancy analysis techniques, behavioral objectives, PPBS (Planning-Programming-Budgeting System), PERT (Program Evaluation Review Technique), method-means selection techniques, and MBO (Management by Objectives).

The technical approach to curriculum planning proceeds from a "systems analysis" or "management" framework. Carroll Londoner defines "systems analysis" as "the total analytical procedure (or blueprint) for progressing from the assessment of an educational need and the specification of the terminal outcome to the actual achievement of that outcome through the logical sequencing of the components comprising the total system."[33] The components of the planning "system" are, in order of

[30] Robert M. Gagne and Leslie J. Briggs, *Principles of Instructional Design* (New York: Holt, Rinehart & Winston, 1974).

[31] Robert B. Thompson, *A Systems Approach to Instruction* (Hamden, Conn.: Linnet Books, 1971), p. 145.

[32] Donald E. Orlosky and B. Othanel Smith, *Curriculum Development: Issues and Insights* (Chicago: Rand McNally College Publishing Company, 1978), p. 106.

[33] Carroll A. Londoner, "The Systems Approach as an Administrative and Program Planning Tool for Continuing Education," *Educational Technology* 12 (August 1972): 25.

sequence: empirical analysis of needs; prioritizing needs; specifying objectives in behavioral or performance terms; selecting content to meet the specified objectives; defining, describing, and sequentializing teaching processes and learning activities; and identifying quantifiable evaluation measures.

Needs assessment, the first step in the planning sequence of technical curriculum development, is described by Fenwick English and Roger Kaufman as a "curriculumless process" since it is independent of any particular curriculum design or subject area. It is empirical in nature and facilitates the specification of outcomes of education, the selection of criteria for the development and assessment of curriculum, the validation of behavioral objectives, and the selection of appropriate evaluation devices.[34] A needs assessment also helps to identify the distance between desired educational goals and present conditions. Jon Wiles calls this "developmental staging," a form of discrepancy analysis which breaks down the gaps between real educational situations and ideal change, displays the comprehensiveness of the anticipated changes, and suggests the instructional objectives needed to achieve desired changes.[35]

Once educational needs or goals are identified, they are analyzed and translated into observable, measurable, and behavioral terms. This is a three-part sequential procedure. The first step is a *task analysis* to specify the desired behavior outcomes of the instructional process. A task analysis is, in effect, an inventory of the components (i.e., knowledge, skills, attitudes) of any topic or job students are expected to master. As early as 1918 Franklin Bobbitt advocated an analytical procedure for identifying educational objectives. Using the concept of "activity analysis," which is analogous to task analysis, he argued:

Human life, however varied, consists in the performance of specific activities. Education that prepares for life is one that prepares definitively and adequately for these specific activities. However numerous and diverse they may be for any social class, they can be discovered. This requires only that one go out into the world of affairs and discover the particulars of which these affairs consist. These will show the abilities, habits, appreciations, and forms of knowledge that men need. These will be numerous, definite, and particularized. The curriculum will then be that series of experiences which children and youth must have by way of attaining these objectives.[36]

The second step in analyzing educational goals is expressing learning tasks and activities as behavioral objectives. They are stated empirically, meaning: (a) The overt behavior that must occur to indicate the attain-

[34] Fenwick W. English and Roger A. Kaufman, *Needs Assessment: A Focus for Curriculum Development* (Washington, D.C.: Association for Supervision and Curriculum Development, 1975).

[35] Jon W. Wiles, "Developmental Staging: In Pursuit of Comprehensive Curriculum Planning," *Clearing House* 50 (February 1977): 274-77.

[36] Bobbitt, *The Curriculum,* p. 42.

ment of the objective is stated in measurable terms, (b) The conditions under which the terminal behavior is to be manifested are specified, and (c) The criteria for establishing minimum levels of proficiency in demonstrating the desired terminal behavior are identified.[37] These behavioral objectives function as guidelines for sequencing instructional activities, selecting appropriate materials, and evaluating the instructional processes and products.

The third step in translating educational goals into instructional objectives is determining the sequential or hierarchical relationship among the behavioral objectives and identifying the order in which they are to be treated in instruction. This procedure is called *structural analysis*.[38]

Once the list of sequentialized behavioral objectives is derived, the curriculum worker moves on to the second phase of the technical curriculum-planning process. This phase is called *synthesis*. First, instructional activities are specified, making allowances for individualization and options in learning processes. A means-ends procedure is used to identify and analyze all viable instructional alternatives for each terminal objective and to select the ones most appropriate for achieving the desired competencies. Second, some decisions are made about evaluation procedures. Techniques are devised to elicit: (a) individual evaluation for monitoring student performance and determining the progressional order of the objectives; (b) formative evaluation for assessing in-process instructional effectiveness and improving the objectives and materials while they are still in the formative stages of development; and (c) summative evaluation for providing an overall impression of the efficacy of the total instructional package.[39]

The third aspect of the "systems" technology of curriculum planning is *operations*. It merely means carrying out the instructional activities as planned and applying the evaluative criteria as specified to systematically collect data on the efficiency and efficacy of the instructional "system." After all data are collected and analyzed, alterations are made in the instructional "system" in accordance with the evaluative data. This process of evaluation, feedback, and modification is iterative in that it is a "continuous and repeated process of evaluating each step with all prior steps and the specified terminal outcomes to insure the systematic development of all system operations for achieving the desired behaviors."[40]

Recent examples of curriculum designs derived from a technical or "systems" planning process are numerous and varied. Computer-assisted instruction, programmed instruction, performance contracting, vocational

[37] Londoner, "Systems Approach."

[38] Bruce W. Tuckman and Keith J. Edwards, "A Systems Model for Instructional Design and Management," *Educational Technology* 11 (September 1971): 23.

[39] Ibid., pp. 21-26.

[40] Londoner, "Systems Approach," p. 30.

educational programs, IEPs for mainstreaming the handicapped, and competency-based teacher education programs are all illustrative of technical models of curriculum. Each in its own way is goal oriented and concerned with attaining specific performance competencies through systematic, empirically based instructional programs. The various examples claim such strengths as: increased relevance of instruction through individualized, continuous reporting of student progress; choices among alternative instructional approaches; objective, data-based educational decision making; high correlations between principles of learning and instructional program planning; and a built-in process for continuous self-renewal of the curriculum-planning process itself. Furthermore, this technical approach takes the guesswork out of curriculum development and replaces it with scientific procedures that maximize the organization, management, and execution of qualitative education programs.

The Pragmatic Model

When Delmo Della-Dora asked, "Who Owns the Curriculum in a Democratic Society?" in his presidential address to the 1976 annual conference of the Association for Supervision and Curriculum Development, he was, in effect, posing the question most fundamental to the pragmatic process of curriculum development. In answering the question he described the interplay of values, interests, demands, and powers of special interest groups in making decisions about educational governance and instructional planning and implementation. Insofar as individuals, groups, and agencies influence the allocation of values in school systems, they are engaging in political activities.[41] The allocation of values and the power negotiations among special interest groups occur with great regularity in curriculum decision making, thereby making it a political process.

While some educators claim curriculum planning is a systematic, logical, and prescriptive procedure, others contend that it is neither systematic nor particularly rational in the sense that the process is predictable, follows prescriptive guidelines, or conforms to a single theoretical framework. Rather, "it is the outcome of a very long and dynamically complex process of social involvement and interaction." [42]

In actuality curriculum planning is an eclectic and political process that often occurs in a reactive, fragmentary, and "patchwork" fashion. Curriculum practitioners frequently employ a combination of selective

---

[41] Jay D. Scribner and Richard M. Englert, "The Politics of Education: An Introduction," in *The Politics of Education,* 76th NSSE Yearbook, ed., Jay D. Scribner (Chicago: University of Chicago Press, 1977), pp. 1-29.

[42] James B. Macdonald, "Curriculum Development in Relation to Social and Intellectual Systems," in *The Curriculum: Retrospect and Prospect,* 70th NSSE Yearbook, ed., Robert M. McClure (Chicago: University of Chicago Press, 1971), pp. 95-96.

concepts and principles from different theoretical models, along with conventional wisdom and common sense, depending upon the particular planning activities being pursued at the moment and the sociopolitical context in which these activities take place. In other words, in the same instructional programs, curriculum workers may use some elements of all three conceptual models (e.g., academic, experiential, technical) discussed earlier. For example, practitioners may appeal to academic rationality in developing a rationale for a proposed instructional program; they may use a combination of ideas and strategies from the experiential and technical models in selecting content, learning activities, and teaching processes; they may draw on the technical model in determining the type of evaluative measures; and they may utilize both pragmatic and technical models in assessing need for an instructional change—i.e., action priorities may reflect the interests and trends presently prominent in the nation's and/or school's sociopolitical milieu. It is not uncommon for local school districts to use different structural arrangements in organizing curriculum-planning committees which represent an intermingling of conceptual principles from different theoretical models of curriculum development. For instance, curriculum-planning committees organized around subject areas tend to operate primarily within the academic planning mode; and those organized around grade level and/or minimum competency testing may function basically within a technical framework. In a sense, then, the pragmatic curriculum-planning process can be considered both as a separate conceptual model of decision making and as a methodological technique for the implementation of *any* theoretical model of curriculum planning.

The pragmatic curriculum model perceives instructional planning as a particularistic, localized process that is specific to the sociopolitical milieu of the school context in which it occurs. It concentrates on what individuals do in the daily operations of school bureaucracies to answer questions about what should be taught and how curriculum should be determined, organized, and evaluated. Of particular interest are the informal political negotiations, power allocations, and consensus building that take place among different interest groups. Decker Walker describes this approach to curriculum development as a "naturalistic model"; [43] John Verduin calls it "cooperative curriculum change"; [44] and Glenys Unruh refers to it as "responsive curriculum development." [45] Lawrence Iannaccone argues that curriculum development is, by nature, a political process, for "answers to 'who shall decide what questions' is always an authoritative allocation of

[43] Decker F. Walker, "A Naturalistic Model for Curriculum Development," *School Review* 8 (November 1971): 51-65.

[44] John R. Verduin, *Cooperative Curriculum Improvement* (Englewood Cliffs, N.J.; Prentice-Hall, 1967).

[45] Glenys G. Unruh, *Responsive Curriculum Development: Theory and Action* (Berkeley, Calif.: McCutchan Publishing Corporation, 1975).

values containing some organization of influences and some distribution of resources." [46]

Curriculum planning is political in at least three other significant ways. First, decisions regarding what instructional programs are actually implemented in schools and how they are prioritized are affected by political events within the social environments of schools. What learning is of greatest worth and who should make this decision are as much political questions as they are value issues. Second, state legislatures and local school boards of education have the regulatory power to determine general educational goals and establish policy for their achievement. Third, within each local school district there exists a hierarchical administrative power structure through which specific curriculum issues and decisions are channeled.[47] According to James Macdonald, these three features comprise an interactive and dynamic political system which subjects the curriculum-planning process "to diverse and sometimes contradicting cultural and social pressures, to the relation of instructional and social living in the schools, and to the personalities and characteristics of those involved in the development and implementation of curricula." [48] What becomes the operational or functional curriculum in local school communities results from the power, influences, and pressures exerted upon the educational decision-making processes from forces both internal and external to the system.

Curriculum planners concerned with practical realities cannot ignore the ways national, state, and regional agencies and mass media affect state and local curriculum policy making. The North Central Association, College Entrance Examination Board, Educational Testing Service, and the National Assessment of Educational Progress are among the most influential accrediting associations and testing agencies affecting curriculum decision making. These "pressure points" establish normative standards which local districts use to assess their own curricular strengths and weaknesses, to institute modifications in those areas of greatest weakness and to generate curriculum alternatives. Within a matter of days, electronic media can escalate a relatively minor or localized educational issue into a national crisis and significantly influence educational priorities and funding patterns in instructional programming.

A case in point where these "pressure points" have converged on a single issue and impacted significantly upon curriculum decisions is the

[46] Lawrence Iannaccone, "The Politics of Curriculum/Educational Decision-Making: Who Should Be Responsible for What," panel presentation given at the Annual Conference of the Association for Supervision and Curriculum Development, San Francisco, Calif., March 1978.

[47] Michael W. Kirst and Decker F. Walker, "An Analysis of Curriculum Policy-Making," *Review of Educational Research* 41 (December 1971): 479-509.

[48] Macdonald, "Curriculum Development," p. 97.

current concern for basics and minimum competency testing. The mass media's discussion of declining scores on standardized tests of basic literacy skills has intensified reactions to this situation almost to the point of hysteria. Pressures from the general public, colleges and universities, professional associations, parents, and business and industry demand that schools be held accountable for delivery of basic literacy skills at minimum levels of proficiency. These interest groups have exerted enough power and pressure to influence 35 states to mandate and/or encourage minimum competency testing for grade promotions and high school graduation. A similar situation has occurred with College Boards. Historically, college and university entrance requirements have exerted an inordinate amount of influence on the form and content of high school curricula.

National, state, and regional educational associations are also powerful determinants of local curriculum priorities. Prestigious associations such as ASCD, NEA, NASSP, AASA, and IRA regularly identify their value commitments and endorse curriculum priorities through publications, conferences, position statements, and resolutions. Usually these associations are content to use these "academic maneuvers" to encourage curriculum policy making in certain directions unless their particular content areas are threatened by financial restraints and instructional reorganization plans. Then they become politically mobilized and assertive. For example, the current movement by aesthetic educators to convince state departments of education and local school boards of the saliency of music and the arts to general education was prompted by the growing tendency of schools to drop these subjects from the curricula because of budgetary constraints.

One of the other most significant groups influencing practical curriculum decisions is suppliers of instructional materials. Textbook authors and publishers, the federal government, private foundations, and civic groups are actively engaged in developing educational materials. The content, conceptualization, value orientation, and structural design of these materials have a powerful effect on curriculum planning. When statewide, single textbook adoptions were in vogue, publishers virtually controlled the functional curricula of schools through the content presented in the books. Despite the decline of single text adoptions and the increase of nonprint instructional technology, textbook authors and publishers continue to be powerful forces to be reckoned with in curriculum planning.

Federal legislation and funding policies of governmental agencies are other major determinants of pragmatic curriculum development. Education is an expensive business. Increasingly, state legislatures and local districts are finding it virtually impossible to finance educational programming without federal assistance. The public is rebelling against growing costs of education as is evident in the difficulty that some districts are having in getting bonds and levies passed, in early school closings that result from depletion of the fund base, and in the passage of Proposition 13 in California. Through the financial support it provides, the federal government has become one of the most influential forces affecting curriculum decisions.[49]

More often than not the monies made available by the federal government are earmarked for special-emphasis instructional programs. Therefore, the degree to which school systems get involved in seeking grants—and the *kinds* of grants solicited—greatly affects the kinds of curriculum priorities emphasized in the districts. For example, a school district soliciting heavy ESEA or Title IX funds will have different curriculum development priorities from one that is concerned primarily with compliance with PL 94-142, vocational education, and programs for the gifted. As Della-Dora has so pointedly observed, as the federal government assumes greater responsibility for financing local education, the roles it plays in determining educational policy are likely to increase proportionally.[50]

On occasion, too, federal and state courts make decisions which impact directly upon curriculum development. *Robinson* v. *Cahill* (minimum competencies), *Epperson* v. *Arkansas* (theory of evolution), and *Lau* v. *Nichols* (bilingual education) are some cases in point.

The growing involvement of the federal government in local education has led to several developments relative to curriculum decision making. Among these are: (a) increasing centralization of authority on curriculum issues; (b) legalization of the curriculum as a result of a growing body of federal legislation, state regulations, and judicial decrees; (c) expansion of the participants involved in curriculum construction, implementation, and evaluation; and (d) increasing complexity and bureaucratization of the hierarchy of governmental authority and chains of command involved in the curriculum decision-making process.[51]

Pragmatic curriculum planners are not immune to pressure politics from disciplinary scholars and learning theorists. It is not uncommon for scholars to lend their expertise to local curriculum planning by serving as content consultants, conceptualizers, process observers, program evaluators, and even curriculum project directors. These functions can shape the entire character of given instructional programs. It is not surprising, for instance, that most of the major national curriculum projects of the 1960s were discipline centered when we recall the pedagogical theory (disciplined inquiry and the structure of the disciplines) in vogue at the time, the political reactions to Sputnik, and the fact that most of the project directors were university scholars. Nor is it surprising to find that many local school districts adopted Man: A Course of Study (MACOS), Physical Sciences

[49] A. W. Sturges, "Forces Influencing the Curriculum," *Educational Leadership* 34 (October 1976): 40-43.

[50] Delmo Della-Dora, "Democracy and Education: Who Owns the Curriculum," *Educational Leadership* 34 (October 1976): 51-59.

[51] William Lowe Boyd, "The Changing Politics of Curriculum Policy-Making in American Schools," *Review of Educational Research* 48 (Fall 1978): 577-628.

Study Committee (PSSC), Biological Sciences Curriculum Study (BSCS), or School Mathematics Study Group (SMSG) and/or used them as models for developing their own curriculum plans and priorities. The prestige of the projects, the scholars associated with them, and the intellectual tenor and political climate of the times demanded these kinds of responses.

Private firms and civic groups are influential forces shaping curriculum decisions, too. Their influence is exerted through advocacy positions on critical educational issues and through the development of instructional materials which are specific to their particular interests and are made available to educators free of charge or at cost. Proctor and Gamble, the Chamber of Commerce, Bell Telephone and Telegraph, and the AFL-CIO are among the most active in these endeavors. Still other corporations are forming mergers with publishing companies and diffusing their production portfolios to include the dissemination of instructional materials. Illustrative of this trend are IBM's purchasing SRA; American Educational Publications' taking over Xerox; RCA's buying Random House; GE and Time's creating General Learning, Inc.; and CBS' owning Holt, Rinehart, and Winston.[52] The League of Women Voters, Civil Liberties Union, Common Cause, Anti-Defamation League, and Nader's Raiders also exert influence on curriculum decisions through the causes they promote. Feminist organizations pressure schools to include examination of sex-role biases, stereotypes, and discrimination in instructional programs. Ethnic groups lobby for accurate portrayals of their historical and cultural experiences in school curricula. Gay liberation, "gray power" groups, the handicapped, and other subsets of society practicing alternative life styles and value systems demand that their presence be felt in the negotiation of curriculum decisions. Teacher unions are becoming increasingly more active in influencing curriculum development through collective bargaining and lobbying at the state and federal governmental levels.

Additionally, the pragmatic-oriented curriculum worker must contend with the political pressures operating within the local school community. However, these pressures are not as systematically and consistently expressed as are the external forces. Local communities tend to become activated in episodic curriculum issues, such as a controversy over a particular textbook or instructional program. The Kanawha County, West Virginia, textbook controversy of 1974, bond levies, Proposition 13, sex education, and moral education are examples of this pattern.

As curriculum leaders plan and implement instructional program changes, they must be particularly sensitive to the chain of command in local districts. Within the school bureaucracy they must operate through an established administrative hierarchy of authority. At the apex of the power structure are the superintendent and his or her immediate subordinates. They are responsible for executing the planning process. The super-

---

[52] Kirst and Walker, "Analysis."

intendent and/or his or her designates organize mechanisms for change, provide general directions and guidelines, facilitate cooperation, and monitor interactions among the individuals and groups actively engaged in curriculum making.[53] They are assisted by a contingency of curriculum coordinators and/or supervisors who help to create and facilitate curriculum-planning committees and generally oversee the planning of instructional program proposals. The curriculum committees do the work of preparing the proposals for change. At the base of the pyramid of authority is a host of study groups and advisory councils. They provide additional input and reviews for the design committees and function as a liaison between community constituencies and the school personnel. Once the curriculum design proposals are completed, the process executor (superintendent and/or designates) presents them to the policymaking body (school board) and explains the validity of the proposed changes; how they will affect the total school program; the extent to which they represent a compilation of different values, interests, and concerns of divergent constituencies; and their possible acceptability and effectiveness.[54]

According to Michael Kirst and Decker Walker, curriculum decision making proceeds *incrementally* through the vertical administrative power structure in local school systems. Value conflicts between educational personnel and community interest groups are "resolved through low profile politics."[55] That is, actual curriculum planning, "rather than being characterized by dramatic crisis policy-making, or by the often prescribed but seldom realized model of *rational* decision-making, generally is characterized by the modest and mundane strategy of *disjointed incrementalism*." [56] David Braybrooke and Charles Lindblom describe this process as a system of "decision-making through small or incremental moves on particular problems rather than through a comprehensive reform program . . . it takes the form of an indefinite sequence of policy moves . . . [and] it is exploratory in that the goals of policy-making continue to change as new experience with policy throws new light on what is possible and desirable."[57]

Although curriculum development as a pragmatic or political process may not necessarily employ sophisticated, highly formalized decision-making strategies that are neatly sequentialized, objective, logical, and systematic, it is nonetheless real, and somehow it works. Pragmatic curriculum planning is a dynamic complex of interactions between individuals and groups wherein many of the political negotiations and power alloca-

[53] Robert E. Jennings, "The Politics of Curriculum Change," *Peabody Journal of Education* 49 (July 1972) : 295-99.

[54] James O'Hanlon, "Three Models for the Curriculum Development Process," *Curriculum Theory Network* 4 (1973/74): 64-71.

[55] Kirst and Walker, "Analysis," p. 487.

[56] Boyd, "The Changing Politics," p. 582.

[57] David Braybrooke and Charles E. Lindblom, *A Strategy of Decision* (New York: Free World, 1963), p. 71.

tions occur at the informal level of operation. Conflicting values, demands, and interests of different constituencies are often argued in private; consensus decisions are often negotiated prior to public debate. This model of curriculum planning—much more than the academic, experiential, or technical models—approximates what happens in daily practice. In many ways it is more an implementation process than a design or construction model.

Conclusion

Whether perceived as a rational, experiential, technical, or political process, curriculum planning is a complex, imprecise, challenging phenomenon. Yet, it is incredibly vital and dynamic. The particular positions individuals take on what is the most viable approach to curriculum planning reflect their personal philosophies of education and the perspectives from which they view the educative and curriculum-making processes. The conceptual models discussed in this chapter are not the only ways of conceptualizing the curriculum-planning process. Others are available in the literature, and even more are likely to be forthcoming. The question, "Which curriculum-planning process is the best or right one to use?" may be the wrong question. A more appropriate query might be, "How can conceptual or theoretical models of the curriculum-planning process help curriculum workers better understand and improve the dynamics of the process?"

When considered independently and conjunctively, these four models —academic, experiential, technical, pragmatic—may provide greater insights into the complex task of curriculum development. Although it is quite unlikely that field-based curriculum practitioners will be able to translate any one of these models into practice in its entirety, understanding theoretical models of curriculum planning can help the practitioners to conceptualize and describe their own planning practices better; to be aware of conceptual planning options; to be able to assess discrepancies between actual operations and idealized planning processes; to determine the potentialities of generalized conceptual models of curriculum planning as guidelines for actual practice in particularized situations; to be somewhat less vulnerable to the politicization of curriculum development; and thus to improve the quality of their curriculum decision making, planning, developing, and implementing processes.

Section Three.
The Way It Is

IN THE THIRD SECTION of the book, the authors attempt to deal with schools and school systems as they are. Reality is always more complex than theory. In the first two sections, we attempted to deal with the culture of the school, which is a way of dealing with the school as it is, and with certain aspects of curriculum theory. Since the function of theory is to clarify reality, the second section also dealt with the way it is. But both the first two sections sought to simplify matters so that they might be grasped. Actuality doesn't come simple. It comes complicated.

In chapter 8, Fenwick English returns to offer a practical plan for mapping curriculum in local school systems. His approach is highly rational; it has been tried, and it works.

Theodore Czajkowski and Jerry Patterson write from the context of one of the more active public school systems. They bring together theory and practice and suggest ways that action may, indeed, be considered. Hence the title of the present book. Theirs is one of the few statements on this basic theme that really unites theories about the way it is with the actuality of the way it is.

The closing chapter, by Joel Weiss, seeks to go behind the classroom door to consider what teachers can in fact do about it all. Acknowledging that in the final analysis the curriculum is what teachers and students do to each other in classrooms, he considers the opportunities and the constraints (some self-imposed, some from outside) that operate as teachers make the curriculum.

The present book might have been called *Theory into Practice,* if that title had not been preempted. *Considered Action for Curriculum Improvement* requires not only that we act but that we have the means for making action considered, deliberate—not faddish, opportunistic, or merely responsive to pressures. Those readers who have reached this point in the book will be able to judge whether it has achieved its purose.

144

8 Curriculum Development Within the School System
Fenwick W. English

ALTHOUGH IT IS POSSIBLE to consider curriculum development and curriculum theory apart from their function within school systems, for the practicing curriculum administrator it makes little sense to do so. The fundamental fact of life about curriculum development *within systems of education* is that the activity occurs *within* a system of schools and *reinforces* that system. Curriculum development as a practice and curriculum per se are designed to perpetuate the existing organizational and managerial structure that controls schooling. To effectively consider how curriculum might be improved within schools, it it necessary that this structure be examined. In this sense curriculum theory cannot be decoupled from current management theory.

Using understanding gained from management theory, we turn now to look at how the prevailing organizational and managerial structure came into being, how it works, and how it affects curriculum development within the school system.

The Preeminence of Management

There was no need for systematic development of curriculum until a *system* of education had been formulated and implemented. Perhaps the classical problem of any organization in terms of management is that of uncertainty of demand for services which results in difficulties meeting the demand. If the demand is regular, then a response is relatively easy to formulate by fixed resources. However, if the demand is irregular, then at certain times too many resources may be created. In the terms of management, slack is a consequence.

Perhaps one analogy is that of the demand for goods and services during the year as a whole compared with holiday periods. One solution for organizations is to overstaff for brief periods of time or to move towards overtime. Both solutions to uneven demand allow the organization

145

to fix its resources and to meet peak demands without substantially raising costs. The solution is called "smoothing."[1] "Smoothing" enables an organization to create an even response to irregular demands.

Now consider the nature of schooling prior to the graded school. In the one-room schoolhouse there was a great deal of uneven demand in terms of learners who had a tremendous range intellectually and physically. The rapid growth of cities and the move toward universal education created excessive staffing and organizational demands upon the one-room school. So the graded school was developed.

The great advantage of the graded school was that it fixed the demand for services, i.e., it "smoothed" out the demand by decentralizing it in self-contained units and defining learning as time spent within the units (grades). All of the coordination problems of the system with ungraded units, and even of the Lancastrian/monitorial school during the brief flirtation with it, were solved. The uncertainty of irregular demand was simply absorbed within the smaller units. The necessity of dealing with learners all together was eliminated. Learning styles, learner differences, motivation, socioeconomic background were absorbed, as well as major considerations for the allocation of resources.

In terms of costs, a minimum level of staff could be formulated much more easily and maintained by simply changing the ratio of teachers to students (class size). The requirement to process information about students laterally and vertically was de-emphasized. In management thinking, demand was evened out and a *system* of education could be built.

In terms of modern management, schools historically have selected one of at least four design alternatives to the problem of "smoothing." One alternative to the graded system with a nine-month schedule was to move toward a longer school year and have some students attend part of the year and others attend another part. While there was some experimentation with year-round schools due to growth demands, such patterns never really took hold. Another alternative was to move toward a modification of the Lancastrian model with team teaching or differentiated staffing and open school approaches. While there was serious experimentation with this design alternative in the sixties, such models are not dominant today. The last design alternative was simply not available at the time of the invention of the graded school because the application of computerized information and instructional systems was not available. This last option was an investment in increased capacity for processing information about students and creation of a technology which could be responsive.

The graded system—the self-contained management design alternative—quickly became dominant and is dominant today. But each solution contains costs. The costs of the graded structure of schooling are a high

---

[1] Jay R. Galbraith, *Organization Design* (Reading, Mass.: Addison-Wesley, 1977), pp. 224-40.

level of duplication among and between the self-contained units and an extremely difficult coordination problem that is created when any system is required to be responsive *as a system*. The level of decentralization in most school systems is not conducive to rapid instructional or curricular change. Both vertical and lateral communication within graded structures is extremely difficult.

The function of curriculum had to be compatible with the function of the management design alternative which was prevalent. The curriculum therefore had to be *time based* rather than performance based. The curriculum had to keep differences within the self-contained units and therefore had to be extremely broad in conception. "Meeting the needs of students" became synonymous with dealing with individual differences *within* the structure rather than altering the structure and forcing a different organizational design selection. Curriculum language had to maintain an elasticity which precluded much specificity about real learning or objectives because the system had precluded much discussion of this nature by its structural decision.

Curriculum therefore filled up time because time is a dependent variable rather than independent one. Since it is by time and absorption that slack is reduced, no curriculum could operate very long on any contrary principles without threatening the design alternative selected and inviting retaliation or extinction. Thus ultimately the structure which was dominant was accepted.

From a management perspective, discussion about humanizing the school falls in the acceptable range as long as humanization *does not mean* forcing a different structural design alternative. As long as alternatives conceptualized reinforce or ignore the existing administration relationships, they are tolerable. Therefore, various strategies to increase classroom teaching effectiveness—by setting performance objectives, defining teachers' duties, altering class size, individualizing instruction, utilizing family assisted instruction, adopting subject-centered or child-centered curricular models, using technology—are acceptable as long as the given or assumed constant is a decentralized, self-contained organizational design decision.

However, when such strategies call into question that design decision, they are confronting a vast army of forces designed to maintain the original decision—including the administrative hierarchy, state regulations, federal legislation, textbook publishers, and certification requirements for teachers. Whether a search for different strategies by those pursuing a different curricular base can be viable depends upon the extent to which the preeminence of management theory and thinking is recognized as a major variable in changing public school curricula. No searches for ways to alter curriculum can be effective without understanding why the system in which the curriculum functions operates as it does.

School Districts as "Loosely Coupled Systems"

For the activity of curriculum development to be accurately conceptualized within school districts, the influence of management theory must be considered. The curriculum is used by the administration to maintain the current organizational design alternative. The model of goverance has been called a "loosely coupled system" by Karl Weick. He has said: "Educational organizations are holding companies containing shares of stock in uninspected activities and subunits which are largely given their meaning, reality, and value in the wider social market."[2]

The fact that school systems have operated without precise mission objectives has been well documented.[3] Much of the accountability movement and the minimum competency movement is aimed at establishing such precise objectives by legislative mandate.

However, it is the absence of such objectives that typifies school district management today. The advantage of this absence is that in organizations which represent "loose couplings" between people—i.e., roles, groups, subunits—there is a wider span of appropriate responses available for role incumbents than if objectives were more precise. "Loose coupling" between subunits creates independencies and reduces the requirement that the overall organization engage in wholesale change. Only pieces or parts of the system must change. The remainder can continue their current range of activities. Coordination costs are kept at a minimum because subunits operate autonomously.

The disadvantage to "loosely coupled systems" is that while they may be able to adopt an innovation quickly, the "loosely coupled" structure presents a large barrier to spread or expansion of innovation. Expansion must be individually negotiated across the subunits or between key influential individuals. Subunit independence also presents an obstacle to political responsiveness. It forces the brunt of political pressure upon a few checkpoints such as the board of education or the superintendent while the rest of the system escapes the brunt of potential or real electoral wrath.

A "loosely coupled system" is a kind of organized anarchy. It is a system with unclear and ambiguous objectives. Curriculum personnel and administrators trying to implement the aims of the organization have a broad range of possibilities for action. However, the compatibility between those actions and attainment of the goals of the organization are unclear and often unknown. What then is effective action? What really makes a difference? These questions are not approachable in the usual means-ends

---

[2] Karl E. Weick, "Educational Organizations as Loosely Coupled Systems," *Administrative Science Quarterly* 21 (March 1976): 14.

[3] Roger A. Kaufman and Fenwick W. English, *Needs Assessment: A Guide to Improve School District Management* (Arlington, Va.: American Association of School Administrators, 1976).

types of frameworks which characterize rational planning and curriculum development in "loosely coupled systems."

If educational systems are not rational and not amenable to the usual approaches to planning, it is clear that the move towards competency-based testing and the imposition of more specific goals will not result in a more rational organization until or unless there is a fundamental change in the management structure that breaks down the barriers which now comprise the "glue" which holds the organization together.[4] This situation seems to be a paradox. The organization is held together in such a way as to be almost a nonorganization, and efforts to alter its method of operating must attack the very survival mechanisms it utilizes to perpetuate itself.

Curriculum Development in "Loosely Coupled Systems"

Let us assume for the moment the correctness of the description of the educational system as "loosely coupled" and examine what the curriculum looks like in an organization that is characterized by imprecise objectives, global job descriptions, ambiguous technology, and no "best way" known to the role incumbents to accomplish any of the major tasks.

Curriculum exists in the form of global kinds of guides which serve as very rough filters for instructional personnel to utilize. Decisions about the inclusion or exclusion of subject or content are assisted by the presence of such generic filters. Curriculum guides assist teachers in knowing that a topic or subject came before or will come after another topic in a particular K–12 sequence; but within those parameters, the amount of time, emphasis, pacing, and iteration are the domain of teachers to decide. Since these are open questions and not even acceptable variations, options, or combinations are specified, there is essentially no control exercised by curriculum guides or the management system. One critic remarked that "it is the kind of system in which everyone is in control but no one is in control."

Most school district personnel in curriculum have no idea of the extent to which any given curriculum spelled out in a guide is being followed; nor do they know, if it were followed, the degree of variation from teacher to teacher, department to department, school to school, or subdistrict to subdistrict of the total system. Drawing together a group of representative personnel who write a new curriculum guide is moving from one hypothetical curriculum to another. As such, a new curriculum guide may have nothing to do with impacting the instructional program. The construction of a new guide does not proceed from a real idea of the baseline of what exists in the schools.

[4] See Thomas F. Green, "Minimal Educational Standards: A Systematic Perspective," paper prepared by CEMREL (September/October 1977).

There is little or no linkage between system goals and objectives and the curriculum guides which contain instructional objectives. Almost any subject area curriculum could include most global educational goals. Global school district goals therefore do not serve as effective operational criteria upon which to construct or select curriculum, since almost any would be capable of delivering the desired goals. Such criteria are usually embodied in a board of education philosophy of education if one exists at all.

> . . . Central classroom activities of teachers—instruction and classroom management—are not primarily determined by high level policy decisions; they cannot be viewed as 'following orders,' and the reasons are not hard to find. The educational goals of school systems tend to be vaguely defined and refer to present and future outcomes that defy easy measurement and specification into readily identifiable goal-directed activities.[5]

Curriculum guides operate in isolation from specific management objectives for the district. Management objectives may relate to improving services by expanding them, reducing class size, or even reducing costs; but until management objectives begin to focus on pupil learning, there is no bridge between the "stuff" in curriculum guides and management action. Management action is expected to help improve instruction, and curriculum is expected to fit into the management system. But they remain unlinked and isolated, or "loosely coupled."

For example, when minimum competency tests or objectives are adopted by management and embraced or integrated into the existing curriculum (or replace the curriculum), it is often assumed that the existing curriculum (the sum of the "loosely coupled" subunits within the system) can somehow *produce* the desired results. The assumption is made that the desired ranges of results are within the capability of the "in place" curriculum and instructional systems to deliver. Or put another way, it is assumed that the imposition of a standard will substitute for a "best way" or most effective approach to engage in instruction if one is not known or has not been defined. Curriculum does not have to be revised. Instruction does not have to be changed. The minimum competency specification will serve the function of both the criterion and the result simultaneously. It is no wonder that so many thoughtful educators are pessimistic about the capability of the minimum competency movement to make a substantial difference in upgrading instruction and/or reducing costs.[6]

---

[5] Robert Dreeben, "The School as a Workplace," in *Second Handbook on Teaching,* ed., R. M. Travers (Chicago: Rand McNally, 1973), p. 453.

[6] Barry D. Anderson, "The Costs of Legislated Minimal Competency Requirements," paper prepared for the Education Commission of the States under a contract with NIE. 12 September 1977. (Mimeographed.); Shirley Boes Neill, *The Competency Movement: Problems and Solutions* (Arlington, Va.: American Association of School Administrators, 1978).

From one end of the school system to the other, curriculum development follows and fits into "loosely coupled" units within districts, schools, departments, and/or grade levels. The production of specific curricula can occur within any of the units, but absorption or movement across the system is made extremely difficult by the fact that negotiations are required to expand a curriculum. Negotiations refer to the process of exploring and exchanging influence in order to affect the opposing negotiator. Negotiations can occur formally in a collective bargaining sense or informally. However, negotiations are time consuming, whether formal or informal. Therefore, curriculum guides or philosophies of education have served a largely symbolic function: they have given the appearance of agreement without the necessity of actual agreement on a precise meaning. Curriculum guides therefore usually do not tamper with existing relationships between organizational subunits.

Considered Action for Curriculum Improvement

The Improvement of Curriculum and Management Theory

Traditional efforts to improve the "mix" of the curriculum usually accept the current management design decision. A design decision relates to the nature of how any organization will group and define work (the division of labor) and how certain classical problems, such as coordination and economy of scale of resource utilization, will be confronted. Once management has made the design decision, no discussion regarding the "what" of curriculum will be likely to exert any real change until the management theory itself is confronted. Simply labeling management considerations as examples of industrialized, assembly line impositions on a humanistic enterprise will not help practicing administrators to deal with the actual variables by which school systems can be changed. The real test is the degree to which any theory is able to explain relationships and then perhaps to predict effects, based upon real or hypothetical causes.

Curriculum theory must include management theory if curriculum is to be implemented in *systems of schools*. Whether the theory is humanistic, existential, self-realizing, personalized, flexible, or individualized, it will make little substantial impact on learning until it is able to generate a practical alternative for *systems of schools*. As long as learning is conceptualized as an idiosyncratic, largely unscheduled, and mostly fortuitous event, *and that assumption* is the *only* alternative held up for school curriculum administrators, we will continue to hold fast to the current design alternative, and current curriculum development efforts will continue to reinforce that alternative.

It is only if the curriculum developer and theorist understands management theory that he or she can offer the practical kinds of directions to fully consider curricular change. The ideology of Romanticism and the notion of "organic management" cannot be viable substitutes for curriculum development in *systems of schools*.[7]

The current management model of schooling has frozen the curriculum. It is preoccupied with time and activities within self-contained units. Uneven learning curves, pupil boredom, excitement, discovery, joy, creativity, are continually "smoothed" out in order to maintain the existing organization design decision. While doing so may be anachronistic to learning, it is *compatible* with the definition of schooling. The type of organizational design schools have selected has brought with it a kind of control that has meant incarceration for many students and teachers.

Toward A Different Design Alternative

Can schools really be different? The first prerequisite is to consider which organization design decision will lead to a different curriculum "mix." If the organization or management design is not considered, a new curriculum which embodies a set of values and constructs different from that of the existing management design cannot last. It will be preempted by the existing structure's contrary set of values.

The problem with curricular alternatives that contain the same set of characteristics as the current set is that no design alternative *has* to be considered. Substituting existentialism for Latin changes the subject "mix" only. Nothing else may be changed.

The Concept of Curriculum Variance

To qualify as a system, any system must create a common set of elements in order to function as an organization. A system creates conformance on some variables or criteria and ignores others. The current curriculum has a great deal of commonality in terms of time, but a tremendous difference in the content, pacing, and ordination or sequencing in actual practice.

Variance refers to the extent to which any array of content in one set or sequence is exclusive to that in any other set or sequence. It is the widest possible difference of nonoverlapping items. Taking the two elements in the most powerful variable relating to student achievement, *time on task,* the current school curriculum has a very low time variance but a large degree of content (task) variance. This situation occurs because historically curriculum guides have been only general references for decisions by teachers regarding content, pacing, and sequence. This type of conformance fits rather nicely into the existing organizational design decision about self-contained units.

---

[7] The notion of "organic management" is addressed as "fallacy of creativity" by Peter Drucker in *Management* (New York: Harper and Row, 1973), p. 267.

A different organizational design decision may reduce the current level of time conformance but require some other kind of conformance in order to continue to function as a system. Therefore, in any design alternative, the curriculum developer must decide where conformance is desired or required and where it is not.

The movement toward competency testing and standards is partially an effort to reduce the perceived level of curricular variance in content and, by so doing, improve the level of curricular concentration. The idea appears to be to reduce the overall level of variance. However, without some consideration of the time constraint, no improvement in pupil performance may really occur. The curriculum that can respond most effectively to a narrow range of outcomes (minimum competencies) may contain exactly the opposite variance-conformance balance between time and content from that present today.

It may well be that an organizational variance on time offers more possible individual variance than the current time and/or task conformance-variance patterns. A greater possible variance in time for teaching and learning response would go much farther in moving school systems *as systems* toward focusing on learning and being more sensitive to the learner; such time variance would also be more effective in delivering any given range of results. More actual content change and consolidation may be prompted by scheduling changes than by efforts to deal first with content and its pragmatic and/or theoretical base. Part of this assertion may be borne out by some of the kinds of curricular changes forced by the movement towards flexible scheduling in the late sixties.

Although the time dimension may be independent of considerations of subject matter discussions, removing the time lid may enable school systems to take a kind of inventory to determine how well any given subject or subjects can serve as the means to achieve specified learner objectives and then to eliminate less effective areas or combine them into fused subjects for any given range of objectives. It may be possible to deal anew with the question of curriculum balance.

Curriculum Mapping and Curriculum Power

An analytical procedure by which the real time and task dimensions of the real curriculum (the one the learner encounters) can be studied has been called *curriculum mapping.*[8] It is based on an old descriptive research technique called "content analysis."[9] Curriculum mapping is a technique to determine the variance in time and/or task delineations from

[8] Fenwick W. English, *Quality Control in Curriculum Development* (Arlington, Va.: American Association of School Administrators, 1978).

[9] Walter R. Borg, *Educational Research: An Introduction* (New York: David McKay Company, 1963), pp. 260-65; Joseph E. Hill and August Kerber, *Models, Methods, and Analytical Procedures in Education Research* (Detroit: Wayne State University Press, 1967), pp. 108-16.

the curriculum guide and to indicate the extent to which what is taught is also congruent with the testing program. The technique is based on the assumption that there is significant variation in content taught and time spent on any set of tasks (objectives, concepts, minimum competencies, etc.) within a school or school system. Another assumption is that once known, such variables can be adjusted so as to reach more effectively any set of outcomes desired. A curriculum sequence is a statement of time and task statements in ordinal form.

Curriculum power is the degree to which a curriculum is able to reach effectively any set of outcomes desired. Power may be enhanced by dealing with task inclusion and exclusion decisions regarding the curriculum and with the level of repetition (time) within types of ordination (sequences.)[10]

One type of summary curriculum map is shown in Table 1. It is a hypothetical compilation from individual classroom teachers as to what they include or exclude in science teaching of 25 possible topics from the curriculum guide.

If we exclude for the moment a breakdown of whether the topics are introduced, reinforced, or expanded (something which is extremely difficult to differentiate in practice), we can show that the most time is actually spent on the following topics (K–12): (a) *magnetism* (5.7 hours per week per semester) over seven grades; (b) *nutrition* (5.0) over five grades; (c) *solar systems* (5.0) over five grades; (d) *human body* (5.0) over four grades.

By grade level the most time spent on various topics was: (a) *tenth grade* (6.5) four topics; (b) *third grade* (5.1) six topics; (c) *twelfth grade* (4.1) eleven topics, *first grade* (4.1) five topics, *second grade* (4.1) five topics, *fifth grade* (4.1) five topics.

Those topics classified as *singletons*—i.e., they appear only once in the entire K–12 sequence—were simple machines, insects, volume and mass, tobacco and drugs, and bonding. One topic included in the curriculum guide—i.e., optical illusions—was not taught at all in the entire K–12 sequence.

What Curriculum Mapping Provides. Using a curriculum map, a curriculum administrator can compare *actual* time on task (objectives, concepts, minimum competencies, etc.) with the *desired* time on task to see the extent of variance between actual teaching content and designed teaching content. This information, in conjunction with the testing program and the existing curriculum guide, can help the administrator do the following:

1. *Determine a Baseline of Actual Time and Task Emphasis.* A curriculum guide provides a hypothetical curriculum. The extent to which it

---

[10] George J. Posner and Kenneth A. Strike, "A Categorization Scheme for Principles of Sequencing Content," *Review of Educational Research* 46 (Fall 1976): 665-90.

Table 1. Curriculum Mapping: Analysis of Data
Science Curriculum of Shady Grove Public Schools

TOPIC	Grades													Total Time by Topic
	K	1	2	3	4	5	6	7	8	9	10	11	12	
1. Simple machines	I/1	0	0	0	0	0	0	0	0	0	0	0	0	1.0
2. Work and energy	0	I/1	R/1	0	0	0	0	0	0	0	0	0	E/1	3.0
3. Locomotion	I/1	0	0	0	0	0	0	0	0	0	0	0	E/.2	1.2
4. Insects	0	0	0	0	0	I/1	0	0	0	0	0	0	0	1.0
5. Magnetism	0	I/1	R/1	E/1	0	0	E/1	0	0	R/1	0	R/.5	E/.2	5.7
6. Weather	I/.5	0	0	E/1	0	0	0	0	0	0	0	I/2	0	2.0
7. Kinetics	0	0	0	0	0	E/1	0	E/1	0	0	0	0	E/1	3.0
8. Temperature	I/.5	R/1	R/1	0	0	0	0	E/.5	0	0	0	0	0	3.0
9. Nutrition	I/.5	0	0	0	R/1	0	0	E/.5	E/.5	0	E/2	0	0	5.0
10. Sex differences	I/.1	0	0	0	R/1	0	0	0	0	0	E/2	0	0	2.1
11. Ecology	I/.1	R/.1	R/.1	R/.1	0	0	0	0	0	0	0	0	0	1.4
12. Solar system	0	I/1	R/1	E/1	E/1	0	0	0	0	0	0	0	0	5.0
13. Gravity	0	0	0	I/1	0	0	0	0	0	0	0	0	E/.1	1.1
14. Radioactive dating	0	0	0	0	0	0	0	0	0	0	0	0	E/.1	.6
15. Volume and mass	0	0	0	0	0	0	0	0	I/.5	I/2	0	0	0	2.0
16. Bonding	0	0	0	0	0	0	0	0	0	0	0	0	I/.1	.1
17. Human body	0	0	0	0	0	I/1	E/1	E/.5	0	0	E/2	0	0	5.0
18. Cells	0	0	0	0	0	I/.1	E/.2	E/1	0	0	E/.5	0	0	1.3
19. Plants	0	0	0	R/1	0	R/1	E/1	0	0	0	0	0	0	3.0
20. Tobacco and drugs	0	0	0	0	0	0	0	0	0	I/1	0	0	0	1.0
21. Atom	0	0	0	0	0	0	0	0	I/1	0	0	0	E/.2	1.2
22. Friction	0	0	0	0	0	0	0	0	I/1	0	0	0	E/.1	1.1
23. Optical illusions	0	0	0	0	0	0	0	0	0	0	0	0	0	0.0
24. Waves	0	0	0	0	I/.2	0	0	0	E/.5	0	0	0	R/.1	.8
25. Quantum theory	0	0	0	0	0	0	0	0	0	0	0	0	I/1	1.0
TOTAL TIME BY GRADE	3.7	4.1	4.1	5.1	3.2	4.1	3.2	3.5	3.5	4.0	6.5	2.5	4.1	

Legend: I=introduced; R=reinforced; E=expanded
Time Delineation: number equals hours per week per semester

may be followed may be only obliquely revealed in a testing program. If there are significant variations from the guide, it becomes extremely difficult to adjust the curriculum to reach more effectively any range of instructional objectives without having a data base upon which to issue intelligent directions. It is almost impossible to use test data as feedback under such conditions. A curriculum map, depending upon the level of detail included, can provide data on what the actual curriculum includes and emphasizes, and in what order. Such assessment of teaching content is one element which is almost universally absent in school districts' attempts to comply with minimum competency requirements.

2. *Provide a Focus for Curricular and Instructional Adjustments.* The time and task ordinal data revealed from a curriculum map can be compared with the desired curriculum design, and directions can be issued to insure greater congruence. If a reference to the testing program is also included in the setup of a curriculum map, a greater level of congruence between objectives, teaching, and testing should occur.

Ordinarily curriculum administrators bounce back and forth between looking at the testing program and revamping curriculum guides, apparently assuming that whatever is spelled out in the guides will insure teacher compliance. What most curriculum maps reveal, often for the first time to practitioners, is the extremely high level of content variance within the same grade level and subject area by veteran teachers who know their areas well. Because teachers work in isolation from each other, midstream adjustments do not usually occur in order to insure any kind of minimal level of compliance with a set of outcomes desired. There is no warning signal to the instructional staff that the level of content and time on task variance is way off from that which will be effective in reaching instructional targets—minimum competency objectives or others—except when test scores begin to slide. At that point it is often impossible to reconstruct any series of events that could be retraced to correct any imbalance in existing time and task emphases. Most often instructional staff turn to the curriculum guide as a solution, never knowing the extent to which it is representative of the actual classroom curriculum.

Toward a Curriculum Breakthrough

In the language of management, a *breakthrough* occurs when a higher level of performance is recorded that becomes a new standard level of performance. In order to be called a breakthrough, an improvement must meet two criteria. The first is that the new level of performance has never before been attained; the second is that the change is the result of a design, not luck.[11] A breakthrough therefore deals with the chronic causes of poor

---

[11] J. M. Juran, R. S. Bingham, Jr., and Frank M. Gryna, *Quality Control Handbook* (New York: McGraw-Hill, 1974), pp. 2-15.

performance. It attempts to deal with those factors which control the largest degree of variance.

It is believed that teaching is the pivotal element in improving learner performance and that the way to improve that performance is to insure the greatest possible congruence between the actual and desired curricula. If both are keyed to the testing program, and it is possible to use the results obtained from testing to make adjustments so teaching will become more effective, a new and superior level of pupil performance should be possible to attain. To do all of this, however, may call into question the structure and emphasis of the existing curriculum and the organizational design alternative selected by management. At that point the practitioner will have arrived at an understanding of the pervasive influence of management theory on curriculum development.

9

Curriculum Change
and the School
Theodore J. Czajkowski and Jerry L. Patterson

*... Any attempt to introduce a change into the school involves some exist-
ing regularity, behavioral or programmatic.* These regularities are in the nature
of intended outcomes. It is a characteristic of the modal process of change in
the school culture that the intended outcome (the change in regularity) is rarely
stated clearly, and if it is stated clearly, by the end of the change process it has
managed to get lost. It certainly was not an intended outcome of the introduction
of the new math that it should be taught precisely the way the old math was
taught. But that has been the outcome, and it would be surprising if it were
otherwise.[1]

Sarason

One conclusion stands out clearly: many of the changes we have believed
to be taking place in schooling have not been getting into classrooms; changes
widely recommended for the schools over the past 15 years were blunted on the
school and classroom door.[2]

Goodlad and Klein

No MATTER at what level curriculum gets initiated or developed,
if it is ultimately to make a difference, it must bear fruit in the school and
its classrooms. This chapter will discuss and analyze school level curriculum change,* and the one that follows will focus on the classroom. Sarason
makes no bones about the necessity of changing behavioral and programmatic regularities within the school if meaningful curriculum change is to
occur. Goodlad and Klein's conclusion underscores the failure of most
major curriculum change efforts of the past several decades to find their
way into schools and classrooms. It appears that most efforts at curricu-

---

[1] Seymour B. Sarason, *The Culture of the School and the Problem of
Change* (Boston: Allyn and Bacon, 1971), p. 3.

[2] John I. Goodlad and Frances M. Klein, *Behind the Classroom Door*
(Ohio: Charles A. Jones, 1970), p. 97.

* We will use curriculum change and curriculum development interchange-
ably since most curriculum development seeks to bring about some more or less
substantive change in a particular educational program. Even curriculum development which attempts to define a new program—for example, career education
—results in curriculum change if only because of its impact on other curricula.

lum change literally fall short of significantly influencing what happens in schools. This seems to be the case even at times when the change is initiated within the walls of the school rather than by some external source. Certain questionable assumptions about schools and teachers and curriculum change processes have contributed to our problems in fostering and guiding school curriculum change.

Assumptions About Schools and Teachers

Two serious criticisms have been leveled by Herzog at typical approaches to the concept of planned change. "These criticisms are *viewing schools as objects to be manipulated* and *failing to recognize that most people are engaged in activities because they see value in those activities, not because they are resistant to change.*" [3] Much of the language we use seems to betray our image of curriculum users: teachers and principals as passive recipients in the curriculum change process at best, stubborn resisters at worst. We talk about "disseminating," "installing," and "transmitting" innovative curricular products. We talk of "change agents," "clients," and "teacher-proof curriculum." Even much of the "involvement" and "shared decision-making" emphasis of the past several years smacks of manipulation and continues to reflect lack of respect for users. The practice of characterizing user groups, often by schools, as more or less innovative or as innovators or resisters is still very much alive in school change circles. This blamesmanship style is very self-serving and indicates a simplistic view of human behavior, both individually and in groups. Even if it might seem to be fair turnabout on teachers and administrators who often blame students for not learning because they "come from broken homes," "aren't motivated," or "have poor study habits," this type of explanation reflects a lack of understanding of and respect for teachers, principals, and the complexity of their school cultures.

Many schools and their inhabitants have good reason for resisting curriculum change. In a historical sense they have probably been lied to, conned, manipulated, and coerced many times by so-called change agents. They have likely learned to ignore, resist, and, if necessary, subvert efforts to change their classroom situations, particularly when they feel their classrooms are operating successfully.

In a recent article which discussed teachers' reasons for resisting innovations in the school curriculum, Delahanty stated:

Teachers fear risk to classroom discipline, pupil achievement, and ultimately their own reputations. Moreover the risks are often unaccompanied by

[3] John D. Herzog, "Viewing Issues from the Perspective of an R and D Center," quoted in K. A. Leithwood and H. H. Russell, "Focus on Implementation," *Interchange* 4 (1973): 15. (Italics added.)

convincing prospects of success. Failure is most often attributed to teachers, not innovators; success to innovators, rarely to teachers.[4]

Sarason emphasized a related point:

> Another factor too lightly passed over by those involved in planning and change is that many of those who comprise the school culture do not seek change or react enthusiastically to it. There are those among the "change agents" whose ways of thinking are uncluttered by the possibility that others see the world differently than they do.[5]

A critical element of any school change process is readiness for curriculum change—that is, a school staff that perceives a discrepancy between *what is* and *what could be* going on in their school and classrooms. It's likely that readiness for change comes about in an idiosyncratic manner in each school and is based on that school's cultural peculiarities. The cultural configuration of any school has many reasons for being the way it is. Some are caused by the particular people who have collected there; some result from formal and informal leadership; some are based on historical occurrences; and so on. These factors contribute to basic cultural features like interpersonal norms, vested interests, and coping behaviors which undergird a school's behavioral and programmatic regularities. In Sarason's words:

> In trying to understand such a complicated human network as a school system, it is insufficient to characterize its organizational structure as more or less authoritarian. There can be many variations in organizational structure, and these variations are important in terms of the pattern of human functioning. Likewise similar organizational structures can be inhabited by different kinds of people, and this too is important. The interaction between structure and individuals must be our focus. Furthermore to make matters even more complicated, *it is precisely this kind of interaction, occurring over long periods of time, that results in something we call a subculture, which is held together by a force not much different and no less powerful than the feelings of morality that bind our larger western culture.*[6]

There is little utility in labeling a particular school's cultural nature simply as innovative or traditional or in planning to use the same curriculum change strategy across several school cultures. Those who seek to provide curriculum leadership must come to understand the complexity and uniqueness of each school culture. They must respect and accept each school culture for what it is and what it represents and seek from it the data and human resources necessary to help plan effective change processes. On the other hand, curriculum leaders who view schools as similar objects to be manipulated and teachers as resisters without reason have a vision of reality which is unlikely to promote successful curriculum change.

---

[4] David B. Delahanty, "Myths About Older Teachers," *Phi Delta Kappan* 59 (1978): 263.

[5] Sarason, *The Culture of the School,* p. 8.

[6] Ibid., p. 231.

Assumptions About Curriculum Change Processes

Assumptions about the change process are often at the root of unsuccessful school change efforts. Some of the more obvious and questionable assumptions about change are illustrated by linear models, sequential steps, and "best" ways to promote change. School curriculum change processes are too dependent upon the unique aspects of the school and its inhabitants to be characterized by linearity or "best" sequential steps. Sarason questions such assumptions as he discusses where to start:

I would suggest that where one starts has to be a problem that is presented to and discussed with the target groups—not as a matter of empty courtesy or ritualistic adherence to some vague democratic ethos but because *it gives one a more realistic picture of what one is dealing with. An obvious consequence of this is that in different settings one may very well answer the question of where to start rather differently,* a consequence that those who need to follow a recipe will find unsatisfactory because there is no one place to start. Still another consequence is that one may decide, indeed there are times one should decide, *to start nowhere,* that is, the minimal conditions required for that particular change to take hold, regardless of where one starts, are not present. The reader should note that the decision not to proceed with a particular change, far from being an evasion, forces one to consider *what other kinds of changes have to take place before the minimal conditions can be said to exist.*[7]

In addition to faulty assumptions about readiness for and initiation of curriculum change, there is often a lack of understanding of and substantive attention to implementation. Most obviously deficient are those processes which seem to expect the transition from planning, adopting, or adapting to implementing simply to occur. Fullan and Pomfret recently published an outstanding review of "Research on Curriculum and Instruction Implementation." Among other things, they conclude:

If there is one finding that stands out in our review, it is that effective implementation of social innovations [those that require role changes] requires time, personal interaction and contacts, inservice training, and other forms of people based support. Research has shown time and again that there is no substitute for the primacy of personal contact among implementers, and between implementers and planners/consultants, if the difficult process of unlearning old roles and learning new ones is to occur. Equally clear is the absence of such opportunities on a regular basis during the planning and implementation of most innovations. All this means is that new approaches to educational change should include longer time perspectives, more small-scale intensive projects, more resources, time and mechanisms for contact among would-be implementers at both the initiation or adoption stages, and especially during implementation. Providing these resources may not be politically and financially feasible in many situations, but there is no question that effective implementation will not occur without them.[8]

---

[7] Ibid., pp. 217-18.

[8] Michael Fullan and Alan Pomfret, "Research on Curriculum and Instruction Implementation," *Review of Educational Research* (Winter 1977): 391-92.

Fullan and Pomfret also supported Sarason's notion that changes in behavioral regularities are necessary if a significant degree of implementation is to be reached. They discussed a series of studies emphasizing such findings as a majority of teachers' inability to identify the essential features of the innovation they were supposedly using, and an innovation's description in abstract global terms with consequent ambiguity on the part of the teachers as to what the change entailed behaviorally. Then Fullan and Pomfret diagrammed their proposition:[9]

Low explicitness	→	User confusion	→	Low degree
		Lack of clarity		of
		Frustration		implementation

It seems reasonable that changes in programmatic or behavioral regularities would be unlikely to occur if users did not know explicitly what the essential features of the curriculum change were and if they could not specify the behaviors they would have to perform to put the change into action in their classrooms.

Whether the locus of initiation for curriculum change is external to the school (for example, national or statewide) or internal (perhaps inspired by a group of teachers), a process can only be effective to the extent that it influences what goes on in schools, classrooms, and their surroundings. It is our contention that curriculum, in a real sense, is what happens in and around schools when kids, teachers, and things interact. Whether that curriculum has been inspired by a professionally bound and slickly packaged curriculum product or by highly personal scratchings in a teacher's plan book, it is successful only to the extent that it enhances the quality of educational experiences that a particular group of youngsters has. To the extent that some written or otherwise established curriculum has become internalized in a school's people, things, and interactions, it is likely to make a difference; to the extent that it hasn't become so, its value to that particular school is at best unrealized.

In summary, it seems that some faulty assumptions about curriculum users as individuals and groups and about curriculum change processes deserve considerable responsibility for the failure of many efforts to extend successfully through school and classroom doors. Inadequate understanding of and attention to the culture of a school and the way it interacts with the stages of curriculum change has been an obvious problem for curriculum leaders. The implementation stage has been particularly slighted in most curriculum change efforts even though it seems critical to changes in behavioral and programmatic regularities and ultimately to the potential for success of any attempted change.

In an effort to help isolate and illuminate some of the "particulars" of school curriculum change, we have developed a descriptive model which we call the Framework for Understanding School Curriculum

---

[9] Ibid., pp. 368-69.

Change. In the following two sections we will introduce it and use it to describe some examples of strategies which could be used as part of a total school curriculum change process. Walker emphasized the need for theoretical integration of the curriculum field and warned against prescriptive models:

> ... Theoretical integration should lead to firmer, more dependable, and more readily interpretable generalizations. But I doubt whether we shall ever see useful wide generalizations about curriculum change because so much depends on the particulars—the particular subject involved and the particular reforms being pursued, the particular climate of the times, what else happens to be going on at the same time, the particular locale with its unique actors. This situation is not cause for despair, but rather for caution and modest expectations ... The image of the technician at the control panel directing the entire operation needs to be replaced with a more realizable one, perhaps that of the mountaineer using all of the tricks of modern science, together with personal skill and courage and an intimate study of the particular terrain, to scale a peak.[10]

Framework for Understanding School Curriculum Change

The purpose of the Framework is to conceptualize and describe practices at the school level which are aimed at curriculum change. The Framework is descriptive, not prescriptive. In other words, it doesn't purport to tell curriculum leaders what they should do or pass judgement on what they did. Rather, it provides concepts and categories for describing the realities of school-based change, trying to simplify without being simplistic. We hope it will arm the curriculum leader as "mountaineer" with some tools for navigating the climbs up future "peaks."

The Framework for Understanding School Curriculum Change will be constructed using four components: *stages, nature, orientation,* and *strategies* of curriculum change. This categorization is offered with the qualification that any effort to describe curriculum change in such form will lose some of the dynamics of change occurring in a school. Perhaps examples of the Framework in action will give some life to the schema.

Stages of Curriculum Change

Numerous models have categorized the process of curriculum change into anywhere from two stages to eight or more.[11] For purposes of this discussion, however, the number of stages is not important; the important point is that the stages as a group accurately describe the curriculum change process. Although the stages represented in Figure 1 are depicted sequentially, the real life of the school curriculum change is less linear and much more dynamic.

---

[10] Decker F. Walker, "Toward Comprehension of Curricular Realities," in *Review of Research in Education*, ed., Lee S. Shulman (Itasca, Ill.: F. E. Peacock Publishers, 1976), pp. 51-52.

[11] K. A. Leithwood and H. H. Russell, "Focus on Implementation," *Interchange* 4 (1973): 10-25

Figure 1. Framework for Understanding School Curriculum Change

The *initiation* of curriculum change usually comes about in one of three ways. In some cases, school staffs note a discrepancy between what they think could be happening within the curriculum and what curriculum practices actually exist. As an example, Belmont Middle School health teachers recently participated in a workshop on physical wellness. The teachers realized that much of their current curriculum centered on the concept of illness and how to treat it. After several planning sessions, the teachers agreed to initiate changes in their health curriculum so that the emphasis shifted from illness to wellness.

Sometimes, an innovation becomes simply an attractive alternative to what's currently being done, and momentum grows to adopt the new idea. The teachers at Sadler Elementary School voted to adopt a program of Individually Guided Education (IGE). The decision was not based primarily on discrepancies between what was and what should be. Rather it was based on the comprehensive nature of the IGE management and reporting system and its value to the Sadler staff.

A third way of initiating curriculum change is to mandate it. For instance, the superintendent of Marsh Hollow School District directed all schools to have a competency-based physical education program within 12 months.

Regardless of the form it takes, the initiation stage usually includes a plan of action aimed toward implementation. Many times plans change as the process unfolds, but the transition from initiation to development frequently occurs with the completion of basic plans.

Development consists of a school staff's readying the curriculum for implementation. At Wells High School it took the form in social studies of modifying a commercially prepared program. More specifically, the teachers spent about a year tailoring a program in law-related education to fit the needs of the Wells students. Tailoring, in this sense, meant omitting student objectives that were covered in other courses and including objectives that had been developed by local law enforcement programs.

In another school, curriculum development involved teachers' generating their own curriculum product, piloting it at two grade levels, then preparing a tentative curriculum to be used by all teachers in the school. The understanding was that further development should occur, based on the results of a one-year trial.

The *implementation* stage begins when one or more of the features of the planned change is put into action by users. One of the more comprehensive conceptualizations of implementation was developed by Hall and

Loucks. They contend that individual users reflect roughly seven different "levels of use"—e.g., mechanical, routine, integrated use—as they become more adept at using the innovation.[12] Without elaborating on the categories, it should be apparent that implementation isn't a static point. In fact, as Fullan and Pomfret point out:

> ... Implementation is a highly complex process involving relationships between users and managers, and among various groups of users, in a process characterized by inevitable conflict and by anticipated and unanticipated problems that should be prepared for prior to attempting implementation and continually addressed during it.[13]

As mentioned earlier, the stages illustrated in Figure 1 represent one way of viewing the curriculum change process as it unfolds. Within each of these stages, change can assume a variety of forms as described below.

Nature of Curriculum Change

In simplest terms a distinction can be made regarding the nature of change between unplanned and planned change. (See Figure 2.) *Unplanned change* encompasses any alteration in curriculum that evolves without deliberate decisions which are goal directed. In one hypothetical instance, Whitmore Elementary School experienced virtually no teacher turnover for almost a decade. As the pendulum of prevailing curriculum change swung toward a basic skills emphasis, teachers found themselves relying more and more on instructional practices they had used years earlier. Staff stability contributed to continual reinforcement of certain biases about what the school's curriculum should be. Over the course of ten years, Whitmore became labeled an extremely traditional school with an outmoded curriculum. The curriculum probably justified the allegation. It seems fair to say that what happened was a natural occurrence and that it was unplanned in the usual sense of the term.

Figure 2. Framework for Understanding School Curriculum Change

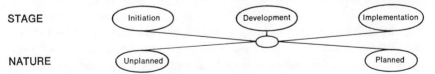

By contrast, *planned change* implies something more than happenstance. Unruh, for instance, offers the following definition: "Planned

---

[12] Gene E. Hall and Susan Loucks, "A Developmental Model for Determining Whether the Treatment is Actually Implemented," *AERA Journal* 14 (Summer 1977): 263-76; Gene E. Hall, S. F. Loucks, B. W. Newlove, and W. L. Rutherford, "Levels of Use of the Innovation: A Framework for Analyzing Innovative Adoption," *Journal of Teacher Education* 26 (Spring 1975): 52-56.

[13] Fullan and Pomfret, "Research on Curriculum," p. 391.

change involves mutual goal-setting and a conscious, deliberative, and collaborative effort to apply appropriate knowledge systematically to human affairs so that procedures can be designed for reaching the goals."[14]

As used in the Framework for Understanding School Curriculum Change, planned change refers to any deliberate attempt to bring about change in the curriculum. The locus of initiation for a change may range from a federal statute requiring nondiscriminatory activities in the physical education curriculum, to a team of science teachers trying to improve their unit on plants and animals, to an individual teacher seeking to improve his/her reading program. In any case, there is a deliberate effort to influence curriculum. Further discussion in this section will address such change. This is not to minimize the effect that unplanned change has on school curriculum, but to narrow the focus to activities planned by curriculum leaders and school staff to improve curriculum.

Orientation of Curriculum Change

As illustrated in Figure 3, most curriculum leaders have an orientation toward curriculum change that can be categorized as either *individual* or *group* oriented. Curriculum change practices, in general, seem to operate on a set of assumptions drawn from a psychology of the individual.

Figure 3. Framework for Understanding School Curriculum Change

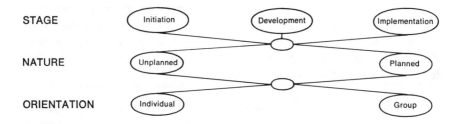

That is, activities geared to bring about change are based on how individuals behave apart from their place in a group. An individual-oriented change strategy, for instance, would take into consideration personality, homeostasis, security, and the like as variables affecting the planned change. On the other hand, a group-oriented strategy tends to focus primarily on social psychological factors. The culture of the group, with its accompanying norms, values, incentives, and power structure, may exert a much greater influence on proposed change than the collection of individuals in the group. In Sarason's words:

[14] Glenys G. Unruh, *Responsive Curriculum Development: Theory and Action* (Berkeley, Calif.: McCutchan, 1975).

Many of us are intellectually reared on a psychology of the individual; that is, we learn, formally or informally, to think and act in terms of what goes on inside the heads of individuals. In the process it becomes increasingly difficult to become aware that individuals operate in various social settings that have a structure not comprehensible by our existing theories of individual personality. In fact, in many situations it is likely that one can predict an individual's behavior far better on the basis of knowledge of the social structure and his position in it than one can on the basis of his personal dynamics.[15]

In summary, one orientation to change emphasizes a psychology centering on the behavior of individuals. A group orientation, on the other hand, assumes that an alteration in the prevailing school culture is necessary for curriculum change to occur.

Strategies for Curriculum Change

Although in the real life of the schools curriculum change strategies may vary according to the conditions of the moment, it is possible to talk about the three general strategies that appear in Figure 4.

Figure 4. Framework for Understanding School Curriculum Change

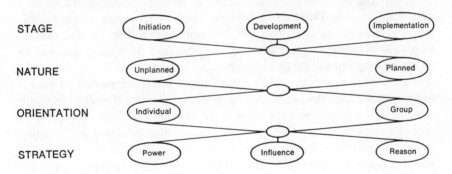

A *power strategy* is one that usually emanates from the "top-down," and the school or teachers have little control over the decision to participate. Usually this strategy takes the form of legislation, court orders, or directives from superordinates. Short of the radical position of nonparticipation with its attendant consequences, teachers usually enter into this form of change with a low level of commitment to the change itself. At best, commitment lies in a derived outcome unrelated to the goal of the change effort. Many times the incentive for participation in a power strategy is to avoid the negative sanctions for noncompliance. The role of the teacher under these conditions is usually passive, reacting to the forces aimed at bringing about some form of curriculum change.

Examples of power strategies would be accountability legislation mandating the testing of students on specific objectives in reading, Title

[15] Sarason, *The Culture of School*, p. 12.

IX regulations, a superintendent's directive requiring all elementary schools to include metrics in the math curriculum within nine months, and a principal's demand that all teachers emphasize grammar as part of their language arts program.

An *influence strategy* is one that is designed to make curriculum change attractive to the participants. Other labels used to describe this strategy are persuasion, manipulation, and utilitarian. The major premise of this strategy is that curriculum change can take place if the conditions for change can be made sufficiently appealing to entice action by a school staff. Thus the commitment to change using an influence strategy is usually based on a perceived benefit to the participant, not on the change per se. For example, if teachers are influenced to attempt the curricular changes involved in changing from a junior high to a middle school organization, and a feature of the new organization is additional planning time for teachers, they may become committed to the change because of the increased planning opportunity. Of course, this type of commitment can be very tenuous; if another set of attractive conditions comes along, commitment could shift quickly.

The role of the school staff within an influence strategy can be passive or interactive. Teachers can choose to participate only at a level sufficient to receive the incentives. Or they can share in the decision making as well as the curriculum change activities because the change happens to be the best option available under the circumstances.

Reason strategies provide the foundation for many models of educational change. In this approach, commitment is to the change itself. Teachers clearly see the need for a given change, and they are willing to take the steps necessary to achieve their goal. The incentive for engaging in the process of curriculum change is the substance of the change. Usually the participant's role extends into leadership, decision making, and active involvement in the process. The reason strategy assumes that with sufficient knowledge, skills, and resources, teachers given the opportunity will move in a reasonably deliberate manner to reduce the discrepancy between what is and what ought to be in the curriculum.

Application of the Framework for Understanding School Curriculum Change

Now that construction of the Framework is complete, an explanation is in order regarding its application in the world of the school. Most models of educational change propose one "best" way, as defined by the author(s), to bring about change. What's neglected is the fact that change in education is buffeted by a variety of forces, both within and outside the school. In order to deal with these forces appropriately, a description of curriculum change needs to take into consideration the realities of curriculum change practices. The Framework for Understanding School Curriculum Change attempts this by recognizing that a given change takes on its particular configuration due to the conditions that go into making a decision regarding effective change.

There are many paths to take using the Framework. It is important to understand that while some paths may be seen as generally more favorable, any of the possible paths may be appropriate for a particular school situation under a particular set of circumstances. Recent research on curriculum and instruction has underscored the variety of practices that have been applied.[16] The Framework is an important step in conceptualizing what these practices actually mean in the realm of school-based curriculum change.

To illustrate the application of the Framework, certain paths are described below. It should be pointed out that these are only representative. In reality, most of the possible combinations have been used in schools, in varying circumstances with varying degrees of success.

Initiation/Power/Individual Path

Frequently schools experience a "top-down" directive requiring changes in school curriculum practices. The following example characterizes what an individual-oriented power strategy would look like.

Title IX of the Education Amendments of 1972 declares, in part, that:

No person in the U.S. shall on the basis of sex, be excluded from participation in, be denied the benefits of, or be subjected to discrimination under any educational program or activity receiving federal financial assistance.

Relating specifically to curriculum, Section 86.34 of the Title IX regulation states that schools may not "provide any course or otherwise carry out any educational program or activity separately on the basis of sex, or require or refuse participation therein of any students on the basis of sex, including health, physical education, industrial, business, vocational, technical, home economics, music, and adult education courses."

Upon receiving notification of these requirements, the director of curriculum in a suburban school district asked each school to see to it that all teachers complied with the regulation within nine months. The curriculum change process set in motion at each school followed along these lines: (a) All teachers were given a copy of Title IX regulations. (b) They were asked to determine to what extent their curriculum was in noncompliance. (c) They were told to submit a plan of action for redressing any noncompliance.

This illustration depicts how the initiation of curriculum change could occur employing a power strategy that focused on changing the behavior of individuals apart from their role in the culture of the school.

---

[16] Fullan and Pomfret, "Research on Curriculum," p. 391.

Development/Influence/Group Path

Curriculum change practices during the development stage are often shaped by a myriad of forces, both within and outside the school, vying for a "best" curriculum as defined in their terms. The example below traces one school's experience in the curriculum development stage.

Burris Middle School recently completed a needs assessment in social studies that showed some problems in curriculum coordination between seventh and eighth grade. The staff agreed some form of action was in order. But the school had just moved to a multiage organizational structure the previous year, and commitment to further energy-draining activities was at low ebb. The principal, sensitive to the norms and power structure of the school, realized that an appeal to reason would cause some staff members to act out of the need to improve curriculum coordination. The principal also realized, however, that the designated leaders of the four teaching teams considerably influenced any staff decision. Another factor the principal noted was the outdated supply of social studies program materials. Consequently, the principal identified some funds that were available to purchase materials and called a meeting of the team leaders with the following proposition: If the staff were willing to meet bimonthly from 3:30–4:30 P.M. to try to resolve the curriculum discrepancies between seventh and eighth grade social studies, new textbooks could be ordered to support any changes in the curriculum.

These incentives made the needed curriculum work more attractive to the team leaders. They, in turn, conveyed to their colleagues that conditions were ripe for beginning curriculum development. The staff was influenced by the opportunity to get new social studies materials, and curriculum development got underway, due in large part to the principal's understanding of the culture of the school in connection with an influence orientation toward the curriculum change.

Implementation/Reason/Individual Path

As cited in Fullan and Pomfret's research, few curriculum change projects ever reach the implementation stage. Even during implementation, though, various combinations of curriculum practices are available. The example below illustrates how a school applied an individual-oriented reasoned approach to implementation.

Stanford Elementary School had spent four years attempting to better individualize its curriculum. Through a series of inservice opportunities funded by a Title IV grant, the entire staff had revamped the curriculum to include learning centers as a central means for individualizing. For the past six months, all teachers had been implementing the learning center concept with varying degrees of success. Even among those still struggling at a mechanical use level, commitment was high. Teachers continued to seek new ideas for centers, and those who were most successful were eager to help those who weren't.

The principal viewed the prevailing curriculum practices as an opportunity to pair teachers in professional growth teams so that help could be made available to those who needed it most. Because all teachers in the school were convinced of the merits of learning centers, the incentive to change was the change itself. Thus, the principal figured that if individual teachers were given opportunities for information and training, they could eventually begin using learning centers in ways that fit their teaching style, rather than continuing the routinized approach some were employing. The staff agreed and used the teaming system to further implement the learning center methods.

Our purposes for sharing the framework and depicting a few of the many possible paths to change are: to underscore the complexity of school curriculum change processes; to provide the reader with some sensible and useful categories for observing and engaging in school curriculum change; and to emphasize that options are not inherently good or bad, only more or less appropriate depending on the "particulars" identified by Walker.[17]

Changing Schools and "Scaling Peaks"

In the first section of this chapter we discussed how certain faulty assumptions about teachers, schools, and the process of curriculum change have interfered with efforts to adopt, adapt, or generate curriculum. We concluded that section with Walker's statement which included an image of the curriculum worker as "mountaineer" rather than "technician." The discussion of the Framework for Understanding School Curriculum Change emphasized the complexity of the process, among other things. Now we will emphasize some useful assumptions and observations in an attempt to enable the curriculum worker as "mountaineer" to understand the nature of some of the "particulars" he/she will face "scaling the peaks" of curriculum change.

For openers we would suggest a new organizing concept for the process—*program improvement*. It seems to us that activities called curriculum development, adoption of innovations, curriculum change, and selection of new materials all represent attempts at program improvement. Further, particularly at the school level, *curriculum* activities, *staff development* activities, and *program evaluation* activities should be interrelated efforts to improve program. These statements lead us to our general assumption, or "particular" if you will. *Schools that meaningfully coordinate curriculum change, staff development, and program evaluation toward specific aspects of program improvement are more likely to reach successful implementation than those that don't.* The "particulars" and discussion that follow elaborate on this assumption.

[17] Walker, "Toward Comprehension," pp. 51-52.

Teachers and Program Improvement

An important lesson of the "Decade of Reform" (1965-1975) is that even the "best" educational practice is unlikely to fulfill its promise in the hands of an inadequately trained or unmotivated teacher. We have learned that the problem of reform or change is more a function of people and organizations than of technology.[18]

McLaughlin and Marsh have done an outstanding job of drawing implications and conclusions from the Rand Study of *Federal Programs Supporting Educational Change*.[19] Some of the assumptions below relating teachers and staff development to program improvement are supported by their article.

In terms of knowledge about the practice of teaching, teachers often represent the best clinical expertise available. This assumption adds another dimension to the argument that teachers must be *substantively* involved in the process of curriculum change. It suggests that we use the clinical expertise of teachers to test and alter curriculum ideas so that they may be more meaningfully applied in school and classroom settings. Not to use the clinical expertise of teachers risks the demise of a perfectly good curriculum idea or procedure only because it was not structured or modified to meet the realities of the school and teachers expected to implement it. Outside experts often hesitate to let teachers manipulate and alter their curriculum ideas and procedures because they fear the teachers will destroy them.

The other side of the coin is more appealing. If teachers in a school do not have the opportunity to manipulate and alter—yes, even destroy— an idea, it is unlikely that they will ever come to understand, own, or implement it.

In a sense, teachers and administrators need to "reinvent the wheel" each time curriculum change is brought to or generated within the school building. So often we hear the comment in educational circles, "We don't (or shouldn't) have to reinvent the wheel." The comment seems to be based on the assumption that once curriculum has been "invented" it can be transferred directly in some manner to other schools. This assumption seems to ignore the implications of differences in school cultures and the complexities of the curriculum change process reflected in our discussion of the Framework for Understanding School Curriculum Change. Just as each geometry student must rediscover, for example, the Pythagorean Theorem if he/she is to understand, apply, and make it his or hers to use, so must the staff of a school rediscover the meaning (to them) of a curriculum idea and be able to understand, own, and use it in their particular

---

[18] Milbrey W. McLaughlin and David D. Marsh, "Staff Development and School Change," *Teacher's College Record* 80 (September 1978): 69.

[19] The findings of this study are reported in eight volumes under the general title, *Federal Programs Supporting Educational Change*. R-1589-HEW (Santa Monica, Calif.: Rand Corporation, May 1978).

situation. Even something which seems relatively simple, like clarifying the purpose for curriculum change, requires complex interactions by a school staff and often a considerable amount of time and energy. Perhaps it is not only necessary for each school staff to "reinvent the wheel" but also to reestablish the purpose for working at "reinventing the wheel" and to determine whether the "wheel," once "reinvented," will contribute to improving their school's educational program. At any rate, it is likely that the "reinventing" process is more important than the "wheel."

Professional learning is a long-term, nonlinear process. School program improvement is based on the quality of the professional learning that occurs as teachers and principals struggle together to define a curriculum idea, acquire the perceptions and knowledge required to make it happen, and incorporate it into their total school program. The meandering path from identifying or recognizing a need to improve, to evaluating the extent to which implementation contributes to the educational experiences of the students is based on many readjustments to data about the staff and where they are relative to the process. "Stages of concern" and "levels of use" information that reflect personal and behavioral patterns are examples of data that could help a curriculum worker plan appropriate interventions in the process.[20]

Staff development should be seen as an ongoing part of the school program improvement process. Staff development can help teachers and administrators sharpen their program improvement goal(s) and establish commitment and ownership gradually as the process unfolds. When school staff come to see staff development as a functioning component of the continuing program improvement process, they have probably reached a self-renewing mode. Using the findings of the Rand Study, McLaughlin and Marsh found:

> Within the most successful projects, the project was not a 'project' at all, but an integral part of an ongoing problem solving and improvement process within the school. In a sense, good staff development never ends. It is a continual characteristic of the school site.[21]

Leadership and School Change

Three levels of leadership seem to have a significant impact on the quality and effectiveness of program improvement. For our purposes we will identify them as principal, district administrators, and project coordinator.

Principals have a significant impact on program improvement through their influence on school organizational climate and their behavior in support of the process. It is often said that the principal sets the tone for a school building. To the extent that the tone of a school reflects good work-

[20] Hall, Loucks, Newlove, and Rutherford, "Levels"; Hall and Loucks, "A Developmental Model."

[21] McLaughlin and Marsh, "Staff Development," p. 90.

ing relationships among teachers and a willingness to struggle openly and honestly with problems, the school is more likely to achieve program improvement. The sense of ownership that usually develops when school staffs have the opportunity to shape specific attempts at program improvement is necessary to promote high level implementation. Principals also send important messages to teachers with their behavior and involvement in the program improvement process. Rand Study results support the following conclusion:

> The importance of the principal to both the short- and long-run outcomes of innovative projects can hardly be overstated. When teachers thought that principals disliked a project, we rarely found favorable project outcomes. Some projects with neutral or indifferent principals scored well, particularly in the percentage of goals achieved; but these projects typically focused on individualization or curriculum revision, and had highly effective project directors who compensated for the lukewarm principals. Projects having the *active* support of the principal were the most likely to fare well. In general, the more supportive the principal was perceived to be, the higher was the percentage of project goals achieved, the greater the improvement in student performance, and the more extensive the continuation of project methods and materials.
>
> The principal's unique contribution to implementation lies not in "how to do it" advice better offered by project directors, but in giving moral support to the staff and in creating an organizational climate that gives the project "legitimacy." [22]

District administrators or "downtown" staff do have a significant impact on program improvement through resource support and other perceivable expressions of interest. Again the Rand Study provides a basis for a conclusion that is helpful:

> The support and interest of central office staff was, as suggested earlier, very important to staff willingness to work hard to make changes in their teaching practices. Though a skilled and enthusiastic project director may be able to effectively implement a special project in the absence of explicit support from downtown, project staff are unlikely to continue using project strategies unless district administrators express interest. [23]

An effective project coordinator has a significant impact on the level of implementation reached in program improvement efforts. The project coordinator may have been employed to perform the role or may be a curriculum coordinator, principal, teacher, or someone else representing another role who has been assigned to or otherwise achieved a position of leadership. It seems critical that the project coordinator be perceived by the school staff as effective. This usually requires that the project coordinator be sensitive to the types of assumptions and information contained in this chapter. This person should be an effective process consultant: she/he should be able to perceive the nuances of group processes

---

[22] Paul Berman and Milbrey W. McLaughlin, *Federal Programs Supporting Educational Change, Volume VIII: Implementing and Sustaining Innovations.* R-1589/8-HEW (Santa Monica, Calif.: Rand Corporation, May 1978).

[23] McLaughlin and Marsh, "Staff Development," p. 81.

and school culture, to encourage the group to ask the difficult questions and follow good decision-making procedures, and to shift gears and plan interventions that respond to complex shifts in the process. The project coordinator may, more than anyone else, be the one who performs the role of the "mountaineer." It should be evident by now that it is not an easy role because the process is so complex and has no precise sequential steps or guidelines. Using the Rand Study data, McLaughlin and Marsh have concluded:

> The Change Agent data show that the more effective the project director (in the view of teachers), the higher the percentage of project goals achieved, and the greater the student improvement observed as a result of the project. An effective project director has significant instrumental value to project implementation—a director's special skills or knowledge can foster staff understanding of project goals and operations, minimize the day-to-day difficulties encountered by classroom teachers, and provide the concrete information staff needs to learn during the course of project operations.[24]

Climbing the School "Peak": Some Closing Comments

Given the realities of school culture and the apparent need to meaningfully involve those most responsible for implementation, the school seems to be the primary unit for program improvement. Whether the curriculum idea being deliberated by a staff comes from some external source or is generated within the school, the idiosyncracies of the particular school culture must be adequately perceived and carefully considered in planning and guiding the process. Some perceptions can be supported by fairly sophisticated data ("stages of concern," "levels of use");[25] others can find support in schema like our Framework; others must remain more subjective and intuitive because there are as yet no conceptual tools or lenses which theoretically integrate them. Many of the tools and skills of the "mountaineer" are as yet relatively primitive, and the school culture is a formidable foe. As Sarason has cautioned us:

> All that I am saying at this point is that when we say a setting is "organized," or that cultures differ from each other, we mean among other things, that there is a distinct structure or pattern, that, so to speak, governs roles and interrelationships within that setting. What is implied, in addition is that structure antedates any one individual and will continue in the absence of the individual. It may well be that it is precisely because one cannot *see* structure in the same way that one sees an individual that we have trouble grasping and acting in terms of its existence.[26]

On the other hand we do have some reasonable, data-based information about "particulars" that can help us in "scaling" program improvement "peaks." We have tried to share such information in this chapter.

[24] Ibid.
[25] Hall and others, "Levels"; Hall and Loucks, "A Developmental Model."
[26] Sarason, *The Culture of the School,* p. 12.

10

The Realities of Curriculum Work: The Classroom Level

Joel Weiss

FEW WOULD ARGUE with the idea that teachers should have the responsibility for what goes on in the class setting. However, there is some question about what role they should play in curriculum decision making, where control should lie. During the twentieth century, one can trace swings from control that is far removed from the classroom (in the form of textbook writers, large-scale reform projects, provincial or state education officials, board curriculum committees) to control that is vested with teachers in their own setting (e.g., progressive and open education movements). But if on the face of things the pendulum has swung from one movement to another, the swings have been of unequal amplitude since most of the formal curriculum development work has occurred outside of the classroom. Publishers, professors, policy makers, and professionals at curriculum making seemingly account for the visible textbooks, packages, guides and source materials that we value as curricular goods. At the school board level, curriculum consultants often decide on the appropriate texts and packages for use in their jurisdiction. Teachers sometimes sit on curriculum committees, but it would appear as if the classroom teacher has little to do and say about curriculum development. *However, I will argue in this chapter that although classroom teachers may not have an overtly large role in curriculum development as we have come to think of it, they actually wield enormous influence on day-to-day curriculum decision making.*

Conditions Affecting Teachers' Curriculum Development Activities

As a means for understanding the classroom curriculum context, let us recall from chapter 3 some of the conditions of professional life for the classroom teacher. At the elementary level, a teacher typically spends

176

most, if not all, of the school day with the same group of approximately 20–35 children. At the secondary school level, teachers may encounter five or more groups of a comparable size passing through each day. For the teacher of younger children, there is the potential for 30 different curricular programs; for the secondary level teacher, the number of programs typically depends upon the number of different courses taught.

Grannis also suggests that schooling imposes restrictions on a child's time. Not only are there formal laws that regulate when a child must be in school, but there are also regulations rooted in tradition as well as statute that help determine how the day shall be spent. The number of hours spent on required subjects, the number of options available, the number of resources available—all potentially temper how teachers and students manage classroom time.

A third influence on classroom life suggested by Grannis is the expectation that teachers will foster literacy. This expectation is regulated not only by governmental authorities but also by many segments of the public, often in a vocal way.[1] This emphasis on basic cognitive skills— usually reading and computing (and sometimes writing)—exerts pressure to find public indicators of achievement, and schools have responded with wholesale use of commercially developed, standardized achievement tests. And more recently, many states have mandated the use of specially developed tests of literacy as a means of certifying the minimum essential skills of high school students.

These three conditions help to provide a framework for understanding the nature of curriculum development activities of teachers. They help to define the world of the classroom, the agenda both hidden and otherwise. Given the complex nature of educational practice, it is simplistic to attribute so much to so few factors, no matter how pervasive they appear in their influence. So I would suggest, additionally, that a teacher's background may loom large as a potential influence on curriculum development activities. For example, pedagogical training might influence a teacher's view of how classrooms work and how children are perceived and treated. Although training in specific curriculum development activities is the exception in preservice education, an emphasis in subject matter training may influence a teacher's willingness to participate in curriculum development activity in that area. Of course, the reverse may be true:

---

[1] The fact of governmental regulations and public concern for basic skills is not, of course, a coincidence. State departments of education, ministries of education, and local boards of education reflect community pressure in the rhetoric and substance of guidelines, goals, and even resource materials. (See, for example: Michael Kirst and Decker Walker, "An Analysis of Curriculum Policy Making," *Review of Educational Research* 41 (December 1971): 479-510.) I cannot neglect public censorship of the curriculum, since this is a very dramatic and painful encroachment not only upon the professional's responsibility but also upon control of decision making.

lack of confidence in a subject area may render a teacher unable to participate in all but a superficial way—leaving choices to others.

Another way that a teacher's background might influence his/her curriculum development activity is the extent of his/her involvement in curriculum activities at the school, board, state, provincial, or even national level. Some of this involvement may be influenced by the political process that helps to delineate the centralization-decentralization mode of educational decision making, i.e., whether teachers and local schools and boards in fact have curriculum-making responsibility or there is centralized control of curriculum work. And the amount of encouragement received from colleagues and administrators can influence the perceived rewards for this type of involvement and possibly deter or encourage future participation.

We can imagine a continuum of teacher involvement in curricular work, all the way from creating the total curriculum to serving as monitor for already developed programs. Neither extreme has much basis in the reality of most teachers' professional lives. What is certain is that teachers are exposed (and expose themselves) to a variety of curricular situations which call for some type of decision making. Just the choice of text or program used (even though such material might leave no room for individual choices) involves teachers in curricular decision making. Let us look at some of the types of programs and consider how they affect the teacher's role in this decision making.

Externally Developed Curricula and Their Effects

In tracing the most recent curriculum history in North America, one encounters the familiar tale of large-scale curriculum projects having their impetus in the launching of the Russian Sputnik satellite. While certainly this interpretation is a part of the story, the part dealing with large-scale public financial support and a renewal of discipline-centered curriculum efforts,[2] it leaves the impression that centralized curriculum work started with this event. But we know that textbooks have always exerted a strong centralizing influence; that is, a few textbook writers have controlled the curricular activities of millions of children. Nevertheless, choices of what programs and instructional strategies should be used involve such complex professional, social, cultural, political, and economic considerations that at any point in time there are any number of options available to teachers. In describing the role of the teacher in implementing the post-Sputnik, discipline-centered curriculum development projects, Grobman points to the very real differences among the projects "on their views of how materials should be taught, how much flexibility should be built into the curriculum, how many choices teachers and students should have, and

---

[2] Daniel Tanner and Laurel Tanner, *Curriculum Development* (New York: Macmillan, 1975).

whether all students should use the same materials."[3] Rather than superficially judging all programs developed during this era as having similar organization, i.e., highly structured with no choice of sequence and scope of activities and materials, Grobman suggests that the differences are great among these projects on their definitions of curriculum and that consequently the role teachers play in using a project's material is varied. So projects that conceive of the curriculum as a text, or as groups of material to be used with all students or for each individual child, or as anything and everything needed to achieve the goals, allow for a variety of curriculum decision making by teachers.

Although Grobman's analysis demonstrates the heterogeneity of approach (or at least of the intentions of the curriculum developers), the net effect of these large-scale curriculum efforts was a move toward teacher-proof activity, i.e., curriculum developed in a preordinate fashion, with little opportunity (perceived or actual) for teachers to influence the learning situation. What is important about this state of affairs, of course, is that teachers as the users have the ultimate word in what they do. They not only have the choice of what materials to use but of how they are used—the subject matter components, the instructional strategies, the motivational aspects. Unwittingly, teachers may not understand the subject matter content or may have difficulty adapting from a direct style of instruction to an inquiry-based approach. There may also be instances where a teacher reacts to the imposition of a predetermined program by consciously adapting it to his/her situation. In myriad ways, teachers alter the intentions of curriculum developers. As Shell Oil would have us believe a few years ago: the final filter has an important influence on performance.

If the large-scale, externally developed curriculum packages have been interpreted as representing a teacher-proof curriculum approach, there is also the extreme of curriculum-proof teachers. This state of affairs occurs with teachers who appear to have a built-in program device—one that allows for remarkably similar implementation regardless of program, text, or guideline used. Herron[4] has documented an example of curriculum-proof teaching with observations on the inservice attempts of several large-scale science projects to familiarize teachers with the rationale of each program.

User-Based Curricula and Their Implications

Textbooks and large-scale, externally developed curricular programs are but a few of the forms that curriculum development activities may take. There is a range of activities that can be collectively viewed as

[3] Hulda Grobman, *Developmental Curriculum Projects: Decision Points and Processes* (Itasca, Ill.: Peacock, 1970), p. 115.

[4] Marshal Herron, "On Teacher Perception and Curricular Innovation," *Curriculum Theory Network* 7 (1971): 47-51.

locally based curriculum efforts. One can view such efforts as part of a trend that waxes and wanes, depending on other influential sources of curriculum-making activity—e.g., decentralization as a reaction to centralized curriculum control. Connelly[5] describes the tension between the two modes (externally and locally based) as "oscillations," with one perhaps being the dominant partner at any particular point in time. Consider this hall of mirrors! The most recent "oscillation" toward a more structured, centralized approach to basic skills is a reaction to the perceived laissez-faire, teacher autonomy-based open schooling of the late sixties and early seventies which in turn was a reaction to the highly centralized, discipline-centered programs of the late fifties and middle sixties, which in turn was a reaction to the dying, progressive education movement of the forties and fifties.

Of course this description is an oversimplification of reality. At any time, there are any number of curriculum efforts taking place: professors of education writing textbooks; foundations sponsoring multicultural curriculum modules; commercial curriculum committees translating state and provincial guidelines; curriculum coordinators working with teachers to develop a program specially suited for a child having perceptual difficulties.

But how are teachers involved in curriculum development? It is naive to expect that teachers should spend their time developing curriculum and program materials. With some exceptions, teachers do not have the time, resources, and training to perform this role. To be sure, teachers are constantly involved in developing outlines, lesson plans, objectives, exercises, enrichment, and remedial materials, but often as a reaction to an administrative directive or a specific problem situation. However, if few out of the many teachers participate in curriculum development work as external developers, all teachers are involved in modifying, adopting, adapting, and otherwise translating already existing programs, materials, and guidelines. It is this function of teacher as user that Connelly[6] contrasts with the external developer.

Considering starting and ending points and methodology, Connelly sees the external developer's function as the elaboration of theoretical notions of society, knowledge, teacher, and learner and the translation of these views into curriculum materials; he sees the user's function as articulation of visions of specific instructional situations and the translation into classroom use. Teachers cannot swear allegiance to a program; they can only be faithful to their own situation. Now there is a problem associated with fidelity to external developer intentions: a misunderstanding of a program may lead to inappropriate use, regardless of how much the teacher knows a setting. But if a teacher knows the setting and is

[5] F. Michael Connelly, "The Functions of Curriculum Development," *Interchange* 3 (1972): 161-77.

[6] Ibid.

able to appropriately adapt a program to that setting, then the user's intentions take precedence over the developer's.

Let us now consider conceptions or models of curriculum development and what effects these have on teachers' curriculum decisions.

Curriculum Development Models and Their Usefulness

Although Gay in chapter 7 has already discussed several models of curriculum development, some attention will be paid here to several of these approaches and some others with an eye toward the classroom teacher. Gay described several orientations toward education that find expression in possible approaches to curriculum development. She presented four models: "academic," "experiential," "technical," and "pragmatic." As Connelly has suggested in chapter 6, the roots of these models grow in the soil of philosophy. Others have developed their own conceptions of orientations toward curriculum that have implications for development. For example, Eisner[7] has posited five conceptions: "cognitive," "technological," "subject matter rationalism," "self-consummatory," and "social reconstructionist." Without much difficulty these can be identified with the four models of Gay.

But as Gay pointed out in chapter 7, none of these models is "functionally operational: curriculum practitioners will not implement the model in its idealized or theoretical form or employ one model to the total exclusion of all the others."

The "Academic" Approach

Of all the models of curriculum development, the Tyler Rationale has received most attention and is an example of Gay's "academic" model. Over the years it has become identified as an objectives-based model (with technical overtones). To read the education literature over the last 15 or so years is to believe that much of the curriculum development work uses the Tyler Rationale[8] as the major determiner. But to say that the objectives-based approach has been influential in the literature is not to say that most curriculum development and teachers' curriculum activity proceed with this model in mind. Theoretical support for this statement can be found in the writings of Eisner,[9] Kliebard,[10] Macdonald-Ross,[11] and

---

[7] Elliot Eisner, *The Educational Imagination* (New York: Macmillan, 1979).

[8] Ralph Tyler, *Basic Principles of Curriculum and Instruction* (Chicago: University of Chicago Press, 1950).

[9] Eisner.

[10] Herbert Kliebard, "The Tyler Rationale," *School Review* 78 (February 1970): 259-72.

[11] M. Macdonald-Ross, "Behavioural Objectives: A Critical Review," *Instructional Science* 2 (1973): 1-52.

Wise.[12] In fact, it might be fair to say that most teachers go about curriculum making in a very intuitive fashion, with little reliance on an overriding model or highly articulated conceptual orientation.

In addition to the rhetoric on what teachers ought to do, there is a small but growing literature on what teachers actually do. Several studies have been conducted that bear on how teachers plan and the extent to which objectives figure prominently in their curriculum planning. Clark and Yinger,[13] in their review of research on how teachers think, summarized several studies that bear on teacher planning and made the point that it is only since 1970 that such empirical work on the preactive phase of teaching has been conducted. The picture that develops from this emerging research is that teachers rely less on objectives than we have been led to expect. In a study of teacher planning in English secondary schools, Taylor[14] found that in general, aims were of lesser importance to teacher planning than were the needs of the pupil and subject matter; teaching methods were viewed as least important. Also of little importance to these teachers were evaluation and how a course fit with the curriculum as a whole. Specifically on curriculum planning a factor analysis of teacher ratings also indicated that aims and purposes of teaching were less important than factors associated with the teaching context (e.g., materials, resources) and student interest. Taylor's general conclusion was that course planning appeared to be unsystematic with teachers who (by my inference) were not certain what was expected of them in curriculum development work. Using a sample of American primary school teachers, Goodlad and Klein found similar results showing the lack of centrality of educational objectives: "We are forced to conclude that the vast majority of teachers in our sample was oriented more to a drive for coverage of certain material than to a reasonably clear perception of behavior sought in pupils." [15]

The role of specified objectives in decisions teachers made prior to teaching was studied by Zahorik.[16] The responses for 194 teachers indicated that from the following categories of decisions (objectives, content, activities, materials, diagnosis, evaluation, instruction, and organization), the greatest number in the sample (81 percent) chose pupil activities. The

[12] Robert Wise, "The Use of Objectives in Curriculum Planning," *Curriculum Theory Network* 5 (1976): 280-89.

[13] Christopher M. Clark and Robert J. Yinger, "Research on Teacher Thinking," *Curriculum Inquiry* 7 (1977): 279-304.

[14] Philip H. Taylor, *How Teachers Plan Their Courses* (New York: Humanities Press, 1970).

[15] John Goodlad and others, *Looking Behind the Classroom Door* (Worthington, Ohio: Jones, 1974), p. 8.

[16] John Zahorik, "Teachers' Planning Models," *Educational Leadership* 33 (1975): 134-39.

decision most frequently made first surrounded content concerns (51 percent), while decisions on objectives were initiated first by 28 percent of the sample. From this research we might infer that teachers do not see that objectives are of prime importance in their curriculum decision making. Zahorik also found, contrary to the integrated ends-means model,[17] seen by some as an alternative to the objectives model, that a miniscule number of teachers actually initiated their planning with a particular activity in mind.

A second point that emerges from this literature on teacher planning tends to support Lortie's[18] contention that craft pride for teachers is found in the success of particular students and teachers' relationships with students. The important professional rewards for a teacher are, for the most part, contained within the limited boundaries of the classroom—especially since the teacher's craft is marked by an absence of concrete models for emulation, unclear lines of influences, multiple and controversial criteria, ambiguity about assessment criteria, and instability in the product. When a teacher finds success with but one student, he/she may believe that his/her day may have been worthwhile after all. Perhaps we should not be surprised that students' needs and pupil activities figure so prominently in the planning of teachers. The payoff for teachers may not be so much in terms of general educational achievement for the greater good as with special experiences for individual children. This finding may be in keeping with Jackson's[19] observation that teachers are more intuitive than rational.

A "Pragmatic" Approach

A decade has passed since Joseph Schwab leveled his charge against the curriculum field, suggesting that progress will be made only by placing less stress on theoretical talk about curriculum and more on the reflexive nature of curriculum problems as exemplified by what practitioners do.[20] What developed from Schwab's diagnosis and prescription has been metatheoretical writing about the methods and principles of curriculum activity.[21] Since the emphasis is on deliberative actions instead of theoretical

[17] Eisner.

[18] Dan Lortie, *School Teacher* (Chicago: University of Chicago Press. 1975).

[19] Philip Jackson, *Life in Classrooms* (New York: Holt Rinehart, 1968).

[20] Joseph Schwab, "The Practical: A Language for Curriculum," *School Review* 78 (November 1969): 1-23.

[21] Ian Westbury, "The Character of a Curriculum for a 'Practical Curriculum'," *Curriculum Theory Network* No. 10 (Fall 1972):25-36; Warner Wick, "Knowledge and Action: The Theory and Practice of 'The Practical'," *Curriculum Theory Network* No. 10 (Fall 1972):37-44; Joseph J. Schwab, *Science Curriculum and Liberal Education: Selected Essays,* eds. Ian Westbury and Neil Wilkof (Chicago: University of Chicago Press, 1978).

inquiry, the major emphasis should be decisions rather than knowledge generation.[22]

As Westbury suggests:

It (the character of the practical) sees doing and making as the products of skills and habits that use existing situations as the necessary antecedents to ends that are in view but not yet accomplished. It offers, and draws upon, an image of a creative and practical reformer discerning problems through an awareness of apparent gaps between what should be and what is, then seeking solutions from his understanding of what might be done, and finally moving to bring about change or improvement.[23]

Reid[24] argues that curriculum tasks should be seen as problem-solving situations, and he suggests that they should be viewed in the wider context of problem solving in public policy-making areas. Illustrations of deliberations in curriculum-making activities are offered by Fox[25] and Walker.[26]

Of what relevance to our concerns with the classroom level is this "pragmatic" approach to curriculum activity? Schwab's own intentions for curriculum decision making include a team of specialists representing the commonplaces (subject matter, milieu, learner, and teacher), as well as a general curriculum person.[27] His model is more appropriate at the board or external project level. But there are implications for the classroom level in viewing curriculum development as problem-solving activity, especially those problems which are not readily ameliorated by research or calculation. Curricular situations confront teachers with uncertain practical problems. The process of deliberation, entered into individually or with others, helps "to identify the questions to which we must respond, establish grounds for deciding on answers, and then choose among the available solutions."[28] To the extent that teachers can become sensitive to this process of deliberation and recognize the situational nature of curriculum making, they may become better decision makers.

But there is for me a problem with the notion that the study of what teachers *are doing* is our road to salvation. My concern lies with whether

---

[22] Lee Cronbach and Patrick Suppes, *Research for Tomorrow's Schools: Disciplined Inquiry for Education* (New York: Macmillan, 1969).

[23] Westbury, "Character of a Curriculum," pp. 30-31.

[24] William Reid, "Practical Reasoning and Curriculum Theory in Search of a New Paradigm," *Curriculum Inquiry* 9 (1979): 187-207.

[25] Seymour Fox, "A Practical Image of 'The Practical'," *Curriculum Theory Network* No. 10 (Fall 1972): 45-57.

[26] Decker Walker, "Curriculum Development in an Art Project," in *Case Studies in Curriculum Change: Great Britain and the United States,* eds. William Reid and Decker Walker (London: Routledge and Kegan Paul, 1975).

[27] Joseph Schwab, "The Practical 3: Translation into Curriculum," *School Review* 81 (1973): 501-22.

[28] Reid, "Reasoning and Theory," p. 6; Reid calls these *procedural* problems since they are amenable to solution by an applicable methodology.

this approach can best inform us of what teachers *ought to be doing* in terms of curriculum practices. While tradition should be honored in some situations, we should recognize that it should not always be revered. Perhaps those who are translating and developing the conception of deliberation will enable us to have a process whereby we might better judge the actions of teachers.

Two Approaches to "Experiential" Curriculum Development

Progressive/Open Movements. This orientation to curriculum has its roots in the progressive education era and has been manifested more recently in the open education movement. Briefly, the argument for this approach to curriculum work concerns the respect that teachers have for the right of children to participate in decisions about their own education, coupled with a belief in the natural development of the child.[29] One of the major dilemmas associated with this orientation is: How do teachers translate their respect for children into allowing them decision-making responsibility? To satirize the point: "Yes, but do I have to do what I want to do today?" In his criticism of the progressive education movement, Bode[30] suggested that unless teachers took the responsibility for creatively channeling children's interests through teachers' own professional experiences and judgements, the movement was doomed to failure. Kohlberg and Mayer[31] made the same point in their rejection of the romantic conception of curriculum in favor of a developmental aim for education.

To what extent do teachers reflect this "experiential" approach to curriculum work? A teacher's program reflects the complex world of the classroom: organization of curriculum; instructional strategies; various roles for each of the actors; and organizational arrangements for bringing together students, teachers, and materials in a specific context. According to Hill,[32] these dimensions of class life fall into two categories: *procedural,* which speaks to the organizational life of the class (such as the size of instructional groups, whether there are bells, where learning takes place); and *normative,* which addresses the amount of freedom students have in making decisions about class life. The distinction between these two concepts has implications for understanding teachers' views of curriculum. It

[29] Charles Silberman, *Crisis in the Classroom* (New York: Random House, 1970).

[30] Boyd Bode, *Progressive Education at the Crossroads* (New York: Newson, 1938).

[31] Lawrence Kohlberg and Rochelle Mayer, "Development as the Aim of Education," *Harvard Educational Review* 42 (1972): 449-96.

[32] B. V. Hill, "What's 'Open' About Open Education?" in *The Philosophy of Open Education* ed. V. Nyberg (Boston: Routledge and Kegan Paul, 1975), pp. 3-13.

is possible for a program to be procedural without being normative, but normative would appear to subsume procedural dimensions. Goodlad and Klein[33] in their investigation of American classrooms have even questioned whether procedural openness was being implemented, since they found few instances of curriculum innovations in use. Traub and Weiss,[34] in their study of the program practices of teachers from 72 schools in Southern Ontario over a three-year period, found evidence of procedural openness but not a trace of teachers allowing students to be involved in decision making, let alone allowing them to be the sole decision makers. What also comes through is that teachers rely heavily on existing curriculum materials, but neither students nor teachers engage in making curriculum material to any appreciable extent.

Grannis[35] has suggested that some form of joint teacher-student control is a far better manifestation of humanistic ("experiential") education than for either teacher or child to be solely in control. What emerges for me at least is that some very exceptional teachers can initiate and maintain an "experiential" approach to their curriculum but that most teachers either do not choose philosophically to follow such an approach, or their understanding of open education, for example, suggests a misunderstanding of what constitutes normative openness.

Understanding Meaning. There is an emerging literature in the curriculum field that has been labeled "reconceptualist" because its proponents differ from "traditionalists" who want to guide practitioners and from "conceptual empiricists" who seem to use the methods and procedures of the social sciences to investigate curricular phenomena, often in a predictive way. Among "reconceptualists" there is a mistrust of current curriculum theory which is seen as influenced by a technological ideology. According to Pinar, the purpose of the "reconceptualist" approach to curriculum theorizing is to understand the nature of educational experience by attending to "the internal and existential experience of the public world" through "temporality, transcendence, consciousness, and politics."[36] The roots for this approach lie with history, philosophy, and literary criticism.

[33] Goodlad and others.

[34] Ross Traub and Joel Weiss, "Dimensions of Procedural Openness in the Programs of Southern Ontario Elementary Schools," paper presented at the Annual Conference of the American Psychological Association, Toronto, Ontario, 1978.

[35] Joseph Grannis, "Task Engagement and the Consistency of Pedagogical Controls: An Ecological Study of Differently Structured Classroom Settings," *Curriculum Inquiry* 8 (1978): 3-36.

[36] William Pinar, ed., *Curriculum Theorizing—The Reconceptualists* (Berkeley: McCutchan, 1975), p. xiii.

Van Manen suggests that hermeneutics, the science of interpretation, allows us to see curriculum as "the study of educational experience and as the communicative analysis of curriculum perspectives, orientations and frameworks."[37] But knowledge of alternative perspectives is not enough. Habermas goes beyond the hermeneutic-interpretive to the critical reflection of possibly distorted ways of communicating meaning. He articulates a critical theory that is self-enlightening and includes "the experience of an emancipation by means of critical insight into relationships of power, the objectivity of which has as its source solely that the relationships have not been seen through. Critical reasons gain power analytically over dogmatic inhibition."[38]

How can a "reconceptualist" view and, specifically, hermeneutics and critical theory help us to address the issue of curriculum work at the classroom level? For the most part, curriculum persons who identify themselves with this orientation have been busy establishing a conceptual basis for their work.[39] At some point, however, the value for teachers of this approach has to be demonstrated in two ways. First, it needs to be shown that teachers can become more conscious of their practices from interpretive and critical perspectives. This goal may not be easily achieved, for it requires individuals to be steeped in the art of criticism and in political ideology. But the study of political ideology may not be enough for "liberation" from inequities in a system that they are so tied to.

Second, even if teachers can readily develop a heightened sense of critical consciousness, there will still be the problem of whether such a consciousness can make a difference in curriculum work. Will programs qualitatively reflect differences and will teachers' heightened critical consciousness lead to increased performance of children on those outcomes most valued (e.g., communication skills)? The answers to these questions will depend on the efforts at translating theoretical conceptions into defensible curriculum materials. Some notable examples at translation are offered by Giroux[40] for writing and the social studies and by Gordon[41] for mathematics. At another level, Vallance[42] offers an example of the use of

[37] Max van Manen, "Linking Ways of Knowing With Ways of Being Practical," *Curriculum Inquiry* 6 (1977): 213.

[38] Jurgen Habermas, *Theory and Practice* (London: Heinemann, 1974), p. 254; see also idem, *Knowledge and Human Interests* (Boston: Beacon Press, 1971).

[39] For example: Pinar, *Curriculum Theorizing;* and Madeleine Grumet, "Curriculum as Theatre: Merely Players," *Curriculum Inquiry* 8 (1978): 37-64.

[40] Henry Giroux, "Writing and Critical Thinking in the Social Studies," *Curriculum Inquiry* 8 (1978): 291-310.

[41] Marshall Gordon, "Conflict and Liberation: Personal Aspects of the Mathematics Experience," *Curriculum Inquiry* 8 (1978).

[42] Elizabeth Vallance, "The Landscape of 'The Great Plains Experience': An Application of Curriculum Criticism," *Curriculum Inquiry* 7 (1977): 87-105.

art criticism as a means of judging curriculum materials. What are other ways we can judge or evaluate curriculum materials or curriculum development? What part do teachers play in such evaluation? In the next section I deal with these and related questions.

Curriculum Development/Evaluation and the Teacher's Role

What is meant by effectiveness of curriculum development can be answered only by asking for whom it is effective and toward what ends. Persons with different roles may have different perspectives of what is important. What might be considered effective by a school board's curriculum consultant may differ from what might be expected by a professional curriculum writer or a classroom teacher. The professional curriculum writer may be happy if a program sells; the consultant may be pleased if a program fits in with the rest of the K–12 curriculum; the teacher may be relieved if it fits his/her subject matter concerns and keeps the children busy.

Each group with an interest in curriculum development may assign different roles to the enterprise and, in turn, to its evaluators. I am defining roles in the same sense that Scriven[43] did when he differentiated between roles and goals in his classic essay on evaluation. Goals refer to questions of worth; roles refer to the purpose for which evaluation may be used. Of course, the two are related since it is difficult to conceive of making a judgment of worth of an entity without knowing the purpose for which it will be used. For example, a curriculum program may serve as useful resource material for inservice work with teachers because it exemplifies a particular approach toward the learner; it need not necessarily be useful as a program for a particular group of students. Again, different individuals may take, and even expect, different things from the same curriculum development activities. Ben-Peretz[44] has suggested the term "curriculum potential" for the phenomenon. For some, creating the ultimate materials is of prime importance; for others, the opportunity to participate in deliberations may be the major purpose for curriculum development.

The evaluation of curriculum development at the classroom level is fraught with some of the same difficulties as curriculum development itself. First, just as teachers are rarely involved in formal curriculum development, they are rarely involved in formal evaluations of it. To be sure, teachers make judgments about programs all the time; at the very least, they have an intuitive sense of what works and what does not work. But

[43] Michael Scriven, "The Methodology of Evaluation," in *Perspectives of Curriculum Evaluation,* ed. R. Stake (Chicago: Rand McNally, 1967).

[44] Miriam Ben-Peretz, "The Concept of Curriculum Potential," *Curriculum Theory Network* 5 (1975): 151-59.

this, of course, is not the whole story; for there may be many reasons why teachers are not compelled to either systematically judge what they are using or even to raise questions about the process of determining how their programs are chosen. For example, teachers may use materials because their board has invested money or time on them. So teachers' involvement in the evaluation of curriculum will be more intuitive than systematic; and this fact may guarantee that the de facto, not the de jure, program will be modified.

A second way in which the enterprises of evaluation and curriculum development are similar is the discrepancy between abstract conceptions and ongoing practices. Over the last 15 years, the number of abstract conceptions (or models) of the evaluation process has dramatically helped to create an "instant discipline." Textbooks on educational evaluation (as opposed to measurement and evaluation texts which concentrate on testing) have helped to consolidate a number of these conceptualizations into several categories of models.[45] Just as with models of curriculum development, examples of their use are not easy to find. Again, usefulness of models for educational practice may reside more in their consciousness-raising attributes than in their imitative powers.

A Variety of Evaluation Models

If not all evaluation models are equally useful as conceptions of evaluation processes in general, it is safe to assume that even fewer are appropriate for curriculum development evaluation at the classroom level. Some are developed for application at a gross or macro level; others require resources far beyond what is available in the typical class setting; others may not be responsive to the idiosyncratic ways of different classroom contexts; still others are more appropriate for some types of evaluation but not others (and of course some are inappropriate for more than one reason). Robert Stake[46] has developed a set of criteria for comparing the different evaluation models. He has classified the many conceptualizations currently available into several approaches: "student gain by testing," "institutional self-study by staff," "blue-ribbon panel," "transaction-observation," "management analysis," "instructional research," "social policy analysis," "goal-free evaluation," "adversary evaluation." To this list I have added the connoisseurship-criticism approach. Table 1 presents my selective adaptation of Stake's chart.

Several of the models are similar in orientation to the curriculum development models described earlier in Gay's chapter. The "student gain by testing" model is, of course, directly related to the most popular example

---

[45] For example: Blaine Worthen and James Sanders, *Educational Evaluation: Theory and Practice* (Worthington, Ohio: Jones, 1973).

[46] Robert Stake, "Program Evaluation, Particularly Responsive Evaluation," in *Occasional Paper Series* (Kalamazoo: College of Education, Western Michigan University, 1975), paper no. 5.

APPROACH	PURPOSE	KEY ELEMENTS	PURVIEW EMPHASIZED	RISKS	PAYOFFS	APPROPRIATENESS FOR CLASSROOM LEVEL
STUDENT GAIN BY TESTING	To measure student performance and progress	Goal statements; test score analysis; discrepancy between goal and actuality	EDUCATIONAL PSYCHOLOGISTS	Oversimplify educ'l aims; ignore processes	Emphasize, ascertain student progress	YES
INSTITUTIONAL SELF-STUDY BY STAFF	To review and increase staff effectiveness	Committee work; standards set by staff; discussion; professionalism	PROFESSORS; TEACHERS	Alienate some staff; ignore values of outsiders	Increase staff awareness, sense of responsibility	YES
BLUE-RIBBON PANEL	To resolve crises and preserve the institution	Prestigious panel; the visit; review of existing data and documents	LEADING CITIZENS	Postpone action; overrely on intuition	Gather best insights; judgment	?
TRANSACTION-OBSERVATION	To provide understanding of activities and values	Educational issues; classroom observation; case studies; pluralism	CLIENT; AUDIENCE	Overrely on subjective perceptions; ignore causes	Produce broad picture of program; see conflict in values	?
MANAGEMENT ANALYSIS	To increase rationality in day-to-day decisions	Lists of options; estimates; feedback loops; costs; efficiency	MANAGERS; ECONOMISTS	Overvalue efficiency; undervalue implicits	Feedback for decision making	NO
INSTRUCTIONAL RESEARCH	To generate explanations and tactics of instruction	Controlled conditions; multivariate analysis; bases for generalization	EXPERIMENTALISTS	Artificial conditions; ignore the humanistic	New principle of teaching and material development	NO
SOCIAL POLICY ANALYSIS	To aid development of institutional policies	Measures of social conditions and administrative implementation	SOCIOLOGISTS	Neglect of educational issues, details	Social choices, constraints clarified	NO
GOAL-FREE EVALUATION	To assess effects of program	Ignore proponent claims; follow checklist	CONSUMERS; ACCOUNTANTS	Overvalue documents and record keeping	Data on effect with little co-option	?
ADVERSARY EVALUATION	To resolve a two-option choice	Opposing advocates; cross-examination; jury	EXPERT; JURISTIC	Personalistic; superficial; time-bound	Info. impact good; claims put to test	?
CONNOISSEURSHIP-CRITICISM	To reeducate one's perceptions	Description; interpretation; judgment	AESTHETIC CRITICS	Overemphasis on personal meaning; elitism	Disclosure of meaning; educative for critic and others	YES

Table 1. Ten Approaches to Evaluation. (Adapted from Stake, 1975, p. 33)

of the "academic" model of curriculum development—the Tyler Rationale. Another approach that probably fits within this rubric is the "institutional self-study by staff." The "technical" model of curriculum development has its counterparts in the "management analysis," [47] "instructional research," and "social policy analysis" models. It is a little more difficult to find evaluation models that are comparable to the "experiential" model of curriculum development; but with an emphasis on disclosure of meaning, perhaps the connoisseurship-criticism approach comes as close as any other. The "transaction-observation" model, which emphasizes the disclosure of conflicts in the values of participants, and "adversary evaluation," which stresses the testing of competing claims, come closest in fit to the "pragmatic" model of curriculum development.

Abundance does not necessarily beget practical riches. At the classroom level, there are constraints of time and even of willingness on the part of teachers to formally use evaluation procedures, no matter how appropriate they might seem. A teacher may employ a variation of the "academic" model by developing objectives and using systematic evaluation procedures if these deliberately test for the teacher's objectives. All too often, however, external examinations intrude upon such plans so that the testing may be of someone else's objectives (usually the test developer), not necessarily those of the teacher. Perhaps the only other approaches that teachers have familiarity with are the "institutional self-study by staff" and the "blue-ribbon panel." Ironically, both of these approaches are concerned less with the outcomes than with the inputs (i.e., antecedent conditions such as staff credentials and available resources) and with the processes or transactions (such as pupil-teacher ratio and instructional strategies employed by teachers). There are many examples of the use of the "self-study" model; but all have in common the purpose of making the staff more aware of the quality of the resources of an institution, presumably as a consciousness-raising device. Teachers have probably had less experience with the "blue-ribbon panel" approach, except as the external component of "institutional self-study." [48] Perhaps the visits of area superintendents are the closest teachers might come to this approach.

There are two basic points that might be raised in considering evaluation of curriculum development at the classroom level. First, what is the

[47] The Phi Delta Kappa Committee on Evaluation has acknowledged the influence of systems technology on its model. In addition, one member of the committee couched a description of the model in terms of an engineering paradigm. See also, William Gephart, "The Phi Delta Kappa Committee's Evaluation Model: One Member's View," in *Curriculum Evaluation: Potentiality and Reality,* ed. Joel Weiss (Curriculum Theory Network Monograph Supplement, 1971-72), pp. 115-31.

[48] The various educational accrediting agencies in the U.S. (e.g., North Central Association) and the Ontario Ministry of Education's Cooperative Evaluation Program serve as examples of a combination of self-study and external committee study of institutions.

focus of evaluation? Usually, we consider materials evaluation and/or evaluation of the outcomes of the program. How much does looking at these two factors tell us about curriculum development? Are there other legitimate aspects to consider, such as fidelity of instruction to program? And certainly there is the ever present problem of whether curriculum programs should be evaluated solely on the basis of student outcomes.

A second basic point concerns a fundamental point of view about the nature of education. Should the evaluation of curriculum development start with preconceived ideas about the nature of the program or materials, or should the program or materials be looked at only in the context of practice? The distinction between these two views lies at the heart of some of the difficulties of a "top-down" approach to development and is more broadly related to distinctions between qualitative evaluation and quantitative evaluation. One view suggests that you know what to look for, regardless of context; the other suggests that each classroom is like a fingerprint with its own individual pattern that won't necessarily be predicted from knowledge of other classes.

Both of these two basic points open up a number of issues and problems worth considering. However, I have chosen to address but one of them, the evaluation of curriculum materials using instruments designed by someone other than the teacher because this area provides an opportunity to explore some difficulties teachers may encounter in evaluation.

Curriculum Materials Evaluation

There seems to be no end to the amount of published curriculum materials available for teachers to choose from. One source has estimated that over five thousand textbooks are available for just the four subject areas of reading, mathematics, science, and social studies; over a half million nonprint materials are on the market.[49] Of course not every teacher or school or board has direct access to these riches. Traditional practices and financial limitations represent constraints on curriculum decision making. Still, the potential choices are staggering.

How does a teacher cope with choice making? Are there readily available procedures for evaluating already developed curriculum materials? There have been two large-scale continuing efforts at informing practitioners about materials. The Social Science Education Consortium (SSEC) has developed elaborate checklists of criteria (e.g., rationale, objectives, evaluation, etc.) for evaluating materials and has published sets of evaluations of published programs as guides for practitioners.[50] The Educational

[49] Educational Products Information Exchange, *Educational Product Report No. 76, Report on a National Study of the Nature and the Quality of Instructional Materials Most Used by Teachers and Learners* (New York: EPIE Institute, 1977).

[50] Social Science Education Consortium, *Social Studies Curriculum Materials Data Book* (Boulder, Colo.: SSEC, 1977).

Products Information Exchange (EPIE) also publishes reviews but is, perhaps, more sophisticated about providing linkages with the personal element of decision making that lies with teachers. For example, one of its publications on early childhood programs provides not only reviews of different materials but also a framework for viewing the different approaches to early childhood. This type of help allows practitioners to select programs that more nearly fit their own context. Thus teachers can become conscious of their own views on education and how different curricula have different assumptions and starting points.[51]

But not only the curriculum programs have different assumptions and starting points; so do the evaluation instruments. All too often the unsuspecting user, assuming evaluation to be a value-free enterprise, accepts wherever an evaluation procedure goes. However, evaluation is not value free, and evaluation instruments do reflect biases of the evaluator. Allow me an example of how such bias may operate with teachers. I teach a graduate level course in evaluation of curriculum and instruction. In one of the class assignments students have to use a rating form to evaluate two social studies programs. One program is highly structured with objectives stated to a high level of specificity and organized sequentially; the other program contains a series of enlarged photos with some broad questions and activities contained in a teacher's manual. The evaluation rating form[52] contains a series of questions on four constructs: objectives, organization of the material (i.e., scope and sequence), methodology, and evaluation. Each series of questions leads to a well-defined, seven-point rating scale for each construct. There is also an overall rating of the materials. Below is a rating scale for objectives, taken from the Eash instrument.[53] The scale illustrates quantitative rating for objectives.

1 7

Objectives vague, unclear or missing. Those included not useful. Fails to distinguish between general and instructional objectives, mixes various types of objectives, confusing to the teacher.	The objectives are stated clearly and in behavioral terms. Both general and instructional objectives are stated in a consistent conceptual framework. Excellent, one of the best, useful for a teacher.

Invariably, the ratings done by each class demonstrate great differences between the two programs, with the more structured program receiving on the average at least two points more than the less structured pro-

---

[51] Educational Products Information Exchange, *Educational Product Report No. 42, Early Childhood Education, How to Select and Evaluate Materials* (New York: EPIE Institute, March 1972).

[52] Maurice Eash, "Developing an Instrument for Assessing Instructional Materials," in *Curriculum Evaluation: Potentiality and Reality,* ed. Joel Weiss (Curriculum Theory Network Monograph Supplement, 1971-72).

[53] Ibid.

gram. This result is no surprise since the criteria for the ratings indicate that the author of the instrument sees virtue in structure.

After the students have completed the assignment, I ask them to close their eyes, envision themselves as teachers contemplating both programs, and choose again which one they would use. Generally more of those who change their choice change from the more structured to the less structured of the two programs. In the ensuing discussion, usually several in the class suggest that they were originally seduced by the rhetoric of the rating form and that if I hadn't asked them to make a second choice, they would have stayed with the structured program. Since every story must have a moral, it is this: if teachers are to use evaluation instruments to adopt and/or adapt curriculum materials, they must be prepared to evaluate the evaluation instruments as well.

Declining Enrollment and Curriculum: The Next Two Decades

We are still thinking and acting as if the educational sector is in a period of expansion. However, in many jurisdictions there is (and will continue to be for some time) a decline in both the school population and the resources made available for the educational sector. Although the two do not automatically go together, it appears as if politicians and educational policy makers prefer to provide fewer financial resources for a smaller student population.

The impact of these two conditions has already resulted in closing schools and hiring fewer teachers in many of the remaining schools. Over the long term, how will this affect school programs?

It seems when professional educators do pay attention to the declining enrollment problem, they usually concentrate on the financial and administrative problems.[54] However, recently a Commission on Declining Enrollment set up by the Minister of Education in Ontario included a Task Force on Curriculum. This fact provides at least one indicator of the importance of program to the complex situation facing schools.[55]

The impact of declining enrollments and resources on curriculum can perhaps be inferred from a consideration of their possible influences on conditions of class life: crowding; emphasis on basic skills; and restrictions on a student's time. What follows are my speculations which are offered as a means of provoking thought on these crucial issues.

Fewer children may mean smaller classes, but not necessarily. If the pupil-teacher ratio is kept constant, the crowding factor does not change. Furthermore, teachers may be responsible for split grades (at the elemen-

[54] Susan Abromowitz and Stuart Rosenfeld, eds., *Declining Enrollments: The Challenge of the Coming Decade* (Washington, D.C.: National Institute of Education, 1978).

[55] F. Michael Connelly and Robin Enns, "The Shrinking Curriculum: Principles, Problems, and Solutions," *Curriculum Inquiry* 9 (1979): 277-304.

tary level) or subject areas in which they may not have had training (at both the elementary and secondary levels). The former situation may demand that the teacher offer a more differentiated set of curriculum offerings within a class, but the latter may have the effect of homogenizing the curriculum. Fewer teachers indicates not only fewer courses or classes but also a more restricted variety being offered. It is likely that one of the consequences of a restricted set of course offerings will be an inclination toward back to basics programming; i.e., schools should concentrate on what they can do best: provide skill training. Those areas that are often seen as "frills," such as the arts and special programs, may be the first to suffer. The amount of class time may be influenced by this reversion to more required courses, leaving less time available for options and choices.

In terms of specific curriculum making, teachers may have to rely on existing materials, particularly on those already available within the class, school, or board since text and program changes are expensive. In turn, there probably will be fewer new texts, programs, and materials since the market for such curriculum goods will shrink. Teachers may also have fewer consultants to call upon since pressure to decrease administrative and resource staffs may be even greater than the call for fewer classroom teachers.

Soothsayers may have difficulty predicting what the net effect of these potential situations will be on teacher curriculum decision making. The movement toward more centralized control of a system, if only to be in a position to deploy resources, could also lead to more centralized curriculum control, or at least to an emphasis on common curriculum programs. This situation might be very tempting for teachers who might find themselves teaching more diverse groups of students in nonfamiliar subjects. But as I have suggested throughout this chapter, even if teachers do not decide upon the programs or materials, they do translate them consciously or otherwise into images that they are comfortable with. While the opportunity for personal growth may be greater under this changing type of educational system, unless teachers are given time and appropriate professional development (made more difficult with decreasing resource staffs), curriculum decision making will continue to be a haphazard activity with teachers no more informed about what they are doing than under conditions of an expanding educational sector. A diminished educational system can provide the basis for quality education. We may never again have this opportunity for teachers to develop and understand their sense of purpose. The time and the conditions are certainly right. But can the various educational publics, including (and perhaps especially) teachers, recognize that teachers have control over curriculum decisions?

ASCD 1980 Yearbook Committee Members and Invited Authors

The 1980 Yearbook Committee Members:

ARTHUR W. FOSHAY (Chairman), Rowe, Massachusetts; Professor Emeritus, Teachers College, Columbia University, New York

THEODORE J. CZAJKOWSKI, N.E. District Coordinator, Madison Metropolitan School District, Madison, Wisconsin

FENWICK W. ENGLISH, Manager, Peat, Marwick, and Mitchell Company, Washington, D.C.

GENEVA GAY, Associate Professor of Education, Purdue University, West Lafayette, Indiana

EVELYN LEZZER HOLMAN, Director, Area III, Board of Education of Frederick County, Walkersville, Maryland

DECKER F. WALKER, Associate Professor of Education, Stanford University, Stanford, California

JOEL WEISS, Professor, Ontario Institute for Studies in Education, Toronto, Ontario, Canada

The Invited Authors:

F. MICHAEL CONNELLY, Associate Professor, Ontario Institute for Studies in Education, Toronto, Ontario, Canada

FREEMA ELBAZ, Doctoral Candidate, University of Toronto, Toronto, Ontario, Canada

JOSEPH C. GRANNIS, Associate Professor of Education, Teachers College, Columbia University, New York

JERRY L. PATTERSON, S.W. District Coordinator, Madison Metropolitan School District, Madison, Wisconsin

ASCD Board of Directors

Executive Council, 1979-80

President: BENJAMIN P. EBERSOLE, *Assistant Superintendent, Curriculum and Instructional Services, Board of Education of Baltimore County, Towson, Maryland*

President-Elect: BARBARA D. DAY, *Coordinator of Early Childhood Education, University of North Carolina, Chapel Hill*

Immediate Past President: DONALD R. FROST, *Assistant Superintendent, Community High School District 99, Administrative Service Center, Downers Grove, Illinois*

JULIANNA L. BOUDREAUX, *Assistant Superintendent, Division of Instruction and Child Advocacy, New Orleans Public Schools, New Orleans, Louisiana*

DOROTHY T. BRYANT, *Coordinator of Instruction, Chicago Public Schools, Chicago, Illinois*

GERALD BRYANT, *Assistant Superintendent, Grand Island Public Schools, Grand Island, Nebraska*

LAWRENCE S. FINKEL, *Superintendent of Schools, Chester Township, Chester, New Jersey*

DIANE GESS, *Assistant Elementary Principal, East Ramapo Schools—Hillcrest School, Spring Valley, New York*

RAYMOND E. HENDEE, *Superintendent, Park Ridge School District #64, Park Ridge, Illinois*

ALICE VIVIAN HOUSTON, *Director of Curriculum Services Department, Oklahoma City Public Schools, Oklahoma City, Oklahoma*

CHON LABRIER, *Elementary Principal, Dulce Independent School, Dulce, New Mexico*

MAIZIE R. SOLEM, *Curriculum Coordinator, Instructional Planning Center, Sioux Falls Public Schools, Sioux Falls, South Dakota*

RONALD STODGHILL, *Deputy Superintendent of Instruction, St. Louis Public Schools, St. Louis, Missouri*

Board Members Elected at Large

(Listed alphabetically; the year in parentheses following each member's name indicates the end of the term of office.)

MITSUO ADACHI, *University of Hawaii, Honolulu* (1983)

JAMES A. BANKS, *University of Washington, Seattle* (1980)

MARTA M. BEQUER, *Dade County Public Schools, Miami, Florida* (1982)

REBA BURNHAM, *University of Georgia, Athens* (1981)

C. LOUIS CEDRONE, *Public Schools, Westwood, Massachusetts* (1983)

VIRGIE CHATTERGY, *University of Hawaii, Honolulu* (1981)

MILLY COWLES, *University of Alabama, Birmingham* (1982)

MATTIE R. CROSSLEY, *Public Schools, Memphis, Tennessee* (1982)

THEODORE J. CZAJKOWSKI, *Public Schools, Madison, Wisconsin* (1980)

BEN M. HARRIS, *University of Texas, Austin* (1980)

JOAN D. KERELEJZA, *Public Schools, West Hartford, Connecticut* (1983)

ARDELLE LLEWELLYN, *California State University, San Francisco* (1981)

ELIZABETH S. MANERA, *Arizona State University, Tempe* (1983)

BLANCHE J. MARTIN, *Boone-Winnebago Counties Schools, Rockford, Illinois* (1982)

MARVA GARNER MILLER, *Public Schools, Houston, Texas* (1983)

MARSHALL C. PERRITT, *Public Schools, Memphis, Tennessee* (1980)

RONALD STODGHILL, *Public Schools, St. Louis, Missouri* (1981)

BOB TAYLOR, *University of Colorado, Boulder* (1981)

WILLIAM R. THOMAS, *Public Schools, Falls Church, Virginia* (1982)

GEORGIA WILLIAMS, *Unified School District, Berkeley, California* (1980)

Unit Representatives to the Board of Directors

(Each Unit's President is listed first; others follow in alphabetical order.)

Alabama: GRACE ROCKARTS, *University of Alabama, Tuscaloosa;* JAMES B. CONDRA, *University of Alabama, Gadsden;* ALVIS HARTHERN, *University of Montevallo, Montevallo*

Alaska: E. E. (GENE) DAVIS, *Public Schools, Anchorage;* ANNA BETH BROWN, *Public Schools, Anchorage*

Arizona: NELSON L. HAGGERSON, *Arizona State University, Tempe;* CHARLES FAUSET, *Northern Arizona University, Flagstaff;* PAT NASH, *University of Arizona, Tucson*

Arkansas: HAROLD MEASEL, *Pulaski County Special School District, Little Rock;* PHILIP BESONEN, *University of Arkansas, Fayetteville*

California: ARTHUR L. COSTA, *California State University, Sacramento;* BILL DRESSER, *San Juan Unified School District, Carmichael;* JESSIE KOBAYASHI, *Murray Unified School District, Dublin;* DORIS PRINCE, *Santa Clara County Schools, San Jose;* KEN SANDERS, *Rio Linda School District, Rio Linda;* HELEN WALLACE, *Cotati-Rohnert Park School District, Rohnert Park;* MARILYN WINTERS, *Las Virgenes Unified School District, Woodland Hills*

Colorado: ROBERT ELLSPERMAN, *Boulder Valley School District, Boulder;* DALE F. GRAHAM, *Adams School District #14, Commerce City;* P. L. SCHMELZER, *Poudre School District R-1, Fort Collins*

Connecticut: NELSON P. QUINBY III, *Regional School District #9, Redding;* EDWARD BOURQUE, *Public Schools, Fairfield;* JOAN D. KERELEJZA, *Public Schools, West Hartford*

Delaware: L. JIM ALLEN, *Appoquinimink School District, Odessa;* MELVILLE WARREN, *Capital School District, Dover*

District of Columbia: ROMAINE THOMAS, *Public Schools, Washington;* PHYLLIS J. HOBSON, *Public Schools, Washington;* ANDREA J. IRBY, *Public Schools, Washington*

Florida: ARTHUR J. LEWIS, *University of Florida, Gainesville;* CHARLES W. GODWIN, *Lee County Schools, Fort Myers;* RICHARD STEWART, *Lee County Schools, Fort Myers;* CHARLOTTE EDEN UMHOLTZ, *(retired—Hillsborough County Schools, Tampa), Tallahassee*

Georgia: LOUISE L. MCCOMMONS, *CSRA/CESA, Thomson;* IRIS GOOLSBY, *De Kalb County Schools, Decatur;* ROSS MILLER, *West Georgia College, Carrollton*

Hawaii: ELAINE BLITMAN, *Punahou School, Honolulu;* ANN PORT, *Hawaii Department of Education, Honolulu*

New Jersey: FRANK B. JAGGARD, *Public Schools, Cinnaminson;* MARY JANE DIEHL, *Monmouth College, Witong Branch;* CHARLES J. GRIPPALDI, *Township of Ocean Schools, Oakhurst;* WILLIAM R. KIEVIT, *Moorestown Township Public Schools, Moorestown;* NICHOLAS J. SFERRAZZA, *Gloucester Township Public Schools, Blackwood*

New Mexico: GARFIELD GUTIERREZ, *New Mexico State Department of Education, Espanola;* PATRICIA CHRISTMAN, *Public Schools, Albuquerque*

New York: MARCIA KNOLL, *Public Schools, Forest Hills;* JAMES A. BEANE, *St. Bonaventure University, St. Bonaventure;* THOMAS E. CURTIS, *State University of New York, Albany;* ANTHONY DEIVLIO, *State University College at Fredonia, Fredonia;* DONALD E. HARKNESS, *Public Schools, Manhasset;* JOHN HINTON, *Riverside School, Rockville Centre;* ROBERT SMITH, *Lawrence Public Schools, Cedarhurst;* GORDON E. VAN HOOFT, *State Department of Education, Albany*

North Carolina: JOYCE F. WASDELL, *Durham County Schools, Durham;* LUCILLE BAZEMORE, *Bertie County Schools, Windsor;* ROBERT C. HANES, *Chapel Hill/Carrboro City Schools, Chapel Hill;* MARCUS C. SMITH, *Public Schools, Salisbury*

North Dakota: QUINN BRUNSON, *The University of North Dakota, Grand Forks*

Ohio: ISOBEL L. PFEIFFER, *University of Akron, Akron;* MICHAEL BARNHART, *Public Schools, Troy;* ROBERT BENNETT, *Public Schools, Gahanna;* ROBERT J. HOHMAN, *Public Schools, Avon Lake;* CAROLYN SUE HUGHES, *Public Schools, Parma*

Oklahoma: DWAYNE COLVIN, *Putnam City Schools, Oklahoma City;* JAMES ROBERTS, *Public Schools, Lawton;* NELDA TEBOW, *Public Schools, Oklahoma City*

Oregon: REA M. JANES, *Public Schools, Portland;* MAX L. BRUNTON, *Parkrose Public Schools, Portland;* TROSTEL WERTH, *Public Schools, Gresham*

Pennsylvania: JOSEPH H. KANE, *Methacton School District, Fairview Village;* PHILIP S. BOGGIO, *Chartiers Valley School District, Pittsburgh;* DAVID CAMPBELL, *State Department of Education, Harrisburg;* ROBERT FLYNN, *Capitol Area Intermediate Unit Schools, Lemoyne;* JOHN R. REITZ, *Wilson School District, West Lawn;* JEANNE ZIMMERMAN, *Eastern York School District, Hellam*

Rhode Island: NORA WALKER, *Public Schools, Warwick;* GUY N. DiBIASIO, *Public Schools, Cranston*

South Carolina: JAMES P. MAHAFFEY, *Horry County School District, Conway;* MILTON KIMPSON, *State Health, Education and Human Services, Columbia;* ELMER KNIGHT, *State Department of Education, Columbia*

South Dakota: RONALD L. BECKER, *Public Schools, Sioux Falls;* PHIL VIK, *University of South Dakota, Vermillion*

Tennessee: ELIZABETH R. LANE, *Shelby County Schools, Memphis;* JACK ROBERTS, *Tennessee Department of Education, Knoxville;* EVERETTE E. SAMS, *Middle Tennessee State University, Murfreesboro*

Texas: GENE BRYANT, *Public Schools, Corpus Christi;* M. GEORGE BOWDEN, *Public Schools, Austin;* RITA BRYANT, *Texas Eastern University, Tyler;* DEWEY MAYS, *Public Schools, Ft. Worth;* GERI STRADER, *Public Schools, Houston*

Utah: RONALD J. HERMANSEN, *Granite School District, Salt Lake City;* FLORENCE BARTON, *Weber State College, Ogden*

Vermont: JEAN STEFANIK, *Public Schools, Barre;* JAMES FITZPATRICK, *Public Schools, Hinesburg*

Virginia: EVELYN GRAHAM, *Public Schools, Chesapeake;* EVELYN BICKAM, *Lynchburg College, Lynchburg;* DELORES GREENE, *Public Schools, Richmond;* BOB L. SIGMON, *Public Schools, Richmond*

Washington: ROY R. DUNCAN, *Public Schools, Pasco;* FRANCIS HUNKINS, *University of Washington, Seattle;* CONNIE KRAVAS, *Washington State University, Pullman*

West Virginia: PHYLLIS OSENTON, *Logan County Schools, Logan;* BETTY LIVENGOOD, *Mineral County Schools, Keyser*

Wisconsin: KEITH WUNROW, *Hamilton School District, Sussex;* MARY ANN ALLEN, *Public Schools, Middleton;* RUSSELL MOSELY, *State Department of Public Instruction, Madison*

Wyoming: ARLO HIEDERER, *Public Schools, Rock Springs;* CHARLENE STOGSDILL, *WINS Facilitation, Cheyenne*

ASCD Review Council

Chairperson: HAROLD G. SHANE, *University Professor of Education, Indiana University, Bloomington*

O. L. DAVIS, JR., *Professor of Curriculum and Instruction, College of Education, University of Texas, Austin*

LUCILLE G. JORDAN, *Associate State Superintendent for Instructional Services, Department of Education, Atlanta, Georgia*

CHARLES G. KINGSTON, *Principal, Thomas Fowler Junior High School, Tigard, Oregon*

GLENYS UNRUH, *Deputy Superintendent, Curriculum and Instruction, School District of University City, University City, Missouri*

ASCD Headquarters Staff

GORDON CAWELTI / *Executive Director*

RONALD S. BRANDT / *Executive Editor*

RUTH T. LONG / *Associate Director*

ROOSEVELT RATLIFF / *Associate Director*

KATHY L. SCHAUB / *Assistant Director for Program and Research*

JOHN BRALOVE / *Business Manager*

VIRGINIA O. BERTHY / *Administrative Assistant*

SARAH ARLINGTON, JOAN BRANDT, CLARA M. BURLEIGH, GAYLE CROSSLAND, ANNE S. DEES, ANITA FITZPATRICK, JO JONES, TEOLA T. JONES, MARJORIE KICAK, INDU B. MADAN, AGATHA DEBORAH MADDOX, FRANCES MINDEL, NANCY OLSON, AMY RUPP, ROBERT SHANNON, CAROLYN SHELL, BARBARA J. SIMS, JUDITH ELIZABETH SNOW, BETSEY THOMAS, JANIS WHITE, COLETTE A. WILLIAMS.

ASCD Publications, Spring 1980

Yearbooks

Considered Action for Curriculum Improvement
(610-80186) $9.75
Education for an Open Society
(610-74012) $8.00
Education for Peace: Focus on Mankind
(610-17946) $7.50
Evaluation as Feedback and Guide
(610-17700) $6.50
Feeling, Valuing, and the Art of Growing:
Insights into the Affective
(610-77104) $9.75
Freedom, Bureaucracy, & Schooling
(610-17508) $6.50
Improving the Human Condition: A Curricular
Response to Critical Realities
(610-78132) $9.75
Learning and Mental Health in the School
(610-17674) $5.00
Life Skills in School and Society
(610-17786) $5.50
Lifelong Learning—A Human Agenda
(610-79160) $9.75
A New Look at Progressive Education
(610-17812) $8.00
Perspectives on Curriculum Development
1776-1976 (610-76078) $9.50
Schools in Search of Meaning
(610-75044) $8.50
Perceiving, Behaving, Becoming: A New Focus
for Education (610-17278) $5.00
To Nurture Humaneness: Commitment for
the '70's (610-17810) $6.00

Books and Booklets

About Learning Materials (611-78134) $4.50
Action Learning: Student Community Service
Projects (611-74018) $2.50
Adventuring, Mastering, Associating: New
Strategies for Teaching Children
(611-76080) $5.00
Beyond Jencks: The Myth of Equal Schooling
(611-17928) $2.00
Bilingual Education for Latinos
(611-78142) $6.75
The Changing Curriculum: Mathematics
(611-17724) $2.00
Classroom-Relevant Research in the Language
Arts (611-78140) $7.50
Clinical Supervision—A State of the Art Review
(611-80194) $3.75
Criteria for Theories of Instruction
(611-17756) $2.00
Curricular Concerns in a Revolutionary Era
(611-17852) $6.00
Curriculum Leaders: Improving Their Influence
(611-76084) $4.00
Curriculum Theory (611-77112) $7.00
Degrading the Grading Myths: A Primer of
Alternatives to Grades and Marks
(611-76082) $6.00
Differentiated Staffing (611-17924) $3.50
Discipline for Today's Children and Youth
(611-17314) $1.50
Educational Accountability: Beyond Behavioral
Objectives (611-17856) $2.50
Elementary School Mathematics: A Guide to
Current Research (611-75056) $5.00
Elementary School Science: A Guide to
Current Research (611-17726) $2.25
Eliminating Ethnic Bias in Instructional
Materials: Comment and Bibliography
(611-74020) $3.25
Emerging Moral Dimensions in Society:
Implications for Schooling
(611-75052) $3.75
Ethnic Modification of the Curriculum
(611-17832) $1.00
Global Studies: Problems and Promises for
Elementary Teachers (611-76086) $4.50
Handbook of Basic Citizenship Competencies
(611-80196) $4.75
Humanistic Education: Objectives and
Assessment (611-78136) $4.75

The Humanities and the Curriculum
(611-17708) $2.00
Impact of Decentralization on Curriculum:
Selected Viewpoints (611-75050) $3.75
Improving Educational Assessment & An
Inventory of Measures of Affective
Behavior (611-17804) $4.50
International Dimension of Education
(611-17816) $2.25
Interpreting Language Arts Research for the
Teacher (611-17846) $4.00
Learning More About Learning
(611-17310) $2.00
Linguistics and the Classroom Teacher
(611-17720) $2.75
A Man for Tomorrow's World
(611-17838) $2.25
Middle School in the Making
(611-74024) $5.00
The Middle School We Need
(611-75060) $2.50
Moving Toward Self-Directed Learning
(611-79166) $4.75
Multicultural Education: Commitments, Issues,
and Applications (611-77108) $7.00
Needs Assessment: A Focus for Curriculum
Development (611-75048) $4.00
Observational Methods in the Classroom
(611-17948) $3.50
Open Education: Critique and Assessment
(611-75054) $4.75
Partners: Parents and Schools
(611-79168) $4.75
Professional Supervision for Professional
Teachers (611-75046) $4.50
Removing Barriers to Humaneness in the High
School (611-17848) $2.50
Reschooling Society: A Conceptual Model
(611-17950) $2.00
The School of the Future—NOW
(611-17920) $3.75
Schools Become Accountable: A PACT
Approach (611-74016) $3.50
The School's Role as Moral Authority
(611-77110) $4.50
Selecting Learning Experiences: Linking
Theory and Practice (611-78138) $4.75
Social Studies for the Evolving Individual
(611-17952) $3.00
Staff Development: Staff Liberation
(611-77106) $6.50
Supervision: Emerging Profession
(611-17796) $5.00
Supervision in a New Key (611-17926) $2.50
Supervision: Perspectives and Propositions
(611-17732) $2.00
What Are the Sources of the Curriculum?
(611-17522) $1.50
Vitalizing the High School (611-74026) $3.50
Developmental Characteristics of Children and
Youth (wall chart) (611-75058) $2.00

Discounts on quantity orders of same title to
single address: 10-49 copies, 10% ; 50 or more
copies, 15%. Make checks or money orders
payable to ASCD. Orders totaling $10.00 or
less must be prepaid. Orders from institutions
and businesses must be on official purchase
order form. Shipping and handling charges will
be added to billed purchase orders. *Please be
sure to list the stock number of each publication, shown in parentheses.*
Subscription to *Educational Leadership*—$15.00
a year. ASCD Membership dues: Regular (subscription [$15] and yearbook)—$29.00 a year;
Comprehensive (includes subscription [$15]
and yearbook plus other books and booklets
distributed during period of membership)—
$39.00 a year.

Order from:
**Association for Supervision and
Curriculum Development
225 North Washington Street
Alexandria, Virginia 22314**